"Which American murderer killed over 200 people?

What bandit was John Dillinger's role model?

Who gave the signal for his own execution?

BLOODLETTERS AND BADMEN will answer these questions and hundreds more."
—*Cleveland Press*

Here are the most notorious outlaws, thieves, brothel keepers, syndicate gangsters, arsonists, rapists, kidnappers, murderers, lovers, forgers, embezzlers, bombers, assassins, bank robbers and hijackers who have punctuated our history with crime. Every story is different. Some are a paragraph; others run several pages depending on the fascination of the crimes and their perpetrators.

"Gaudy and gorgeous . . . Nash has a lively eye, an inquiring and skeptical mind . . . a keen sense of the absurd . . . distinct flair for dramatic exposition"
—*Kansas City Star*

"A definitive document of America's criminal past . . . an illuminating book."
—*Buffalo Courier-Express*

"Filmmakers, writers, researchers, lawyers and sociologists should be interested in this fascinating gallery . . . a must for libraries."
—*Publishers Weekly*

"One of the year's best."
—*American Libraries*

JAY ROBERT

BLOODL
AND B

Abridged

WARNER BOOKS

A Warner Communications Company

NASH

LETTERS ADMEN

BOOK 1

Captain Lightfoot To Jesse James

This book is for Bob Abel, who thought it necessary; for Jack Conroy, novelist and friend to young writers; and in memory of two great reporters—William L. "Tubby" Toms of the *Indianapolis News* and Ray Brennan of the *Chicago Sun-Times*.

FOREWORD

The concept for these books began more than fifteen years ago when, as a reporter and editor, I began out of necessity and curiosity to write about American criminals. My occupation led to seemingly endless documents, clippings, books, pamphlets, a storehouse of crime in America and the bizarre, sometimes lunatic, fascinating creatures who lived and moved on the other side of the curtain.

In the beginning, criminals of note came with the bark on and were, in their own untrustworthy way, much the pioneers in highway robbery and murder; one entry in this volume describes John Billington, who landed with the pilgrims and was executed by that pure-living band for murdering a neighbor out of vengeance, thereby setting historical precedent as well as earning for himself dubious distinction as one of America's first bloodletters.

As the fabric of crime knitted its way across the land with those traveling west, the criminals of the period flourished with the wagon trains, cutting their way through wild territories at the side of our famous pathfinders. In that family-oriented society, the first notorious miscreants were brotherhood bands like the six terrible Doane brothers of the 1780s and the vicious Harpe brothers a decade later who became as savage as the wilderness they sought to tame.

Highway robbery was their specialty and vicious killing their instinct. Perhaps one of the few exceptions was the gallant Michael Martin, known as "Captain Lightfoot," who was always the perfect gentleman when looting a stage.

As each successive state became settled and joined the union, the brotherhoods of blood, banded together for mutual protection and trust through family ties, spawned and increased, their dedication to robbery handed down, often, from one generation to another like that of the infamous Loomis brothers of upper New York State.

In Indiana, the Reno brothers controlled half the state and committed the first train robbery at Seymour, Indiana, in 1866. Jesse and Frank James and the four Younger brothers terrorized Missouri and several neighboring states for eighteen years. The Burrow brothers, once simple farmers, took to the gun in Arkansas. The Farrington boys leaped into outlawry in Mississippi and worked their way northward to infamy and death. In Kansas, an entire family named Bender—mother, father, brother, and sister Kate who gave lectures—slaughtered guests at their inn by the score. California had the Sontag brothers, and Texas gave birth to an army of gunfighters all related by blood whose most prominent member was John Wesley Hardin, credited with shooting down forty men.

(The most destructive gunfight between outlaws and lawmen, fought at Tombstone's O.K. Corral in 1881, was strictly a family feud conducted by the three Earp brothers and Doc Holliday on one side and the McLowery brothers and the Clanton clan on the other.)

With the exceptions of Black Bart, Cherokee Bill, John Murrel, Print Olive, Henry Plummer, Jack Slade and some others, crime in America was a family affair, robbery and killing conducted as a business by brothers whose loyalty was unyielding. Even the loners like Sam Bass and Billy the Kid (William H. Bonney) were aided, supplied, fed, bedded and protected by women and gunslingers who were as emotionally bound to them as kin. The hard-scrabble people they lived among, even those they victimized, somehow came to excuse and sometimes admire them for their shoddy fame. In the grime, poverty and ignorance that was the frontier, there was little else beyond the Bible and the land to inspire sundown conversation.

There were the crazies, of course, secret poisoners like Cordelia Botkin and Thomas Thatcher Graves who killed by mail for love and loot, assassins like John Wilkes Booth and Charles Julius Guiteau who did away with presidents out of warped loyalties and ambitions, even America's all-time mass slayer Herman Webster Mudgett (alias H. H. Holmes) who took the lives of more than two hundred women, but the early days of American crime were dominated by the brotherhood gangs, the last of which was led by the indomitable Butch Cassidy whose Wild Bunch was studded with groups of brothers, the McCartys, the Logans.

These fierce blood ties continued on into the twentieth century, but the latter paled by comparison with the previous era, one in which the American family mightily contributed to the burgeoning ranks of outlawry. The word "outlaw" in itself was a softer version of criminal, an almost kindly appellative that embodied sympathy for the wrongdoer's plight and empathy for his lonely life, which is, no doubt, the reason why a cold-blooded murderer such as Jesse James emerges in our historical legends as a man driven to crime (by the railroads, the Yankees, the Pinkertons, etc.), a man deserving of our deepest understanding and left-handed admiration. Close scrutiny of his life and the lives of others in the volume, however, reveals something else, something pervasively sinister that has been with our society since the beginning, our own sly tolerance of criminals, a shrug and a snicker, perhaps, at their ability to outwit and outlast the law and subtle remorse over their capture or demise.

People by the scores wept at the grave of Clay Allison, an alcoholic killer; town folk flocked to bury Belle Starr and on the spot translate her cattle-thieving and whoring into purer acts, nobler deeds. She was no longer the hatchet-faced tomcat, but a vision of beauty on horseback. Ben Thompson and Dallas Stoudenmire, lawmen turned

9

gun-killers, became local heroes, for they had struck out on their own against society, the American way since we broke with the English monarchy.

When the gun-crazy Dalton brothers and the Bill Doolin gang went to death and dust in the 1890s, there was public outrage at their obliteration at the hands of the law because they had, in the words of Bob Dalton, "died game." It was a broad attitude that would die hard and linger long inside our own time. These, then, were the forefathers of American crime, a breed not so much apart or severed from the so-called average man, but distant cousins and uncles who sat occasionally at the hearthstone of our very history warming their hands and telling their stories along-side any worthy pioneer. They drank from the same cup, ate from the same bowl, always outlaws but never outcasts. They were ours.

Jay Robert Nash
Chicago, 1974

ACKNOWLEDGMENTS

I wish to thank the following people and organizations for their extensive assistance in helping me research this book and for the wonderful cooperation they extended in providing photos, information, and encouragement: Kevin John Mosley Collection; Roland Restle Collection; Henry Scheafer and Faytonia Fair of UPI's Chicago office; William and Edie Kelly of Wide World's Chicago office; Peter A. Evans, Librarian of the California Historical Society; James H. Davis, Picture Librarian of the Denver Public Library (Western History Department); Mrs. Leona S. Morris, Editorial Secretary of the Missouri Historical Review (State Historical Society of Missouri); G. F. O'Neill, Director of Personnel, Pinkerton's, Inc.; Jack D. Haley, Assistant Curator, Western History Collections, University of Oklahoma; New York Historical Society; Wyoming State Historical Department; Kansas State Historical Society; Arizona Historical Society; Terry Mangan, The State Historical Society of Colorado; Holly B. Ulseth, Curator of Special Exhibits & Collections, Detroit Historical Museum; Malcolm Freiberg, Editor of Publications, Massachusetts Historical Society; William M. Roberts, Reference Librarian, University of California, Berkeley; Ken Burton, *Tucson Daily Citizen;*

James, John, and Patrick Agnew; Prof. Andre Moenssens; Raymond Friday Locke, Editor, *Mankind Magazine*; Robert Connelly; Thomas Buckley; Richard Case of the Chicago Historical Society; Jack Paul Schwartz; Mrs. Jerrie L. Klein; Neil H. Nash; Jack J. Klein, Jr.; Ray Puechner; Peter Kotsos; Stan Kaiser; Dr. Richard Talsky; Barry Felcher of the *Chicago Daily News*; Curt Johnson; Leonard Des Jardins; Al Devorin; John Gehlman; Mike Berman; James Small; James Stein; Arthur Von Kluge; Brett Howard; Sidney Harris; Arnold Edwards; Jerry Goldberg of the *Los Angeles Free Press*; Warren Stamer; Arnold L. Kaye; Joseph Pinkston; James McCormick of *Chicago Today*; Jack Lane, Jeff Kamen; Herman Kogan of the *Chicago Sun-Times*; William Kirby, Associate Director of the Louisiana Division of the New Orleans Public Library; the dozens of police force officers of all ranks, criminologists, and penologists across the country who gave their time and information; and to my intrepid typist and friend, Carolyn Zozak, whose fingers ceaselessly danced across her typewriter's keyboard on my behalf.

ADAMS, CALEB
Murderer • (1785–1803)

Adams was a "street youth" of Windham, Conn., where a five-year-old neighbor boy, Oliver Woodworth plagued Adams with too many questions and was in the habit of following him.

One day the eighteen-year-old Adams took an axe to little Oliver, striking him on the head. Adams then produced a knife and slit the boy's throat because, as Adams later explained: "He annoyed me."

Adams was promptly convicted and sentenced to hang. On the day of his hanging, November 29, 1803, the youth stood for close to an hour on the gallows before a great throng as the Rev. Elijah Waterman delivered a sermon, pointing out Adams' dissolute life, recounting every crime the boy had confessed to over his brief life span, which included stealing twenty-five cents.

After Adams' spirit had been properly cleansed by Waterman's sermon, he was hanged.

ALLISON, CLAY
Gunman, Outlaw • (1840-1877)

BACKGROUND: BORN IN RURAL TENNESSEE. MINOR PUBLIC EDUCATION. ORIGINAL OCCUPATION, COWBOY. HIRED OUT AS A GUNMAN TO VARIOUS CATTLE BARONS IN NEW MEXICO IN THE 1870s. DESCRIPTION: 6', BLUE EYES, BROWN HAIR, SLENDER. ALIASES: NONE. RECORD: SHOT AND KILLED AN ESTIMATED FIFTEEN GUNMEN MOSTLY IN THE NEW MEXICO TERRITORY IN A TEN-YEAR SPAN, BEGINNING ABOUT 1867.

No historian ever doubted Clay Allison's ability as a fast gun. What most historians either refuse or neglect to state is that this handsome daredevil of an outlaw, popularized as a champion of justice, was a roaring alcoholic who seldom if ever gave his opponents a chance in a standup fight.

Allison was a bully who delighted in terrorizing small towns and aging sheriffs. One story had Allison, drunk to the marrow, charging up and down the main street of Canadian, Texas, naked except for his wide-brim hat, boots and six guns, shooting out store windows.

Another is not as capricious. The deputy sheriff of Las Animas, Colo., once attempted to disarm Allison and his brother John, and nervously squeezed the trigger of his shotgun. John Allison was shot in the arm and Clay, swearing vengeance, sent a bullet into the deputy's forehead. The killing was ruled self-defense.

Most of Allison's time was spent trying to nurture his small ranch on the Washita River in New Mexico. To make extra money, he would hire out his gun to enforce the boundary rights of large ranches. His reputation as a fast gun stemmed from run-ins such as those he had with Chunk Colbert and Francisco "Pancho" Griego.

In Colbert's case it was a matter of two old friends getting together for dinner to murder each other. The two gunfighters sat down to dinner one night at the Clifton House at Red River Station in Texas. One biographer claims the two stirred their coffee with the muzzles of their six guns as they eye-balled each other.

When Allison saw Chunk drop his hand from sight, he tilted his chair back, firing as he fell and hitting Colbert between the eyes. Getting up, Clay finished his steak without even glancing up to see his enemy's body hauled away.

Clay Allison, an alcoholic gunslinger who terrorized New Mexico in the 1870s. (Western Historical Collections, U. of Okla. Library)

Griego went faster and without any ceremony. Allison thought it peculiar that the Mexican outlaw fan himself with his large sombrero during one of Cimmaron's coldest days. Obviously Griego was going for his gun hidden behind the hat and, just as obviously, Allision drilled him dead.

The stories of Allison backing down lawmen Wyatt Earp and Bat Masterson in Dodge City are apocryphal; Clay Allison was not a man to face marshals in open combat. He was clever and his fame with a gun was earned through stealth and guile.

It was probably fitting that this border terrorist met with an inglorious and ironic end. While on his way to kill John McCullough, a neighbor, Allison got drunk and fell out of his wagon. He was killed when the heavily-loaded vehicle rolled over his neck.

Supposedly Allison respected his grisly occupation. "I never killed a man who didn't need it," he once said, claiming that in the course of shooting more than a dozen men he was "protecting the property holders of the country from thieves, outlaws and murderers."

ALMY, FRANK C.
Murderer, Burglar • (? -1892)

For years, Almy operated as a burglar in the New England area under the name of George Abbott. He was apprehended and was sentenced to serve a fifteen-year term in the New Hampshire State Prison, but he escaped.

After having a marriage proposal turned down, Almy murdered Christie Warden July 17, 1891, near Hanover,

N.H. Curiously, while armed bands of men sought him, Almy hid out for almost a month in the Warden barn. He was ultimately discovered and brought to trial in 1892, convicted following his confession, and sentenced to death.

ANDERSON, WILLIAM ("BLOODY BILL")
Guerrilla, Murderer • (? –1864)

Anderson was one of the ruthless lieutenants who served under William Clarke Quantrill's guerrilla band which raided the Missouri-Kansas border towns during the Civil War, ostensibly for the Confederacy. In reality, Quantrill's band, never exceeding 450 men, were terrorists, robbers and murderers. Anderson was the bloodiest of the lot, a raider who enjoyed shooting down unarmed men and boys he thought loyal to the Union.

When Quantrill led his guerillas into Lawrence, Kansas, on a bloodthirsty raid August 23, 1863, Bill Anderson was at his side directing a column of men which included Frank James and Cole Younger. For two hours, Quantrill and Anderson led their marauders through Lawrence's unprotected streets, shooting every man and boy in sight, almost all of whom were unarmed. Only one young boy was spared. Anderson took great pride in compelling the women and girls of the town to watch the slaughter as a "lesson."

Bloody Bill always insisted on a display of violence. He himself was a walking arsenal advertising death and war. At times he carried eight revolvers stuck around his belt, a hatchet, and a saber. On his horse were four rifles and two saddle bags full of pistols.

William "Bloody Bill" Anderson led Civil War guerrillas in murderous raids into Missouri and Kansas. (State Historical Society of Missouri)

In the fall of 1864, Anderson split away from Quantrill to lead his own raid against Centralia, Missouri. With him went thirty of his most ruthless killers, including a seventeen-year-old beardless youth named Jesse Woodson James. They struck Centralia on September 26, 1864, destroying the stores and burning the railroad station. A train pulled into the small town at noon carrying twenty-five Union soldiers. They were quickly disarmed; Anderson ordered them to strip to their underclothes. He then lined them up and asked if any were officers. One Thomas Goodwin said he was (he was only a sergeant) and Anderson ordered him out of the rank. He alone was spared the fate of his comrades.

Turning to his most trusted executioner, Arch Clement, a good friend of Frank and Jesse James, Anderson said: "Muster out the rest of these men, Arch."

Delighted with his task, the diminutive Clement stepped forward smiling. At point blank range he shot dead each man in the line. Some of Anderson's men helped him kill the helpless troopers. Young Jesse James stood and watched.

In October, 1864, Anderson ran into a troop of regular Union soldiers while fleeing through Ray County, Mo. Commander S. P. Cox led a charge against the guerrillas, personally shooting Anderson dead from the saddle.

[ALSO SEE Jesse Woodson James, William Clark Quantrill.]

APACHE KID, THE
Murderer, Robber • (1867- ?)

At age twenty, the Indian known as the Apache Kid was the pride of his nation, a fearless sergeant of scouts on the San Carlos, N.M. reservation. He worked under the command of Indian fighter and scout Al Sieber, and his exploits concerning the arrests of rum-runners and gun smugglers were legendary in that part of the West.

When the Kid's father was killed by a renegade, he took tribal revenge by slaying the murderer. The Kid then surrendered to Sieber but later, justly fearing shabby treatment in the white man's courts, fled with some followers. For two years the Kid hid out; he was finally captured, tried, and convicted of murder, but President Cleveland pardoned him.

The running had changed the Kid, and he turned away from the lawful life, angrily killing a whiskey drummer who

The Apache Kid, cavalry scout gone wrong. (Arizona Historical Society Library)

attempted to sell fire water to his people. He was tried a second time and received a seven-year jail term. On his way to the Yuma jail, the Kid broke away and killed two of his guards, deputies Glen Reynolds and Bill Holmes, on November 1, 1889. Eugene Middleton, a survivor, staggered back to Globe, Ariz., badly wounded, with the news.

Authorities placed a $5,000 reward for the capture of the Apache Kid dead or alive, but no one ever collected the bounty. For two years the Kid and some members of his tribe roamed the New Mexico territory, robbing gold and horses from prospectors, and raping a number of defenseless settlers' wives. The Kid took a wife and lived high in the hills of the Sierra Madre in Mexico, crossing the border when in need of supplies and money.

In 1894, a prospector named Edward A. Clark, reported shooting two Indians, a man and woman, who had invaded his camp one night, just north of Tucson, Ariz. He had killed the squaw, he reported, and wounded the man. He claimed it was the Apache Kid and was positive the Indian's back wound was fatal.

"He crawled away to die somewhere, I know," Clark stated.

Clark may have been right. The Apache Kid never appeared after that, though some historians claim that it was another Indian Clark wounded and the Kid, a practical soul, merely settled down in Mexico, raised a family and lived unknown into the twentieth century.

20

ARNOLD, STEPHEN
Murderer • (Circa 1775- ?)

Slightly touched with lunacy, Stephen Arnold, as a schoolteacher in Cooperstown, N.Y., flew into a rage every time a pupil made a mistake. He found it intolerable, therefore, when his own niece, six-year-old Betsy Van Amburgh, could not spell the word "gig."

Arnold, who was taking care of Betsy for his brother, beat her wildly with a club, killing her. Regaining his senses, the schoolteacher fled to Pittsburgh, Pa. There he was captured and returned to New York for trial in 1805.

Quickly convicted, Arnold was sentenced to hang. His public execution was bloated with pomp. Thousands came to Cooperstown to view the hanging; bands played as Arnold marched to the gallows. He was preceded by a battalion of infantry and a company of artillery, their caissons gayly bedecked with bunting and flowers.

Quavering, with the rope about his neck, Arnold listened to a minister give a lengthy sermon admonishing his evil deed, the speech sprinkled with Arnold's own words of caution to young men warning them to curb their tempers.

Just before the trap was sprung, the sheriff stepped forth and ceremoniously flung the rope from Arnold's neck while the stunned spectators blinked. The sheriff then produced a reprieve from the governor, a document he had kept in his pocket all morning. His explanation for concealing the document was that he wanted Arnold to experience the dread of death for his sin and also that he did not wish to disappoint the crowd of some excitement. (The throng was disappointed.)

Arnold, for reasons of temporary insanity, later received a pardon.

BAKER, JOSEPH
Murderer, Pirate • (? -1800)

Canadian by birth, whose real name was Boulanger, Baker mutinied against his captain, William Wheland, aboard the U.S. schooner, *Eliza* in 1800. Leading two other sailors, LaCroix and Berrouse, Baker killed the ship's first mate and wounded Captain Wheland. The captain was allowed to live after giving his promise that he would navigate the ship into pirate waters.

Biding his time, Wheland finally managed to trap LaCroix and Berrouse below deck, locking them up. Wielding an axe, Captain Wheland drove Baker into the rigging of the ship, where he stayed aloft for sixteen days until the captain brought the *Eliza* to port.

April 25, 1800, Baker was tried in Philadelphia along with Berrouse and LaCroix, for murder and piracy committed on the high seas. All three were sentenced to hang and they mounted the gallows May 9 of that year, confessing their crimes to priests.

BANKS, JOHN
Murderer • (? -1806)

Most murderers find themselves killing out of passion, or for money. John Banks killed for food.

Banks resided in New York City with his wife Margaret, whose cooking and general housekeeping left much to be desired. She also drank heavily and was usually found staggering about by the time Banks came home from his labors.

One spring evening in 1806, Banks returned home to find Margaret blind drunk. When he asked for some coffee, he later related at his trial, May 29, 1806, she gave him "pot-liquor." This was too much. Banks grabbed a coal shovel and beaned his wife, and then, the furies upon him, slit her throat with a butcher knife.

One account stated that Banks "had brought some peanuts and ordered her to brown them . . . and that when he did return with some eggs, he found she had done nothing. These were his provocations [for killing her]."

Banks was speedily tried, and executed July 11, 1806.

BARTER, RICHARD
("RATTLESNAKE DICK")
Robber • (1834-1859)

Born in England, Barter immigrated to the U.S. as a youth and traveled to California shortly after the great Gold Rush period. There, tiring of panning gold for syndicates, he became a petty thief. In 1856 he hit upon a scheme to steal $80,000 in one swooping robbery. He and his gang would stop the gold convoy that regularly traveled by mule down from the Trinity Mountains.

For Rattlesnake Dick it was a gigantic undertaking. The robbery succeeded, but never netted Barter a dime, oddly enough. The outlaw did not deign to perform the deed himself but sent an accomplice, George Skinner, and two other members of his band out to stop the convoy. After Skinner made off with the gold, half-way down the mountain trail near Ureka, the mules gave out and Skinner buried most of the treasure.

Carrying what he could, Skinner and two others straggled down the mountain to keep a rendezvous with Barter. The outlaw chief didn't show up; he was already in jail with Skinner's brother Cy, imprisoned for stealing mules.

A posse intercepted George Skinner and killed him following a wild gunfight. When Rattlesnake Dick and Cy Skinner escaped jail, they fruitlessly searched for the gold taken in the robbery Barter had designed; they never found it (nor has anyone else) and the bandit returned to robbing stages. He was shot and killed by lawmen in 1859.

BASS, SAM
Stagerobber, Trainrobber • (1851–1878)

BACKGROUND: BORN IN WOODVILLE, INDIANA, ONE OF TEN CHILDREN. NO PUBLIC EDUCATION. FOLLOWING THE DEATH OF HIS MOTHER AND FATHER WHEN HE WAS 13, BASS WAS, ALONG WITH HIS BROTHERS AND SISTERS, BOARDED OUT TO AN UNCLE DAVID SHEEKS. ORIGINAL OCCUPATIONS FARMER, MILLHAND, FREIGHTHANDLER, COWBOY. DESCRIPTION: 5'9", BROWN EYES, BROWN HAIR, HEAVY MUSTACHE, SOLID. ALIASES: NONE. RECORD: ATTEMPTED TO ROB THE DEADWOOD STAGECOACH JUST OUTSIDE OF DEADWOOD, S.D. IN THE SPRING OF 1876 AT WHICH TIME ITS SHOTGUN RIDER JOHN SLAUGHTER WAS KILLED; ROBBED SEVERAL STAGECOACHES IN THE BLACK HILLS AREA IN 1876–77 FOR PIDDLING AMOUNTS; ROBBED WITH JOEL COLLINS, JIM BERRY, TOM NIXON, AND OTHERS THE UNION PACIFIC TRAIN NEAR BIG SPRINGS, NEB., 9/18/77 (TAKING $60,000 IN GOLD PIECES BEING SHIPPED EAST FROM THE SAN FRANCISCO MINT, $458 FROM THE RAILROAD SAFE AND $1,300 FROM THE PASSENGERS); ROBBED THE STAGE NEAR MARY'S CREEK OUTSIDE OF FORT WORTH, TEX. IN OCT., 1877 ($43); ROBBED THE HOUSTON & TEXAS CENTRAL EXPRESS WITH HENRY UNDERWOOD, FRANK JACKSON, SEABORN BARNES, AND TOM SPOTSWOOD, 2/23/78 ($1,280); ROBBED TWO MORE TEXAS TRAINS THAT SPRING WITH THE SAME BAND FOR SMALL AMOUNTS; ATTEMPTED TO ROB THE BANK AT ROUND ROCK, TEX. 7/19/78 BUT WAS BETRAYED BY A MEMBER OF HIS GANG; WOUNDED IN THE RAID AND DIED ON A CABIN PORCH NEAR BUSHY CREEK.

Sam Bass, as outlaws go, was not a man blessed with luck. From the beginning of his young life on a farm in Indiana, events were against him. His mother, Elizabeth Sheeks Bass, died giving birth to her tenth child. Sam was only ten then. His father Dan died three years later of illness. His uncle, David Sheeks, a petty tyrant, took in the Bass children and worked them like day laborers on his farm. Sam's scant legacy from his parents consisted of a bull calf and a worn-out saddle, both amounting to $11.

At eighteen, Sam ran away and took odd jobs in his wanderings. He worked as a millhand in Mississippi, earning enough money to stake him to a trip West where he longed to become a cowboy. By 1874, he made it to Denton, Texas, where he became a freighthandler for Sheriff William "Dad" Egan. He did some cowpunching, too, for the local ranchers.

Acquiring a fast pony, Bass entered her in all the local races for small prize money and won. He and his friend, Henry Underwood, then rode through Southwest Texas, the Indian territories, and Mexico, pitting the animal against local entries and easily winning races. On a trip to San Antonio, Bass befriended Joel Collins, a one-time bartender and cowboy, who convinced him that race-horsing for prizes was penny-ante. It also amounted to hard labor, Collins argued. He had a six-gun. All Bass had to do was draw it from his holster to earn big money.

While helping to drive a large herd of Texas cattle to Kansas in 1876, Bass and Collins deserted and entered the Black Hills. There they attempted to stop the Deadwood Stage, but failed. Someone fired a shotgun in anger at the stage's guard, Johnny Slaughter, and killed him. (One of their confederates fired the shot and Bass and Collins drove him away; they didn't want trigger-happy outlaws in their band.)

Bass soon realized that stage robbing proved to be a dirt cheap way of starving. His gang never seemed to hit a stage carrying any gold shipments. The passengers were as impoverished as the outlaws. One stage had no passengers at all. Four passengers on the next stage could offer only $30 between them. Another stage brought the bandits only $3 and a gold watch.

Sam could not resist the gallant *beau geste* during these sorties. He had known poverty and he never let his victims ride off without returning $1 each to them for breakfast. It became his trademark. Though the outlaws were masked, as soon as their leader coughed back eating money passengers knew they had been robbed by Sam Bass.

Bass grew tired of the whole scheme. Stage robbing was a bust. He and Collins thought they'd try holding up a train. Collins set forth his plan to rob the Union Pacific express coming from San Francisco. He and Bass collected four other outlaws, the toughest in the Nebraska territory—Jim Berry, Tom Nixon, Jack Davis and Bill Heffridge.

The six men, following the railroad's timetable, rode out

Sam Bass at sixteen. (Western History Collections, U. of Okla. Library)

to Big Springs on the morning of August 18, 1877, and stopped the train as it was going up a steep grade. Collins and Bass jumped into the Wells Fargo freight car and ordered clerk Charles Miller to open the safe. He said it couldn't be done, that the safe had a time lock on it. Infuriated, Bass grabbed an axe from the car's wall and began to hammer heavy blows on the safe. He couldn't dent the solid iron structure.

Pausing from his labors, Bass wiped the sweat from his brow and, at that moment, happened to see clerk Miller nervously eyeing three boxes on the floor. "What's in them?" Bass asked, resting his hand on his pistol.

Miller stammered ignorance. "I think some kind of hardware," he finally managed.

Bass swung down his axe on one of the boxes caving in the top. He staggered back, amazed. The box was jampacked with $20 gold pieces, fresh from the mint in San Francisco, scheduled for delivery to New York banks.

"My God," Bass exclaimed, realizing that with one swing of the axe his fortunes had changed. Quickly, he broke into the other two boxes. They, too, were brimming with $20 gold pieces, $60,000 in all (a great fortune in that era).

Collins ordered Berry and Nixon to stand guard over the treasure. Collins and Heffridge then went to work on the regular Wells Fargo safe (they never did find out what the bigger safe contained) from which they finally extracted $458.

Bass and Jack Davis raced through the coaches, scooping up about $1,300 from the wealthy trans-continental passengers. With their saddle bags full and jingling, the outlaws then rode away whooping with joy.

The Big Springs raid was a sensation in the press and it brought down dozens of posses, railroad detectives, and the greatly feared Pinkertons on Sam Bass's trail. He had not been recognized but someone on the train identified the much-wanted Tom Nixon. He was well-known in the Black Hills as an outlaw friend of Joel Collins and Sam Bass.

The six men rode southward for their lives, each carrying about $10,000. The men split into pairs just after the raid, all heading back to Texas by various routes. Collins and Heffridge were jumped by a troop of soldiers near Fort Hays, Kan. After the two were wounded several times, the soldiers demanded their surrender.

"I'm going down with my six-guns!" Collins bravely yelled out. In minutes he and Heffridge were dead.

Berry and Nixon were next. A posse trapped them outside of Mexico, Mo. Nixon escaped but Berry stood his ground and was killed by Sheriff Walter Glasscock. Nixon apparently took most of Berry's money with him because only $3,000 was found on the dead outlaw. With his saddle bags bursting with gold, Tom Nixon rode out of Western history forever. No one ever found him again, despite a nationwide manhunt conducted for years by the dogged Pinkerton Detective Agency.

Sam Bass and Jack Davis rode through Texas, dodging lawmen all the way. There, Davis also disappeared forever. It is quite likely that he and Nixon, both frugal cowboys, settled down to inconspicuous living to end their years in comfort and peace.

Sam Bass alone went on with his larger-than-life reputation staked openly and defiantly against the law. At Denton, Tex., he raised another outlaw band which included his old friend Henry Underwood and some other local boys—Frank Jackson, Seaborn Barnes, and Tom Spotswood.

These five hit the Houston and Texas Central express February 23, 1878, near Allen Station, Tex. The take, compared with the Big Springs job, was petty: only $1,280. Two more train robberies that spring involving the same band netted only $600. Train robbing for Sam Bass was proving as meagerly profitable as stopping stages. He decided to turn to banks.

Holed up in his almost impregnable lair, a natural fortress of steep hills and bluffs known as Cove Hollow near Denton, Bass and his bandits planned the robbery of the Round Rock, Texas bank. The outlaw chieftain had taken in a new recruit, Jim Murphy. Seaborn Barnes didn't trust Murphy and told Bass so. Sam was a loyal sort and refused to think ill of his new addition to the gang.

Barnes was right. Murphy, a local boy whose family had been pressured by the authorities to turn over Bass (on threat of prosecution for once harboring him), decided to become a traitor. Murphy's deal with Texas Ranger Major John B. Jones also included a considerable reward.

Another ranger, Captain Lee Hall, in the true tradition of the West, wanted no part of the sellout, branding Murphy a "veritable Judas in every sense of the word." But Jones had his way and Murphy waited for his chance.

When Bass and his band rode out of Cove Hollow to raid the Round Rock bank, Murphy went with them. They stopped in a small Texas town to water their horses. Murphy managed to get off a wire to Jones: "We are on our way to Round Rock to rob the bank. For God's sake get there."

By the time Bass arrived in Round Rock, the rangers were waiting. Murphy said he was going "to look around for lawmen" and quickly vanished. Bass, followed by Barnes and Jackson, went into a grocery store for tobacco. They planned to familiarize themselves with the town and rob the bank the next day.

Two local lawmen then walked into Koppel's store. Deputy Sheriff A. W. Grimes approached the outlaws. "Now you know you men ain't supposed to be wearing sidearms in town," he said. Deputy Sheriff M. Moore stood behind Grimes, fingering his six-gun.

With one nervous look between them, Bass, Barnes, and Jackson went for their guns. Grimes went down with six bullets in him. A bullet hit Moore in the chest and he went down firing; one of his shots hit Bass in the stomach. The outlaws ran from the store just as a swarm of rangers ran up the street toward them.

Barnes was shot dead while mounting his horse. Jackson pushed Bass up onto his mount and the two raced down the street. Jim Murphy watched them from hiding. He saw Sam Bass' saddle coated with blood and reported to the rangers that his leader had been severely wounded. His story was supported that night when a local farmer came into town and told authorities that an outlaw was dying on the front porch of his cabin near Bushy Creek.

Ranger Jones and his men rode to the farmer's place and found Sam Bass. His right hand had been smashed by a bullet and he had lost a great amount of blood from the stomach wound. A doctor who rode out with the posse stated that Bass' case was hopeless.

Jones begged the outlaw to tell him who was with him on the raid. Sam Bass responded in a fashion that was to become part of the Code of the West and, generations later, that of the modern American criminal. "It's agin my trade to blow on my pals. If a man knows anything, he ought to die with it in him."

Jones kept asking for names.

"Let me go," Sam Bass said. "The world is bobbing around."

Then he was gone.

BEADLE, WILLIAM
Murderer • (? -1783)

For a long period of time, something had been troubling William Beadle of Weathersfield, Conn. He seldom spoke to his wife Lydia or his four children in the last year of his life, and developed the habit of taking an axe and a carving knife to bed with him each night. (Ominous as this sign might be, Mrs. Beadle failed to realize that all was not right with Mr. Beadle.)

On the morning of December 11, 1783, Beadle slaughtered his entire family and then slit his own throat.

BEAUCHAMP, JEREBOAM O.
Murderer • (1803-1826)

BACKGROUND: BORN IN KENTUCKY, 1803. BECAME AN ATTORNEY AT LAW, 1823. MARRIED ANN COOKE, 1824. DESCRIPTION: TALL, ROBUST. ALIASES: NONE. RECORD: MURDERED COLONEL SOLOMON P. SHARP IN 1826; CONFESSED AT HIS TRIAL, SENTENCED TO THE GALLOWS; HANGED 7/7/26 at FRANKFORT, KY.

A woman's honor meant everything to Jereboam Beauchamp, born and raised after the genteel tradition in the antebellum South. Beauchamp would do anything to defend that honor, including murder.

Ann Cooke, an aging belle from Virginia, became engaged to Beauchamp when he was only twenty-one years old (she was thirty-eight). Before she would marry the promising young attorney, however, Ann insisted that her honor be avenged. She had been seduced and made pregnant, she claimed, by Colonel Solomon P. Sharp, a member of the Kentucky House of Representatives and a former attorney general of the state.

The heated political campaign of 1826 also involved Ann Cooke. Solomon's political foes used her seduction story against him, openly branding him a scoundrel. The Colonel remained mute on the subject but Jereboam Beauchamp did not. Two years after marrying Ann (there was no child) Beauchamp, no doubt brooding about Ann Cooke's charges then rekindled in the election, confronted Sharp, demanding that he meet him in a duel. The Colonel declined.

Days later, wearing a red hood over his head, Beauchamp appeared at Sharp's estate. When the Colonel opened the door, Beauchamp plunged a dagger into his chest several times until the politician fell dead.

Beauchamp, however, was recognized and his apprehension followed almost immediately. He was imprisoned in the Frankfort jail, a dungeon-like affair with no windows, pitch-black, which had to be entered by letting down a ladder. Here, Ann visited him to pour out her gratitude for effecting her revenge.

After his confession, Beauchamp was speedily tried and sentenced by the Frankfort Circuit Court in May, 1826. He was sentenced to die on the gallows in July. While waiting for the hangman, Jereboam and Ann decided they would commit suicide together. Ann smuggled poison into Jereboam's cell and both took large doses, but they only succeeded in getting sick.

On July 7, 1826, the day of the hanging, the two ate a final breakfast of chipped beef and tea. Then each took turns with a knife, plunging it into each other's stomachs. As Ann died in Jereboam's arms, thousands of people from all over the county gathered outside the jail to await the hanging.

When jailers entered the cell, Jereboam, still alive, dramatically cried out: "Tell my Father that my wife and myself are going straight to Heaven—we are dying." But, severely wounded that he was, Jereboam was not dying. Angry jailers dragged him from his cell, his dead wife clasped in his arms.

Jereboam's last moments on earth were intended to entertain the thousands of spectators who had come to the execution, many with picnic baskets, kites, and small children. He had been expected to sit on top of his own coffin in an open cart and be led ceremoniously to the gallows in a nearby field while bugles, fifes, and drums heralded his last ride.

But Jereboam Beauchamp was too weak for that; he disappointed the crowd by riding in a closed carriage, wrapped with a blanket soaked with blood from his wound. He clung to the body of his dead wife in the carriage, saying to her: "Farewell, child of sorrow! For you I have lived; for you I die!"

Jailers and hangman had to help the weakened man up the stairs of the gallows where the rope was placed about his head with much ceremony. Following the custom of the day, hangman, jailers, the crowd, and the condemned man paused from their ghastly chore. They stood silently for moments, Beauchamp supported in a half-swoon, while a band played a popular air of the day, "Bonaparte's Retreat from Moscow," Beauchamp's last request.

Then the hangman kicked open the trap door and Jereboam joined his "child of sorrow." His body was quickly taken down and Beauchamp was placed in his coffin. His wife, Ann, was placed next to him, her head resting on his shoulder.

They were both buried that day outside of Frankfort. A giant flat slab of Kentucky River sandstone was placed above their common grave as a marker. On the stone was chiseled a poem Ann Cooke Beauchamp had written in the Frankfort jail:

He heard her tale of matchless woe,
And burning for revenge he rose,
And laid her base seducer low,
And struck dismay to virtue's foes.

Daughter of virtue! Moist thy tear.
This tomb of love and honor claim;
For thy defense the husband here,
Laid down in youth his life and fame.

BECKER, BARENT
Murderer • (? -1815)

Becker, a farmer living in Mayfield, New York, grew tired of his wife Ann and disposed of her by following an age-old tradition. Becker prepared his specialty, stewed tomatoes, and served it to her loaded with enough arsenic to annihilate a regiment. She consumed the dish with relish and promptly died.

The farmer confessed and was hanged October 6, 1815, after he delivered a maudlin farewell to his relatives from the gallows. A special hymn, which Becker had composed, was sung.

BENDERS, THE
Murderers, Robbers

BACKGROUND: THE BENDER FAMILY, CONSISTING OF FATHER AND MOTHER, AGES APPROXIMATELY 60 AND 50, ONE SON IN THE LATE TWENTIES, AND A DAUGHTER NAMED KATE, ABOUT 23, ARRIVED NEAR CHERRYVALE, IN LABETTE COUNTY, KANSAS, IN 1872 ESTABLISHING AN INN AND GENERAL STORE. DESCRIPTION: ALL FOUR MEMBERS OF THE FAMILY WERE TALL, LARGE-BONED PEOPLE, THOUGHT TO BE GERMAN IMMIGRANTS (THEY ALL SPOKE WITH HEAVY, GUTTURAL ACCENTS). ALIASES: UNKNOWN. RECORD: THE BENDERS FROM 1872–73 KILLED AND ROBBED AT LEAST ELEVEN TRAVELERS WHO STOPPED AT THEIR INN, THE MOST NOTABLE VICTIM BEING DR. WILLIAM YORK; THE

The Benders of Kansas have become the classic American family of murder but when they rode quietly into Cherryvale, in southeastern Kansas in the spring of 1872, no one took any special notice. Like many immigrants of the period, they had come west to make new lives and new fortunes. Their methods were different from those of most homesteaders.

Between the towns of Thayer and Cherryvale, Kansas, the Benders erected a small log cabin, twenty feet long and sixteen feet wide. The one room was divided by a canvas curtain which separated the living room-grocery store-inn from the family bedroom. Old man Bender, his wife, and their dull-witted son spoke little to the strangers who passed their way, selling them canned goods and coffee, with an occasional grunt for a greeting.

Their tall, buxom daughter Kate, however, was outgoing and aggressive. She fancied herself a spiritualist who could contact the dead and cure serious illnesses (for a price). As "Professor Miss Kate Bender," she eventually held public seances.

Kate appeared in several small Kansas towns with her spiritualistic show. She became quite popular with the more rakish members of the audience. Some of these unfortunate men traveled out to the Bender Inn to visit her and never returned.

The alarming aspect of the living arrangements at the Bender inn was a canvas wall. Some travelers complained that as they sat with their backs to the canvas they heard odd noises behind them. One man insisted on sitting on the other side of the table to eat his meal. Kate suddenly grew angry and began to shout at him—"you sit where you are!" He heard whispers behind the canvas and, frightened, jumped up and ran from the inn.

Others were not as intuitive. If an overnight guest appeared to be wealthy, he was given a hearty meat-and-potatoes meal by Kate and as he ate, Old Man Bender or his son, wielding a sledge hammer, would direct a savage blow against the spot of canvas where the traveler's head rested, instantly crushing his skull.

The body was then dragged beneath the canvas and the corpse was stripped. A trap door leading to a small earthen cellar was thrown open and the body was then dumped into this area until the Benders could find time to bury the victim on the prairie.

This murder system worked well for eighteen months. Then Dr. William York stopped at the inn in the spring of 1873. He had stopped there before and had informed his brother, Colonel York, whom he had been visiting at Fort Scott, that he would again stay with the Benders on his return trip.

Dr. York never reached his home. Shortly after his disappearance, Colonel York arrived at the Bender home, asking about his brother. He knew his brother had stayed with them. Had they seen him?

Father Bender said no, Dr. York never visited their humble inn. "Maybe it's the Indians," he muttered. "And Jesse James is about, you know."

To allay Colonel York's suspicions, Bender and his son offered to help drag a stream not far from the inn.

Colonel York thanked them and rode away. The Benders were now alarmed; one of their victims had been trailed right to their doorstep. They wasted no time. On May 5, 1873, they cleared out, taking their cattle with them.

York, still suspicious, returned to the Bender place five days later with a posse. Finding the inn deserted, York entered the building. He inspected the cellar, noting with alarm that the earthen floor was coated with dried blood. The stench was overpowering.

Then York inspected the open fields about the inn. He found eleven oblong mounds of earth. "Boys," he said slowly, "those look like graves." The posse began to dig and Colonel York was proved correct. The mutilated corpse of his brother was in the first grave opened.

A frantic search by dozens of posses throughout Kansas then began, but the Benders had too much of a head start and were never officially found. They had robbed close to $10,000 from their victims, it was estimated, a small fortune for those days, one which could take them anywhere in comfort. Authorities searched for fifty years for the Benders without success. Once, in 1889, two women identified as Kate and Ma Bender were extradited to Kansas from Detroit but their identification was incomplete and a trial was never held.

It was later claimed that a small posse did catch up with the bloodthirsty family and killed them, shooting them and then burning their bodies, saving Kate for the last and burning her alive—a deed so horrible that the posse members vowed silence. This report was never confirmed.

BILLINGTON, JOHN
Murderer • (? -1630)

John Billington's singular though infamous distinction as an American criminal was permanently established when he became this country's first murderer, arriving with the original band of 102 pilgrims on the *Mayflower* at Plymouth Rock in 1620.

Billington and his family came from London—a rowdy, foul-speaking lot who more than once on the voyage over had been reprimanded by Captain Miles Standish. The good Captain, finding Billington's blasphemous harangues more than he could stand, had the offender's feet and neck tied together as an example of a sin-struck man possessed of a Devil's tongue.

This humiliating and painful punishment did not soften Billington's rough ways. He continued to be the black sheep of the Pilgrim colony at Plymouth, starting violent arguments and fights. One of John Billington's bitterest enemies was John Newcomen, a neighboring settler. Their feud raged for a number of years until 1630 when Billington decided to end it with murder.

Hiding behind a rock, Billington waited in the woods until Newcomen, hunting for game, appeared. Leveling his blunderbuss, Billington shot and killed him at close range. He was quickly tried by the little band of pilgrims and hanged.

Ironically, dozens of present-day Americans lay claim to being related to Billington, murderer or not.

BOISE, THOMAS
Murderer • (? –1864)

Normally Thomas Boise was only a common drunk whose antics in Wood County, West Va. served to annoy local residents. One night, however, Boise, while in the company of Mortimore Gibbony and Daniel Grogan, drank himself into a rage and, following a chance remark, shot Abram Deem, a local farmer.

The three men were tried; Gibbony escaped. Boise and Grogan were scheduled to hang in Parkersburg, West Va., but a curious problem developed. Each prisoner argued passionately with the sheriff that the other should be hanged first. The sheriff attempted to hang them both at the same time but the rope broke. Grogan, yelling he had a right to watch Boise die, was then hanged first while his partner laughed madly. Gibbony was apprehended later and hanged.

BOLTON, CHARLES E.
("BLACK BART")
Stagerobber • (Circa 1820- ?)

BACKGROUND: BORN AND RAISED IN RURAL UPSTATE NEW YORK. MOVED WITH HIS PARENTS TO THE WEST AT AGE 10. LEGITIMATE OCCUPATION UNKNOWN. DESCRIPTION: TALL, BLUE EYES, WHITE HAIR, ERECT MILITARY BEARING. ALIASES: BLACK BART. RECORD: ROBBED THE WELLS FARGO STAGE OUTSIDE OF FORT ROSS, CALIF. NEAR THE RUSSIAN RIVER 8/3/1877 ($605.52 IN CASH AND CHECKS); STOPPED AND ROBBED THE QUINCEY TO OROVILLE, CALIF. STAGE 7/26/78 ($379 IN CASH AND COIN, A $200 DIAMOND RING AND $25 WATCH); ROBBED THE WELLS FARGO STAGE MONTHS LATER BETWEEN SONORA AND MILTON NEAR COPPEROPOLIS ($4,800); TRACED THROUGH A LAUNDRY MARK AND ARRESTED WEEKS LATER; CONFESSED AND SENTENCED TO A SHORT PRISON TERM IN THE STATE PENITENTIARY; DISAPPEARED UPON BEING PAROLED; DATE OF DEATH UNKNOWN.

He was a tired old man, almost sixty, when he began stopping stages, but he was a joker at heart. Charles E. Bolton, better known to the West as "Black Bart," always had enough energy to scribble out some insulting doggerel which he left to vex his pursuers.

Little is known of Bolton's beginnings or even middle life. He moved West with his family at age ten around 1830–31. He was believed to have been first a farmer and then a medicine drummer. He finally settled for city life, moving periodically between Los Angeles and San Francisco with occasional trips into the gold fields to seek his fortune.

The gold fields were panned out by the time Bolton got there and his dreams of luxury were fast fading. Yet Bolton still emulated the rich in dress and manner; he read good books, lived in fancy hotels, wore stylish clothes. To finance these pleasures, Bolton had simply become

Charles E. Bolton, best known along the California trails of the late 1870s as the hooded stagerobber, Black Bart. (Western History Collection, U. of Okla. Library)

Black Bart, the terror of California's Wells Fargo stages, a strange-looking robber who never fired a shot.

Bart first struck August 3, 1877, when he stopped the stage from Fort Ross. His appearance, rather than the rifle he pointed, frightened the driver. Bart was wearing a long, ghostly-looking white duster. Over his head was a flour sack with holes poked through for his eyes.

At this time, as upon all other occasions, Bart snorted only one order: "Throw down the box!" The Wells Fargo box—a small safe made of wood, reinforced by iron and padlocked—was thrown down and Bart joyfully scurried off to his horse with its contents, $300 in cash and a check for $305.52.

A posse found the box days later while combing the brush near the site of the holdup. Inside it, they discovered a note written by the bandit. It read:

I've labored long and hard for bread,
For honor and for riches
But on my corns too long you've tred,
You fine-haired sons-of-bitches.

Beneath this bit of doggerel was the odd signature, "Black

Bart, PO-8," which served to only further mystify the lawmen.

The meager haul was apparently enough to satisfy Bart for almost a year. He did not strike again until July 26, 1878, when he stopped the stage to Oroville, Calif. He wore the same outfit, the duster and flour sack. His voice, as during the previous holdup, was described by the driver as "hollow and deep." He made off with the strong box which contained $379. This time he took a passenger's $200 diamond ring and a $25 gold watch.

Again, lawmen found a note waiting for them in the empty box. Black Bart had written:

Here I lay me down to sleep
To wait the coming morrow,
Perhaps success, perhaps defeat
And everlasting sorrow,
Yet come what will, I'll try it once,
My conditions can't be worse,
And if there's money in that box,
'Tis munney in my purse.

It would be Bart's last jeer at the law and the Wells Fargo express stages. While attempting another holdup, the Sonora stage bound for Milton, Bart ran into trouble. Moments after the strongbox had been thrown down to him he cut his hand while trying to break it open. He covered the wound with a handkerchief. Just then a lone rider came down the road.

Using the rider's gun, the stagedriver fired at Bart and he barely managed to get away with the $4,800 cash shipment. But he had dropped his handkerchief and the Pinkertons, finding a laundry mark on it, traced it to a laundry (they checked through ninety establishments before having any success). It belonged to an elderly gentleman named Charles E. Bolton.

He was quickly taken into custody. Bolton confessed to the robberies but became indignant when detectives called him an outlaw. "I am a gentleman," he said, and twirled his gold-knobbed cane for good measure.

Bolton was sent to the California State penitentiary but, because of his advanced age, was soon released. The last report of him came from Nevada where he was seeking a new fortune.

BONNEY, WILLIAM H. ("BILLY THE KID")
Robber, Murderer • (1859-1881)

BACKGROUND: BORN IN NEW YORK CITY, 11/23/1859. MOVED WITH HIS PARENTS TO COFFEYVILLE, KAN. IN 1862, AND THEN TO COLORADO UPON THE DEATH OF WM. BONNEY, SR. NO PUBLIC EDUCATION. MOVED WEST WHILE STILL A TEENAGER THROUGH TEX., ARIZ., N.M., AND MEXICO. ORIGINAL OCCUPATION, COWBOY. DESCRIPTION: 5'7", BLUE EYES, LIGHT BROWN HAIR, SLENDER. ALIASES: NONE. RECORD: REPORTEDLY SHOT AND KILLED TWENTY-ONE MEN BY THE TIME OF HIS TWENTY-FIRST BIRTHDAY, INCLUDING AN UNKNOWN GUNFIGHTER IN COFFEYVILLE WHEN HE WAS FOURTEEN, THREE APACHE BRAVES ON THE CHIRACAHUA RESERVATION IN ARIZONA A FEW YEARS LATER, A NEGRO BLACKSMITH IN CAMP BOWIE, THREE CARD DEALERS IN MEXICO, TWO MORE INDIANS IN THE GUADA-LUPE MOUNTAINS, COWBOYS BILLY MORTON, FRANK BAKER, AND ANDREW L. "BUCKSHOT" ROBERTS in 1876, SHERIFF WILLIAM BRADY AND HIS DEPUTY GEORGE HINDMAN 4/1/78 CATTLEMAN ROBERT W. BECKWITH 7/17/78, GUNMEN JOE GRANT AND JIMMY CARLYLE SOMETIME IN 1879; INDIAN AGENT JOSEPH BERNSTEIN; DEPUTIES AND WARDENS J. W. BELL AND ROBERT W. OLLINGER AS HE ESCAPED FROM THE MESILLA, N.M. JAIL 4/28/81. SHOT AND KILLED BY SHERIFF PAT GARRETT 7/14/81 ON THE MAXWELL RANCH NEAR FORT SUMNER, N.M. A LITTLE MORE THAN FOUR MONTHS BEFORE HIS TWENTY-SECOND BIRTHDAY.

Of all the legends of the Old West, that of Billy the Kid is the most confusing and impenetrable, so laced is it with dime novel romance, heroic embellishments, and fabulous fiction created by his own friends and enemies. Almost from birth, Billy was a migrant, a drifter who aimlessly rode through the West without roots, family, or purpose. His travels were rarely documented, and attempting to record his life is similar to watching the flashing, powdery cards of an old crank-

Billy the Kid, the great legend of the West. (Western History Collection, U. of Okla. Library)

handled penny peep show machine: the image is there but it is only a fascinating blur, devilishly designed, it seems, by those who insist on perpetuating a sort of noble glory of the Old West, Billy's West. This is the story, shored up with the shaky timbers of the Kid's own legend.

The New York City tenement in which William H. Bonney was born November 23, 1859 was crowded and seamy with poverty and disease; it was no wonder that Bill Bonney moved his wife and son to Coffeyville, Kan. in 1862 to escape. He died there and his widow moved again to Colorado where she married mine-worker William Antrim.

Antrim was a wanderlusting man who yearned to strike it big on his own. He moved the family to Silver City, N.M., where he again worked the mines. Mrs. Antrim ran a small boarding house. Little Billy played in the mud-caked streets, learning the rough ways of streetfighters and gunslingers at an early age. There was no school in Silver City; Billy's education consisted of petty thefts, bloody, knockdown streetfights, and visions of violent, drunken men shooting each other to death.

According to one of Mrs. Antrim's boarders, Ash Upson, a rowdy gunfighter named Ed Moulton took a liking to wild little Billy. He became the self-appointed protector of Billy and his mother while old man Antrim was away working the mines. One day, when Billy was fourteen, a drunk called his mother a name. The boy hit him and then tried to club him with a rock. But the bully was too big to fight and Billy ran. The drunk after him. Ed Moulton stepped in and knocked the man flat.

The boy showed his gratitude to Moulton weeks later when he found two men fighting with his protector. Using a pen knife, Billy repeatedly stabbed one of the men in the back until he died. Even in the free-wheeling Silver City of 1871, Billy's action was branded murder; he needed Moulton's help to escape capture, riding out alone into the Wild West to seek his fortune.

The years between Billy's fourteenth and seventeenth birthdays are sketchy. Information about his whereabouts and activities is documented only by pamphleteers whose facts concerning the Kid were fanciful and unreliable. Ash

Upson, who later collaborated with Pat Garrett, Billy's killer, on a highly romanticized version of the Kid's life, portrayed him as a one-man army of righteous wrath slaying hordes of venomous Indians and crooked Mexican card dealers.

Upson and Garrett insisted that the teenager would take offense from no man in these apprentice-gunslinger years. A Negro blacksmith, they stated, was playing cards with Billy in Camp Bowie and the Kid caught him cheating. "You're a Billy Goat," the blacksmith roared when Billy confronted him. The Kid's gun roared and the blacksmith was sent to eternity with a bullet in his forehead.

When the Government opened up public lands in Southeastern New Mexico, the rush was on. Along with armies of bad men from Texas and points north who came to fleece and rob the homesteaders, cattlemen and farmers raced for their parcels of earth. Billy went with them, showing up in Lincoln County around 1875 where he went to work for an immense ranch owned by L. G. Murphy and J. J. Dolan. These men were in open battle with another giant ranch run by Alexander McSween and an Englishman, John Tunstall. McSween and Tunstall had the support of the great cattle baron, John Chisum.

The Kid's work for the Murphy-Dolan forces consisted of rustling Chisum's cattle from his Jinglebob Ranch. These Murphy sold to the Indians.

Billy probably would have continued being nothing more than a rowdy ranch hand, had it not been for his accidental meeting with the sophisticated John Tunstall. The Englishman was refined, educated, and humane: something new to the West. He was a gentleman rancher who told Billy he would have a great future in cattle. Billy idolized him and went to work at his ranch near the Rio Feliz.

There was nothing Billy wouldn't do for Tunstall. The Kid once remarked that "he [Tunstall] was the only man that ever treated me like I was free-born and white." According to George Coe, a cowpuncher in the area, Tunstall gladly repaid the compliment, stating: "That's the finest lad I ever met. He's a revelation to me every day and would do anything on earth to please me. I'm going to make a man of that boy yet."

Tunstall never got the chance. A so-called posse made up of Murphy-Dolan riders stopped him on the morning of February 18, 1878, as he was returning to his ranch from Lincoln. Sheriff William Brady, a Murphy-Dolan man, had deputized a band of gunslingers who rode against the McSween-Tunstall combine, most of them Billy's friends before he switched sides—Billy Morton, Frank Baker, Jesse Evans, and Jim McDaniel.

Evans told Tunstall they had orders to take a part of his herd, that the cattle belonged to Murphy. When the Englishman objected, the posse men pulled out their guns and ordered Tunstall to surrender. The Englishman told them that he did not want any bloodshed. He dismounted and handed over his six-gun but as he did so, Jesse Evans sent a bullet into him. Then, as he pitched forward, Billy Morton fired a shot into Tunstall's head, killing him.

Billy the Kid was roaring mad at Tunstall's murder; the gentle Englishman had been a father-figure to him, the only man for whom he had felt genuine love. Vengeance hissed through his gritted teeth as he watched Tunstall lowered in his grave: "I'll get every son-of-a-bitch who helped kill John if it's the last thing I do."

The Murphy-Dolan clan heard of Billy's oath and did not take it lightly. The slender, buck-toothed boy was fast on the draw, awfully fast; this they knew. He was cagey, too, an expert bushwacker. Some reported that the phony possemen still believed Billy was their friend. He had ridden with them and that should count for something.

In the Kid's mind, it added up to nothing. He caught up with Baker and Morton at a place aptly called Dead Man's Hole, a watering spot between Lincoln and Roswell, N.M. Billy sent each to his Maker, firing only one bullet at each man. Next came Andrew L. "Buckshot" Roberts, a Murphy lieutenant.

The Kid, along with Dick Brewer, Charlie Bowdre and George Coe, trapped Roberts at Blazer's Sawmill. The doomed man, just before the Kid's gang rode up, picked this unfortunate moment to answer nature's call and he found himself surrounded in an outhouse. Roberts, however, hadn't neglected to take his rifle and six-gun with him and he put up a great fight from the unlikely bastion. Brewer was killed outright. Bowdre and Coe were wounded.

Such was the intensity of Roberts' gunfire that he actually drove off the band, but Billy fired a parting shot which proved lucky and fatal to "Buckshot" Roberts.

Tunstall's murderers were dying right and left before the Kid's guns, but the man who engineered the Englishman's murder, Sheriff Brady of Lincoln, was still alive. Billy the Kid announced that he would correct this oversight.

On April 1, 1878, waiting in ambush behind an adobe wall in Lincoln, the Kid and some others watched as Sheriff Brady and his three deputies—George Hindman, George W. "Dad" Peppin and Billy Matthews—walked out into the noonday sun, heading for the courthouse.

Billy took aim at Brady's back and then fired several shots into the Sheriff who toppled forward, dead. Hindman was next and the Kid's shots hit him several times. He crawled to the front of the Church of San Juan. Dad Peppin and Matthews took cover and began answering the rapid fire unleashed by the Kid and his gang.

Suddenly, Billy leaped over the wall and darted for Brady's body. As he ran he heard the mortally wounded Hindman cry out for water but kept going: the sheriff's expensive weapons were the Kid's goal, especially Brady's shiny new Winchester rifle. A few moments after he picked up the rifle, a well-aimed shot from Billy Matthews slammed into his hand. The Kid dropped the weapon and raced back to the cover of the adobe wall: After a final glance at his victims, he ordered his gang to retreat.

Brady and Hindman brought the count of Billy's dead to seventeen; he was eighteen years old. There were four more deaths to go, according to the legend, and three more years to live.

Sixteen days after Brady and Hindman were murdered, Peppin became the new sheriff and led a huge posse against the Kid's fourteen-member gang, who were barricaded in Alexander McSween's mansion. Thousands of rounds of ammunition were spent as each side shot it out for three days. (Some say five days.)

A troop of cavalry from Fort Stanton then arrived under the command of Col. Nathan Dudley to make peace. The colonel ordered a small cannon trained on the McSween home before calling for a cease fire. During the lull, Peppin's men sneaked behind the mansion and put it to the torch. The Kid, seeing the mounting flames, told his men to run for it.

McSween dashed from the rear of the building carrying only a Bible. Bob Beckwith, a cattleowner deputized by Dad Peppin, shot McSween down in cold blood. The Kid came upon the scene and cursed wildly as he emptied his six-shooter into Beckwith, killing him. Somehow the Kid escaped both posse and cavalry.

Billy was running fast now, indicted for the murder of Sheriff Brady and wanted all over New Mexico. He stopped long enough to steal horses from the Mescalero Indian Reservation; when government agent Morris J. Bernstein tried to stop him, he was shot dead in his tracks.

The Lincoln County war had spread throughout New Mexico, and an anxious President Hayes replaced Governor Axtell with Lew Wallace. Just after Wallace took office, the Kid was watching when Huston Chapman, a lawyer for the McSween faction, was shot down on the streets of Lincoln; William Matthews, William Campbell and James Dolan did the killing. But instead of going for his six-gun, Billy unexplainably rode to see Governor Wallace, offering himself as a witness against the three murderers.

Perhaps the Kid's move was not so puzzling after all, but a shrewdly thought-out plan. When Wallace took over the state, he declared a general amnesty for all those who had participated in the Lincoln County war. This applied to everyone except those who had been indicted for murder, which meant Billy the Kid. By turning state's evidence, however, the Kid hoped to obtain a full pardon.

Wallace and Billy met on March 17, 1879, in the home of one John B. Wilson. The Kid walked through the front door promptly at 9 a.m., the designated time. In his left hand was a menacing Winchester rifle, in the other a six-gun.

"I was sent for to meet the Governor at nine o'clock. Is he here?"

Wallace looked the boy over, finding it hard to believe that he was the most devastating killer in the far West. "I'm Governor Wallace."

"Your note gave me a promise of absolute protection," Billy said glancing about.

"Yes," Wallace nodded. "And I've been true to my promise." Wallace pointed to John Wilson. "This man, whom, of course, you know, and I are the only persons in the house."

The two men then made a deal. If Billy would surrender and testify against Huston Chapman's killers the Governor promised to set him free with a full pardon.

Billy didn't like the idea of surrendering. It was against his personal code, he said. It would look terrible to the folks in Lincoln.

He would be arrested then, the Governor said. The arrest would be phony but appear genuine to the residents of Lincoln. Billy agreed on that condition.

In a matter of weeks, Billy was arrested in Lincoln. As a star witness he was wined and dined in a local store where he was kept prisoner. The Kid testified against Matthews, Dolan and Campbell, but he didn't stop there. He provided lawmen with complete details on the operations and identities of dozens of outlaws then in New Mexico. His non-stop tongue defied the code of silence, but with all the publicity he was receiving, William Bonney must have realized he was above such breaches of criminal conduct; he was Billy the Kid and he did as he pleased.

He also ignored part of his bargain with Wallace. He had agreed to stand trial for the shooting of Sheriff Brady. The Governor had promised that he would be set free, but Billy distrusted Wallace. One day he merely walked out of the store where he was kept "prisoner," and rode off on somebody else's horse, heading for Fort Sumner where he had friends.

At Fort Sumner, Billy ran smack into a Texas gunman named Joe Grant. Billy's reputation as a gunfighter had spread throughout the West by then and Grant decided to face him down. First, the two got roaring drunk, or, at least, Grant did. Billy, pretending to be drunk, praised Grant's courage and told him how much he admired Grant's expensive six-gun. Grant, at Billy's request, showed the Kid his weapon. While fondling it, the Kid turned the barrel around to an empty chamber, so the story goes, and when the two did draw on each other, Grant's gun only clicked and Billy's went off with a roar. Scratch Joe Grant.

After making some raids for horses and a few dollars

around White Oaks, N.M., Billy and his band were holed up in a ranchhouse. A posse rode up and a terrific gun battle ensued. Hours later, the Kid shouted from a window: "I want to talk about surrendering."

Gunslinger Jimmy Carlyle, who knew Billy, said he would negotiate for the posse and stepped from cover. The Kid shot him dead. This was enough to scare off the posse and Billy's gang leisurely rode out of the area.

Until Pat Garrett was elected sheriff of Lincoln County in 1880, the residents despaired of ever ridding the area of Billy the Kid. Garrett had known Billy well when they had run steers for old Pete Maxwell near Fort Sumner. They had been pals (Garrett later stated), drinking and gambling in town together on their days off.

Garrett went after the Kid almost from the moment he pinned on his badge. Governor Wallace wanted him brought in, offering a $500 reward for his capture. Garrett came close one night after setting a trap near Fort Sumner.

The Kid's right-hand man, Tom O'Folliard, was riding point that night and he ran straight into Garrett's posse. A dozen guns barked and O'Folliard toppled from his horse dead. Billy and the others reined up when they heard the shots and rode off in a different direction.

But the six-foot-four-inch Garrett was a determined man and days later, on December 21, 1880, his men surrounded a deserted farmhouse at Stinking Spring. Trapped inside were Billy the Kid, Tom Pickett, Charlie Bowdre, Dave Rudabaugh and Billy Wilson. Garrett called for their surrender. The Kid and his gang answered with a roar of guns. The posse let them have it, peppering the house with intense fire from rifles and six-guns. There was a scream. Charlie Bowdre was hit several times as he tried to cross in front of an open window.

Brutally, Billy propped Bowdre up and threw open the farmhouse door, shoving his wounded friend outside. The Kid shouted after Bowdre: "They have murdered you, Charlie, but you can get revenge! Kill some of the sons-of-bitches before you go!" Charlie Bowdre wasn't killing anyone. He barely had the strength to take a few steps forward before he fell on his face, murmuring, "I wish . . . I wish . . . I wish . . ." Both sides resumed firing over Bowdre's corpse.

Garrett finally called off the siege and withdrew a hundred yards or so where he and his men made camp. The big sheriff decided to starve out Billy and his band. Days later, panting for water and food, the gang surrendered. Garrett brought the Kid and his gang into Santa Fe where he was thrown in jail and placed under heavy guard.

Billy fired off a letter to Governor Wallace reminding him of his promise to set him free. Wallage ignored the Kid's plea and told newsmen that Billy had run away before standing trial for the Brady killing. All deals were off. The Kid was soon taken to Mesilla, N.M., where he was tried for killing Buckshot Roberts.

Mesilla looked to be the end of the line. Billy was convicted of the Roberts murder and Judge Warren Bristol dramatically sentenced him to hang until "you are dead, dead, dead."

One story reports that Billy, upon hearing the sentence, turned defiantly in court while being led away and shouted: "And you can go to hell, hell, hell."

The famous bandit consented to give the *Mesilla News* an interview at which time he said that "mob law" had convicted him, that he hadn't anticipated a fair trial nor a proper execution. "I expect to be lynched," he said sarcastically. "It's wrong that I should be the only one to suffer the extreme penalties of the law." He was referring to all those who had fought in the Lincoln County war, and he was proved right. Billy the Kid was the only warrior surviving that battle who was tried and convicted.

Two of Garrett's top guns, J. W. Bell and Bob Ollinger, were sent to bring Billy back to Lincoln. The two guards brought him back in an open buckboard. Ollinger, who had fought with the Murphy-Dolan faction during the Lincoln County war, hated Billy and kept poking him with a shotgun.

Somewhat of a sadist, Ollinger encouraged his prisoner to escape. "I can save you from the hangman," he reportedly urged the Kid. "Just make a run for it . . . I'd love putting a load of buckshot in your back!"

Bell had to keep telling Ollinger to "leave the Kid alone" on the trip back to Lincoln. Billy sat quietly in the buckboard taking Ollinger's insults without comment. In Lin-

Garrett bringing in
Billy the Kid.
(Mercaldo Archives)

coln, he was placed in the old Murphy Store which was used as a courthouse and jail. He was shackled hand and foot and placed in a second-story cell.

Ollinger sat outside the cell taunting him every day, telling him how it would be with the hangman. Billy said nothing.

Early in the afternoon of April 28, 1881, the Kid somehow got hold of a pistol and shot Bell dead. How he managed this is speculative. One story reported that he asked Bell to help him to the outside latrine and, when returning to the courthouse, pushed Bell down with his shoulder. While wearing leg irons, the Kid hobbled into Garrett's gun room, snatched up a pistol, and shot Bell dead as

he came running inside. Another story reports that a Mexican girl who was in love with Billy had hidden the gun in the latrine.

Ollinger, who was drinking beer in a local bar down the street, heard the shot and went on the run to the courthouse. As he approached the building, he heard a friendly voice call out "hello, Bob." He turned to see Billy the Kid holding his shotgun straight at his head. The manacles on Billy's hands clanked as he pulled back the triggers. Ollinger, petrified, could only wait for the blast. When it came he was hurtled far into the street. A handyman walked in on Billy and the Kid ordered him to find an axe; when the man returned with the tool, Billy grabbed it and smashed the irons from his legs and arms. He took a Winchester and several pistols from the gun room.

Mounting a horse tethered outside, the Kid rode up to Ollinger's body and dropped the shotgun next to it. The few townspeople who had dared to come onto the street did nothing but stare at the boy bandit. He smiled at them, swept off his hat and shouted: *"Adios, compadres!"* Then he rode off.

The daring escape received thunderous press, most of the newspapers off-handedly praising the Kid for getting away and doing in his tormentor, Ollinger. Billy escaped two weeks ahead of the hangman, but he could not put enough distance between himself and Pat Garrett.

The sheriff was a strong-jawed lawman who prided himself on fair play and his ability to enforce the laws of New Mexico. He organized a posse and once again rode after Billy the Kid. For three months he tracked and re-tracked the Kid's movements. Finally, on the bright moonlight night of July 14, 1881, following a tip, Garrett had his man. He found Billy on the old Maxwell ranch where they had spent so many good days together in the past.

According to Garrett, he went into a bedroom which opened on the front of the main ranch house and sat waiting on the bed. Some of his possemen waited outside in the front, lurking in the shadows.

Billy came out of another room facing the long front porch and moved down the porchway trying to distinguish the figures in the shadows. He carried, according to Garrett, a pistol and a long hunting knife. Posseman John Poe heard him call out *"Quien es?"* (Who is it?) No one answered.

Billy kept moving down the porch. *"Quien es? . . . Quien es?"* he repeated in a loud whisper. A figure moved in the shadows and the Kid suddenly backed into the front bedroom where Garrett waited. Two shots rang out. Garrett stated that Billy had turned when inside the room and saw him: ". . . he came there armed with a pistol and knife expressly to kill me if he could . . . I had no alternative but to kill him, or suffer death at his hands."

Garrett's first shot ploughed into Billy slightly above the heart, killing him instantly. The second shot missed.

In a few moments, the possemen were startled to see Sheriff Pat Garrett run from the bedroom, screaming, "I killed the Kid! I killed the Kid!"

Garrett stood in front of the house and trembled. Then he returned to the bedroom. Pretty Deluvina Maxwell was cradling the lifeless body in her arms. She looked up at Garrett and spat: "You didn't have the nerve to kill him face to face."

Some called it murder but a coroner's jury acquitted Garrett's act as "justifiable homicide." The $500 reward for Billy's capture did not come easy. Garrett had to have his friends in the state legislature pass a special act before he received it. The lawman lived an up and down life after that and was himself shot to death on February 29, 1908, by an angry tenant who had been working on his land.

Billy was buried first at the Maxwell ranch. Deluvina dressed him in a borrowed white shirt five sizes too big for him. The girl had a cross made for his grave. The marker bore her words *Duerme bien, Querido* (Sleep well, beloved). His body was later removed, to avoid the thousands of curious souvenir hunters, to a common grave near Fort Sumner where his remains were placed with two of his old gang, Tom O'Folliard and Charlie Bowdre. The word "Pals" was etched into the stone years later.

Lawman Pat Garrett: "I had no alternative but to kill him . . ." (National Archives)

Whether or not Billy the Kid killed twenty-one men in his twenty-one years is no longer important; neither is debate over his slayings and his fast draw. What is important is that history, in his case, insists upon a legend gigantic and solid, romantic and dashing. So be it.

BOOTH, JOHN WILKES
Assassin • (1839-1865)

BACKGROUND: BORN AND RAISED IN MARYLAND. TRAINED AS AN ACTOR FROM CHILDHOOD BY FATHER JUNIUS BRUTUS BOOTH AND OLDER BROTHER EDWIN BOOTH, THE MOST RENOWNED ACTORS OF THE ERA. DESCRIPTION: 5'7", DARK BROWN EYES, BLACK HAIR, SOLIDLY BUILT. ALIASES: UNKNOWN. RECORD: SHOT AND KILLED PRESIDENT ABRAHAM LINCOLN AT FORD'S THEATRE IN WASHINGTON, D.C., 4/14/1865 AS PART OF A CONSPIRACY TO ELIMINATE UNION LEADERS PURPORTEDLY ON BEHALF OF THE CONFEDERACY; FELLOW CONSPIRATORS INCLUDED GEORGE ATZERODT, LEWIS PAINE, MARY E. SURRATT, DAVID E. HEROLD (ALL HANGED AFTER BEING TRIED AND CONVICTED BY A MILITARY COMMISSION; LINCOLN'S ASSASSINATION WAS CONSIDERED A MILITARY CRIME AT THE TIME SINCE HE WAS COMMANDER-IN-CHIEF OF THE ARMY ESSENTIALLY STILL AT WAR); PAINE (BORN LEWIS THORNTON POWELL) ALSO ATTEMPTED TO MURDER SECRETARY OF STATE WILLIAM SEWARD ON THE NIGHT OF LINCOLN'S ASSASSINATION BUT ONLY SUCCEEDED IN WOUNDING HIM WITH A KNIFE; BOOTH TRACKED DOWN BY UNION TROOPS IN A BARN OWNED BY RICHARD GARRETT LOCATED BETWEEN PORT ROYAL AND BOWLING GREEN, VA., 4/26/65, WHERE HE WAS SHOT AND KILLED. BOOTH'S CO-LEADER IN THE CONSPIRACY, JOHN H. SURRATT, A CONFEDERATE SPY, ESCAPED THE COUNTRY UNDER MYSTERIOUS CIRCUMSTANCES AND WHEN ULTIMATELY CAPTURED AND RETURNED TO THE U.S. WAS SET FREE AFTER AN EQUALLY MYSTERIOUS (AND DUBIOUS) TRIAL.

He was mad with his own ego, possessed of a theatrical vanity that gnawed incessantly for fame. As an actor, John Wilkes Booth already owned national recognition, but he lusted after a kind of immortality completely unrelated to his profession. He desperately wanted to be remembered as a political and military hero, a savior of his romanticized version of the Old South.

John Wilkes Booth, the actor turned assassin who thought of himself as the South's avenging angel. (National Archives)

His assassination of President Lincoln earned him the contempt and wrath of the country and a perpetual infamy husbanded by all succeeding American generations. His was a fatal miscalculation of history's judgment.

As a young man—he was twenty-six years old at the time of the assassination—Booth's acting career soared whenever he played the theaters of the South before the war. He enjoyed a popularity few actors could claim with discerning Southern audiences. He was the darling of the plantation owners whose linen-suited, cultured, leisurely lives he wished to emulate. Swimming through the cream of Southern society, Booth became convinced that slavery was necessary and good.

When the Civil War broke out, Booth, however, did not rush to enlist in Confederate ranks, but stayed in the North. There, though he continued to act, his success was not equal to the flowery, pompous praise once showered upon him by his Confederate friends. He grew bitter. Then angry. As the Union forces steadily crushed the Southern armies, his words of sympathy for the South became louder; he flaunted his support for Jefferson Davis and Robert E. Lee. His public dismissed his remarks as those typical of an eccentric but talented actor.

Some did not shrug off Booth's Southern sympathies so lightly. Samuel B. Arnold, 28, and Michael O'Laughlin, 27, two of Booth's boyhood friends, listened intently to Booth's ravings against Lincoln after he sought them out in Baltimore, Md. in September, 1864. Booth hatched an insane plot to kidnap President Lincoln and turn him over to Confederate authorities, so that the President could be ransomed for Southern prisoners and possibly a negotiated peace.

Arnold and O'Laughlin had once served in the Confederate army—Arnold had left because of illness, O'Laughlin had deserted—and both agreed that John Wilkes Booth had a plan that might bring their side victory. Booth's plot had been developed slowly, until he became convinced that it could bring success. He had written a relative months before: "My love (as things stand today) is for the South alone. Nor do I deem it a dishonor in attempting to make for her a prisoner of this man [Lincoln], to whom she owes so much misery."

Booth's successful theatrical career had made him a rich man. He threw money about wildly while discussing his kidnapping plan with Arnold and O'Laughlin, promising them small fortunes if they would participate. They agreed and waited for the actor to enlarge his group of conspirators.

The next recruit was the mysterious John H. Surratt, 20, a wily, highly intelligent Confederate spy whose mother owned and operated a boarding house in Washington, D.C.

Mary E. Surratt, in whose boarding house the Lincoln conspirators met; many argued for her innocence but she was hanged nevertheless. (U.S. Signal Corps, Brady Collection)

Booth had met Surratt through a Maryland landowner, Dr. Samuel A. Mudd. The spy agreed to work with Booth and enlisted two more men, George Atzerodt, 33, and David Herold, 23.

Atzerodt was a coachmaker who knew the waters of the Potomac River well; he had ferried contraband to the South at Port Tobacco which was along the route Booth intended to take the kidnapped President. Herold had no special ability but he idolized Booth and his role seemed to be that of soothing the actor's megalomania. Herold had been a drugstore clerk in Washington but was incapable of holding that or any other job. Doctors examining him later reported that he was feeble-minded, possessing the mental age of an 11-year-old.

The last, and perhaps the most important addition to Booth's kidnapping ring was Lewis Paine, 20, a giant of a man who had broken away from the domination of his father, a Baptist minister. Paine, born Lewis Thornton Powell, was mentally disturbed and has been described as a "half-wit" by doctors and historians. The only subject that seemed to jar him from his melancholy moods was the kidnapping of President Lincoln. He hated the Union and Negroes.

Paine had fought on the Confederate side at Gettysburg, had been severely wounded and captured. After a daring escape, he went to Baltimore. There police answered the screams of a Negro maid who was beaten half to death by Paine on a dark street. He was ordered by authorities to leave the city.

Booth met with these six men on the night of March 17, 1865, in a Washington saloon. The actor was careful to pay for all the food and liquor consumed by the group, which enthusiastically debated the plot. At this time, John Surratt began to argue that abducting Lincoln was too risky; there were guards all around him. Booth insisted that his kidnapping plan was sound. He had learned that the President would visit the Soldier's Home in three days. They could waylay and take him there, he told the group.

Surratt finally agreed to this plan and the plotters assembled to kidnap Lincoln three days later. The President, who had been having "premonitions," however, changed his plans and the kidnapping fizzled.

The next month Lee surrendered to Grant in Virginia. Booth was incensed. He now concluded that the only way

Lewis Paine botched his assignment to kill Secretary of State Seward. (U.S. Signal Corps, Brady Collection)

to deliver the South from the Union was to kill Lincoln. Hastily, he summoned the conspirators together. His plan called for the assassination of Lincoln by himself, the killing of Vice President Johnson by Atzerodt and the murdering of Secretary of State William Seward by Paine.

The conspirators struck on the evening of April 14, 1865. Ten days before, the President had had a dream where he saw his own assassination. He joked about it later, telling his wife, Mary: "What does anybody want to assassinate me for? If anyone wants to do so, he can do it any day or night, if he is ready to give his life for mine. It is nonsense."

As the light comedy *Our American Cousins* was being played out on the stage of Ford's Theater, John Wilkes Booth walked quietly down a Washington Street and into Taltavul's bar. Hours before, in the darkened theater, he had bored a small hole in the door leading to the Presidential box, knowing Lincoln would attend that night. He had also arranged to have a horse waiting for him outside the theater. An illiterate chore boy, "Peanuts" John Burrough, was, at the moment, holding onto the horse's reins at the theater's side entrance.

There was, incredibly, no guard outside of the President's box. Lincoln's protector that night, John F. Parker, had left his position. He later explained that the play bored him and he went to a nearby saloon for a drink! (He was never reprimanded, dismissed, or prosecuted for this gross misconduct.)

Booth drank heavily until a little after 10 p.m. Then he casually walked to Ford's Theater, where he was well known, and entered. An actress, Jennie Gourlay, spotted him. Though she called out, Booth walked past her without comment with what she later described as "a wild look in his eyes."

The assassin was greatly disturbed as he made his way upstairs. The thought of killing Lincoln did not alarm him. The fact that Atzerodt had backed out of his promise to kill Vice President Johnson did. Only hours earlier, the conspirators had met, holding a frenzied conversation. Atzerodt was visibly shaken by their plan.

He hung his head and murmured, "I cannot kill Johnson, I cannot perform such a deed, I cannot become a murderer."

"You're a fool," Booth lashed out at him. "You'll be hanged anyway." He and Paine then set out to complete their gruesome tasks.

When Booth came up to the unguarded door of the President's box it was 10:15 p.m. He peered through the peep hole he had made. Inside, he could see Lincoln sitting in a rocking chair, his wife Mary close by, and to their right Clara Harris and her fiance, Major Rathbone. He opened the door noiselessly and entered, clutching a small pistol and a knife.

In a moment he had fired a single shot into the back of Lincoln's head. Rathbone leaped up and struggled with Booth but the assassin's knife slashed out at him and severely wounded him in the arm. Booth stood for a second on the box's railing as the audience screamed in terror. *"Sic semper tyrannis!"* (Ever thus to tyrants) boomed Booth, ever the actor, and with that he leaped to the stage. His spur caught a flag draped next to the box and he landed with a crash, badly injuring his leg. He staggered up and hobbled off the stage, yelling above the pandemonium: "The South is avenged!"

As Booth stumbled from the theater's side entrance he realized that his left shinbone was fractured. "Peanuts"

John Burrough was saucer-eyed at seeing the actor in his condition but obediently helped him to mount his horse. Booth dashed away down the street.

Lincoln's horrible headwound was untreatable. He died the following morning at 7:22 a.m. in a small room near the theater.

While Booth was enacting his self-designed drama, Lewis Paine clumsily attempted to kill Secretary of State Seward. Paine, who had learned that Seward had been injured in a fall from his carriage days earlier, arrived at the Secretary's home, stating that he had brought medicine and "must deliver it personally to him."

He was halted at the foot of the stairs by Frederick Seward, the Secretary's oldest son. Frederick told him that under no circumstances could Paine see his father. The would-be assassin meekly turned to leave and then suddenly whirled about and brought the butt of his pistol crashing down on young Seward's head, knocking him senseless. Paine then dashed up the stairs three at a time and rushed into the Secretary's bedroom.

The helpless Seward could only let out a weak cry as Paine drove a knife into him several times. Seward's young son and a male nurse ran in and pushed Paine from the bedroom. The wild-eyed conspirator then ran down the stairs past servants and Frederick Seward, then just staggering to his feet. Paine was screaming hysterically, "I'm mad! I'm mad!"

Paine had no horse awaiting him; he merely ran up the street and into Mary Surratt's boarding house, where he hid beneath a bed. He was taken prisoner a short time later, as were Edman Spangler, the stage hand who had arranged to have Booth's horse waiting for him at Ford's theater, Atzerodt, Arnold, O'Laughlin and Mrs. Mary E. Surratt, 48, John's mother. Mrs. Surratt's case was odd in that authorities never proved that she was in any way part of the conspirators' plot to kill Lincoln, yet she was executed on the claim that the plot had been hatched in her boarding house.

Three of the plotters were missing. Booth had ridden furiously southward with David Herold into Virginia, first stopping at Dr. Mudd's Maryland home where his injury

The mysterious John H. Surratt, Booth's co-conspirator, escaped to Europe and was finally returned to the U.S. from Egypt; his trial was a farce and he was eventually freed. (U.S. Signal Corps, Brady Collection)

was treated (Mudd placed splints about his leg and sent him on his way). He and Herold finally hid out in a barn on a large farm owned by a Confederate sympathizer Richard Garrett.

John Surratt could not be found anywhere.

Thousands of Union troops spread through Maryland and Virginia following each report of Booth's escape route, questioning hundreds of persons who claimed to have seen the frantic rider pass. A Lieutenant Baker, leading a company of troops hot on Booth's trail, tracked him to the Garrett farm on April 26, 1865.

Baker told Booth and Herold to surrender or be burned out of the barn.

Booth yelled: "Let us have a little time to consider it."

Baker gave them five minutes.

Then Booth shouted: "Captain, I know you to be a brave man, and I believe you to be honorable; I am a cripple.

I have got but one leg; if you will withdraw your men in one line one hundred yards from the door, I will come out and fight you!"

"We will do no such thing," Baker shouted back.

"Well, my brave boys," Booth yelled, "prepare a stretcher for me . . . one more stain on the old banner!"

Inside the barn, David Herold was cracking, pleading with Booth to surrender. Baker and his troopers heard the actor shout at his hapless follower: "You damned coward! Will you leave me now? Go, go, I would not have you stay with me!" Then, to the troops: "There's a man in here who wants to come out!"

The barn door creaked slowly open and Herold, shaking with fear, walked out and surrendered.

Baker ordered the barn set afire and troopers brought dry brush and piled it against the building. The flame soared upward with great speed. The men outside watched Booth's shadowy figure hobble toward the open door. Just as he reached it a shot rang out and Booth toppled forward. Who fired this shot was never learned. Some claim it was self-inflicted, others point to a Union zealot, soldier Boston Corbett.

Booth's body was dragged from the flames. The actor, barely alive, managed before he died to whisper the words: "Tell my mother I died for my country."

Lieutenant Baker searched the assassin and withdrew Booth's diary. It revealed a tormented mind haunted by the image of his pursuers, a self-pitying chant seeking to justify the assassination. Excerpts: "After being hunted like a dog through swamps, woods, and last night being chased by gunboats till I was forced to return wet, cold, and starving, with every man's hand against me, I am here in despair and why? For doing what Brutus was honored for—what made Tell a hero. And yet I, for striking down a greater tyrant than they ever knew, am looked upon as a common cutthroat. My action was purer than either of theirs. One hoped to be great. The other had not only his country's, but his own, wrongs to avenge. I hope for no gain. I knew no private wrong. I struck for my country and that alone. A country that groaned beneath this tyranny, and prayed for this end, and yet now behold the cold hand they extend me. God cannot pardon me if I have done

With troops and civilians witnessing, four of the major conspirators (left to right)—Atzerodt—were hanged on July 7, 1865. (Alexander Gardner, National Archives)

wrong. Yet I cannot see my wrong, except in serving a degenerate people. The little, the very little I left behind to clear my name, the government will not allow to be printed. So ends all. For my country I have given up all that makes life sweet and holy, brought misery upon my family, and am sure there is no pardon in the Heaven for me, since man condemns me so. I have only heard of what has been done (except what I did myself), and it fills me with horror. God, try and forgive me, and bless

Mrs. Surratt (the first woman in U.S. history to die on the gallows), Paine, Herold,

my mother. Tonight I will once more try the river with the intent to cross. Though I have a greater desire and almost a mind to return to Washington, and in a measure clear my name—which I feel I can do. I do not repent the blow I struck. I may before my God, but not to man. I think I have done well. Though I am abandoned, with the curse of Cain upon me, when, if the world knew my heart, that one blow would have made me great, though I did desire no greatness. Tonight I try to escape these bloodhounds once more. Who, who can read his fate? God's will be done. I have too great a soul to die like a criminal. Oh, may He, may He spare me that, and let me die bravely. I bless the entire world. Have never hated or wronged anyone. This last was not a wrong, unless God deems it so, and it's with Him to damn or bless me. As for this boy with me [Herold], who often prays (yes, before and since) with a true and sincere heart—was it crime in him? If so, why can he pray the same? I do not wish to shed a drop of blood, but 'I must fight the course. 'Tis all that's left to me.' "

On July 17, 1865, George Atzerodt, Lewis Paine, David Herold and Mary Surratt were taken up the steep gallow steps in the grimly bare yard of Washington's Old Penitentiary, ironically being shaded from the sun by umbrellas. There they were hanged. Mrs. Surratt's execution was never fully justified. She was convicted on the testimony of an infamous drunk and a known liar. On the scaffold, big-boned Lewis Paine pleaded with the executioner for the woman's life. "If I had two lives to give, I'd give one gladly to save Mrs. Surratt," he begged. "I know that she is innocent, and would never die in this way if I hadn't been found in her house. She knew nothing about the conspiracy at all . . ." Paine's death prattle was ignored. Mrs. Surratt was hanged anyway, the first female executed by the rope in the U.S. (Arnold was sentenced to life imprisonment and was paroled in 1869. O'Laughlin went to jail for life and died there; Dr. Mudd began serving a life sentence and was pardoned by President Johnson in 1868; Spangler got six years of hard labor.)

Her son John Surratt fled the country to Canada. His escape has baffled and confused historians to this day. He was seen several times on his way through New England to freedom but government agents sent to follow him were given contradictory orders emanating from that curiously truculent Secretary of War, Edwin Stanton.

The Secretary's actions immediately following the assassination appeared to be as hysterical as that of Washington's mobs. He ramrodded the conspirators' trials and hastened their execution. Stanton, who at times had acted more as an adversary to Lincoln than as one of his cabinet members during the President's administration, did strange things following Lincoln's death. For one, he confiscated the only photograph showing the President in his coffin, a photo taken while Lincoln lay in state in New York's City Hall. He had the master plate destroyed and burned all but one print of this picture, keeping it among his personal effects. The photo was accidentally found eighty-seven years later.

What was more peculiar was the way Stanton handled the case of John H. Surratt. Several times government agents located the fugitive and informed Stanton of his whereabouts. The Secretary refused to order his arrest or delayed decision. Tracking down Surratt developed into a world chase. He was located in Italy where he was serving in the Swiss Guards. He escaped. He was finally found in Egypt and was returned to the U.S.

Surratt's eventual trial was a farce. His lawyers, who were oddly enough, friends of Stanton's, cleverly picked apart the law and through various loopholes (the absence of certain key witnesses also helped), got him off. Surratt lived out an inconspicuous life in Baltimore where he died, just after the turn of the century, unidentified to his neighbors as the co-chief of the great plot to murder Abraham Lincoln.

BOSTON, PATIENCE
Murderer • (1713-1735)

Patience Boston, in her short twenty-three years of life had, according to her final confession, committed every kind of sin conceivable in early Puritan Maine—lying, stealing, swearing, drunkenness and finally, murder.

She senselessly killed eight-year-old Benjamin Trot in Falmouth, Maine. As if by whim, Patience picked up the child and threw him down a well in which he drowned.

Patience, who was part Indian, was executed for this murder in York, Me., July 24, 1735.

BOTKIN, CORDELIA
Murderer • (1854-1910)

BACKGROUND: BORN AND RAISED IN CALIFORNIA. MINOR PUBLIC EDUCATION. MARRIED WELCOME A. BOTKIN OF STOCKTON, CALIF., A BUSINESSMAN. GAVE BIRTH TO ONE SON, BEVERLY. DESERTED HER HUSBAND IN THE EARLY 1890S, LIVING A BOHEMIAN LIFE IN SAN FRANCISCO. DESCRIPTION: 5'2", BROWN EYES, BROWN HAIR, HEAVYSET. ALIASES: NONE. RECORD: MURDERED MRS. ELIZABETH DUNNING AND (BY ACCIDENT) MRS. JOSHUA DEANE BY MAILING THEM A GIFT OF HOME-MADE BONBONS LOADED WITH ARSENIC; APPREHENDED THROUGH HANDWRITING AND TRIED IN THE STATE OF CALIFORNIA IN 1898; FOUND GUILTY AND SENTENCED TO LIFE IMPRISONMENT, FIRST IN THE BRANCH COUNTY JAIL IN SAN FRANCISCO AND THEN IN SAN QUENTIN WHERE SHE DIED IN 1910.

John Presley Dunning led an enviable life in 1895. To some he had the best of two worlds—a lovely wife and child and a responsible, well-paying job as Bureau Chief of the Associated Press in San Francisco. He also had a mistress with whom he enjoyed the seamy side of life.

The wife was patient, Edwardian-bred Elizabeth Pennington Dunning, the pretty daughter of a U.S. Congressman from Dover, Del. Elizabeth married John Dunning in Dover in 1891 and gave birth to a daughter later that year. For four years the couple lived quietly but when

Dunning was offered the post as head of the AP office in San Francisco, he jumped at the offer. Then life changed radically for the Dunnings.

Enter the mistress, one Cordelia Botkin, a dumpy pigeon-breasted woman a full ten years older than Dunning. Cordelia was a promiscuous soul who had left her husband, businessman Welcome A. Botkin, in Stockton, Calif. several years past and moved with her obese son, Beverly, to San Francisco. There Cordelia hurtled herself into the wild revelries of the Bohemian quarters, drinking and partying all night, sleeping during the day, living off the money her simple-minded husband sent to her.

Dunning and Cordelia met in one of San Francisco's small parks. He was riding a bicycle, then fashionable, to his office when it broke down near the park bench upon which Cordelia sat. The frowsy little woman rolled her dark eyes just once and Dunning was lost. What drew him to this woman is unknown. Cordelia was rather a dull person as well as being homely.

But there was a hidden wild streak in Dunning which apparently pronounced itself every few years. He admitted later that he was prone to gambling, drinking, and whoring binges that went on for months. Dunning met Cordelia secretly for a year and then, ignoring all propriety, the journalist moved into an apartment with Cordelia, Beverly, and Beverly's mistress, 40-year-old Louise Seeley, his mother's best friend. They were a merry group, drinking and dancing into the early hours of the morning, every morning. Cordelia would dance wildly about the small apartment, leaping awkwardly and, to the consternation of the tenants below, landing with heavy crashes on the floor. Her specialty was telling the other three "racy stories," as she later termed them, while all four stretched out across two beds.

Mrs. Dunning, meanwhile, was left to sit and wait at home with her daughter. Her husband's ridiculous affair went on for more than a year. He lost his job and lived off the money Cordelia kept receiving from cuckolded Welcome Botkin. Elizabeth finally called it quits in 1896. She sold her furniture and jewels to obtain passage money for her journey back East to her parents' home in Delaware. John Dunning did nothing to prevent her from leaving;

he was elated by her decision. Now he would have no guilty feelings at all, he told himself. To earn money he concentrated on gambling, but his racetrack losses mounted and his life with Cordelia became a hit-and-miss proposition.

Elizabeth settled down with her daughter and parents to live a quiet life in Dover, waiting for John Dunning to come to his senses. In the summer of 1897, the journalist's long-suffering wife received the first of many letters from San Francisco, but not from Dunning. The missive described how her husband was cavorting with an "interesting and pretty woman . . . an Englishwoman . . . a lady by birth and education" who was introducing Dunning to "the extreme delight of a quiet Bohemian life." The writer warned Elizabeth not to "renew living" with her husband and signed the letter, "A friend."

Mrs. Dunning received letters written in the same handwriting all summer long but turned them over unread to her father for safekeeping. Her husband was sent a copy of the first letter and he identified the handwriting as Cordelia's but, upon confrontation, the slatternly Bohemian shrieked an emphatic denial.

The affair ended when the Associated Press contacted its former employee in 1898. The Spanish-American war had broken out and the news service was in desperate need of experienced reporters. Would he go? Would he! Dunning left Cordelia and her friends flat, departing for what was then called Porto Rico.

Cordelia's loneliness for her missing lover was acute. She insisted on being by his side and to that end applied for a position as a front-line nurse but was rejected. For weeks Cordelia sank into depression. She listlessly walked the streets of San Francisco, brooding. She thought much of sweet Elizabeth Dunning. Jack Dunning had talked lovingly about her before leaving for the war zone. She would be the one he returned to, Cordelia concluded. He had had his fling. Now work and war would sober him. He would return to his wife and child, that was certain.

Then the mistress developed a plan. She had deviled Elizabeth by mail. Why not let the Post Office eliminate her competition? Cordelia went to a drugstore and purchased two ounces of arsenic. The clerk asked her why

San Francisco's Cordelia Botkin chose poison to eliminate her rival, John Dunning's wife, in 1898.

she was buying the poison (signing a register for the purchase of poison did not become mandatory until 1907 when The Poison Act went into effect).

"I want to clean a straw hat," Cordelia replied.

Though the clerk had never heard of using arsenic for such purposes, he shrugged and sold the woman the poison. He did keep an informal sales record and entered a "Mrs. Bothin," of the Hotel Victoria, in his book.

Next, the lovesick woman went to George Haas's candy store, where she bought a box of candy. Cordelia returned to the Hotel Victoria and, to the puzzlement of the servants, did not emerge from her room for several days. When she did, she carried a large box wrapped securely for mailing.

She walked to the Ferry Post Office in San Francisco and sent her "gift" east to Elizabeth Dunning.

The Pennington family were cooling themselves on their front porch on the blisteringly hot day of September 9, 1898, when the package arrived.

Elizabeth opened the parcel. Inside a glazed and colorful box marked "bonbons," she found a cheap lace handkerchief with a twenty-five cents price tag still affixed to it, and beneath that some odd-looking candy. This she passed around to those on the porch. Her parents declined, but her sister, Mrs. Joshua Deane, Mrs. Deane's child, and Elizabeth's daughter tasted some. Mrs. Dunning and Mrs. Deane ate several pieces. They made a few unkindly remarks about the gritty lumps inside the chocolates. At the bottom of the box, Elizabeth found a scribbled note which read: "With love to yourself and baby, Mrs. C."

"Oh, it must be from that lovely Mrs. Corbally," she remarked, thinking of a close friend in San Francisco.

The following day, the two women and children were taken ill. The children, who had only nibbled at the chocolate, recovered. The sisters grew worse and finally, after suffering violent spasms of pain Mrs. Dunning and Mrs. Deane died, September 12, 1898.

A physician had first diagnosed the illness as "cholera morbus," (a medical catchall) as a result of eating corn fritters. When a specialist was called in, he told Mr. Pennington that he believed the women had been poisoned. By then it was too late to save them. Pennington, fortunately, had saved the box of candy, the wrapping, and the note. The handwriting on the wrapping was the same as that in the letters Elizabeth had received from San Francisco the previous year.

Dunning, who had been contacted, rushed to Dover from the front lines and, upon seeing the letters and the note in the candy box, insisted that they were all penned by the same person—Cordelia Botkin.

Isaiah W. Less, San Francisco's Chief of Police, personally tracked down Cordelia and arrested her. A thorough search of her room at the Hotel Victoria unearthed a wrapping from the George Haas candy store.

On the strength of Dunning's statements, the wrapping, a sales clerk who worked at the City of Paris department store where the lace handkerchief was purchased, and the drugstore clerk, Cordelia was identified as the murderer of Mrs. Dunning and her sister. (Handwriting was not then admissible as evidence in California.)

The pathetic woman was sentenced to life imprisonment in December, 1898. Oddly enough, the judge who sentenced her, Carroll Cook, was amazed to see Mrs. Botkin alight from a cable car in San Francisco in which he was riding in the summer of 1901. He followed her to the Branch County Jail where she was supposed to be a prisoner.

Cook became enraged when he learned that Cordelia had employed her considerable feminine charm with her jailers to obtain special favors. Her cell was made up like an apartment where she received gentlemen callers at night: her wardens. In return for her favors, Cordelia was permitted to take "two days off" during each week, at which time she could freely travel through San Francisco.

Judge Cook put an end to this and Cordelia was moved into an ordinary cell. Following the mass devastation wreaked upon San Francisco by its now famous earthquake, the old Branch County Jail was destroyed. Cordelia survived the holocaust, however, and was sent to San Quentin. She died there in 1910 without ever confessing her terrible deed.

BOYD, JABEZ
Murderer • (? –1845)

B oyd, who was thought to be a deeply religious man in his community, practiced highway robbery at night. One evening, in Westchester, Pa., he robbed Wesley Patton. When the victim put up a fight, Boyd beat him to death with a club.

Boyd was recognized and found the next day in church. According to one report, Boyd was sitting in a pew "with a hymn book in his hand, and from which he was singing with apparent composure."

He was hanged in 1845.

BRAND, SAMUEL
Murderer • (? -1773)

Following an argument, Samuel Brand set fire to his farmhouse while his elderly parents slept. He entered the flaming building with a loaded gun and confronted his brother, who sat in the kitchen staring at him.

"I'll shoot thee," one narrative reported Brand as saying.

"Shoot if thou wilt," replied Brand's stoic brother. The narrative continues, "This simple and inconsiderate answer did but the more provoke his fury, so that he fired off, and the poor victim fell dead on the spot."

Brand was quickly apprehended, convicted, and hanged December 18, 1773, in Lancaster, Pa.

BROCIUS, WILLIAM ("CURLY BILL")
Cattle Rustler, Gunfighter • (1857–1882)

Born William B. Graham, this Arizona outlaw belonged to the McLowery-Clanton faction that faced Wyatt Earp, his brothers, and Doc Holliday in the legendary gunfight at Tombstone's O.K. Corral in 1881. Brocius was not present for this fight but he had participated in several cattle raids and shoot-outs in and about Tombstone earlier.

Brocius is best remembered for his shooting and killing of Tombstone's Sheriff Fred White in October, 1881, when he used a new and deadly trick that later gunfighters (notably John Wesley Hardin of Texas) employed—the gun spin.

One abysmally hot evening, Sheriff White and his deputy, Virgil Earp (Wyatt's brother), stepped out onto Tombstone's streets to quell a minor riot. Dozens of cowboys from nearby ranches were whooping up a gun party, racing up and down the streets on their ponies and shooting wildly into the air.

White and Earp drove the boisterous cowboys from town. But one, Curly Bill, remained standing defiantly in the middle of the street. White walked up to Curly Bill and asked him to turn over his six-gun. Brocius smiled and, according to the story, held out his weapon butt first. As the Sheriff reached for it, Curly Bill spun the gun around his index finger holding the guard, the butt winding up in his hand.

At this moment, Curly Bill later stated in court, Earp jumped him from behind, attempting to lock his arms, and his gun's hair trigger went off, sending a bullet into Sheriff White and killing him. Another version, Earp's, reported that after spinning the gun back into position, Brocius merely squeezed off a round, murdering White in cold blood.

Some witnesses to the shooting claimed that the sheriff caused his own death when, after being angered by Brocius' fancy gun-spin, he grabbed the cocked six-gun by the barrel and set it off himself.

Brocius was tried days later. The prosecution had to admit that Curly Bill's pistol had five shells in it after White had been shot, and that he was therefore not "hurrahing" the town with the other cowboys and so not guilty of prompting White's action. The gunfighter was released and White's death was ruled an accidental homicide.

When the Clanton-Earp war erupted months later, Curly Bill Brocius was mixed up in several forays, always lined up against the Earps. In another bushwacking following the dramatic gun battle at the O.K. Corral, Earp's brother Morgan was ambushed and Virgil crippled for life. Wyatt tracked down, according to his own version, all of the outlaws responsible for the attacks. Curly Bill, one of his prime suspects, was no exception.

The end was a strange affair. Earp and his men met another posse led by Brocius at Iron Springs outside of Tombstone, in the shadow of the Whetstone Mountains. Both groups had stopped at the spring to water their horses. Brocius claimed he had been deputized by Tombstone Sheriff Johnny Behan, an Earp rival, to bring in the Earp posse for violating certain local laws. When Wyatt refused to turn over his six-guns, Brocius went for his irons. Earp was faster and drilled the young outlaw dead. He was the last serious foe Wyatt Earp faced in Tombstone.

[ALSO SEE O.K. Corral]

BUCK GANG

Rufus Buck and the four young men who followed him into a thirteen-day nightmare of murder and rape were illiterate part Creek Indians who suddenly and inexplicably rose against the law in the old Indian territory of Arkansas-Oklahoma on July 28, 1895.

The outrages committed by the five youths (the others included Luckey Davis, Lewis Davis, Maomi July, and Sam Sampson) were sporadic and unthinking. First, the five turned their rifles on a deputy who was looking at them suspiciously and shot him to death. Then, between Muskogee and Fort Smith, Ark., the band held up ranchers and small store owners with lightning speed. Coming upon a widow named Wilson driving to town in her wagon, the gang raped her. Next they invaded the Hassan Farm and put the farmer under guard while they took his wife, Rosetta, into the bedroom.

The woman begged the boys not to part her from her children. Luckey Davis only snorted: "You'll have to go with me," and pointed to the bedroom, threatening her that if she did not comply, they would "throw the goddamn brats into the creek."

The next day they held up a drummer named Callahan and shot in the back a Negro boy who worked for him. The boy died instantly. A giant posse aided by a company of Creek Indian police surrounded the gang in a cave and, following a gun battle, took them into custody August 10, 1895.

Their fate was already sealed by the time they appeared before Judge Isaac Parker in Fort Smith. Parker, known as the "hanging judge," appointed five attorneys to defend them. In a whirlwind trial, all of the members of the Buck Gang were found guilty and sentenced to hang.

The words uttered by defense attorney William Cravens were lame-dog terse: "You have heard the evidence and I have nothing to say."

Neither did Rufus Buck or any member of his gang and

They were hanged high—The Rufus Buck gang in captivity on 7/1/96 before members went to the gallows at Fort Smith, Ark. for murder, robbery, and rape (left to right): Maomi July, Sam Sampson, Rufus Buck, Luckey Davis, and Louis Davis. (Western History Collection, U. of Okla. Library)

they were led, one by one, to the gallows and hanged. A warden found a picture of Buck's mother on the wall of his cell after the execution. The bandit had written a poem (entitled "My Dream") on the back of the picture which read:

I dreamt I was in Heaven
Among the Angels fair;
I'd ne'er seen none so handsome,
That twine in golden hair.
They look so neat and sang so sweet
And played the Golden Harp.
I was about to pick an angel out
And take her to my heart:
But the moment I began to plea,
I thought of you, my love.
There was none I'd ever seen so beautiful
On earth or Heaven above,
Goodbye my dear wife and Mother.
Also my sister.

BUNCH, EUGENE
Trainrobber • (?–1889)

An obscure country school teacher, Eugene Bunch, decided to better his lot in 1888; he began to rob trains in Louisiana, Mississippi, and Texas. Always the Southern gentleman, Bunch introduced himself to his victims as "Captain Gerald," and spoke in a soft, melodious voice when demanding express car guards to open their safes or have their "brains blown out."

He is credited with robbing at least six trains for a total of $18,000. His biggest haul came in November, 1888, when he took $10,000 from the New Orleans Flyer.

After a brief spell of the "straight" life (he edited a newspaper in Dallas, Texas for six months) and a quick love affair with the daughter of a former governor of the Lone Star State, Bunch was off to Mississippi, where he recruited a gang of toughs and resumed robbing trains.

Pinkerton and train detectives trailed the Bunch gang to Jefferson County, Mississippi in 1889, and trapped them on a small island in the swamps. Bunch and two others were killed in a gunfight with the posse.

BURROW GANG

For many years Alabama-born Reuben Houston Burrow was a tiller of the soil in Arkansas where he lived on a small farm with a wife and two children. In 1887, Rube Burrow decided to change all that and take

Trainrobbers Rube and Jim Burrow

his chances with the gun. Collecting his brother Jim and the neighboring Brock brothers, W. L. and Leonard (already a wanted felon who traveled under the alias of Waldrip), Rube led the gang in their first holdup outside of Genoa Station, Ark., December 9, 1887. They boarded the St. Louis, Arkansas, and Texas R.R. bound north for St. Louis, and forced the Southern Express Company messenger to open the safe. They took $3,500.

The gang next struck near Bellevue, Tex., where the bandits stopped a train in early January, 1888, forced open the Fort Worth and Denver Express car, and looted the safe. While Jim Burrow held the express guard at bay, Rube and the Brock brothers ambled through the passenger cars scooping up wallets and watches at gunpoint; the total take was $3,000.

Weeks later, the same gang stopped a Texas and Pacific express train and got $2,000. One of the bandits left behind a brand new black raincoat which the Pinkertons traced to a Burrow confederate. For months, the detectives raced after the fast-moving Burrow gang and finally caught up with them in a mountainous retreat near Nashville, Tenn. Jim Burrow and the Brock brothers were captured, but Rube shot his way to freedom.

Pacing in his cell, Jim Burrow growled to reporters: "Give

us Burrows a gun apiece and we will not be afraid of any man alive." But Jim never got his hands on another gun and died of consumption within a year inside the jail at Little Rock, Ark.

For a short while his brother became the subject of a desperate manhunt. Hundreds of detectives and possemen searched the Southern wilds for him. Elaborate "Wanted" posters in which every minute habit of Rube Burrow was detailed were printed up and distributed by the thousands.

The Pinkerton Detective Agency outdid itself with their own flyer on Burrow:

"REUBEN HOUSTON BURROW is about 32 years of age, 6 feet in height, weighs about 160 pounds, blue eyes which do not look a person full in the face, round head, wears 7¼ hat, full forehead, face broad under the ears but thin near the mouth, short, inclined to pug-shaped nose, swarthy or sandy complexion, light sandy hair, thin light moustache, uses Hair Vigor to darken hair; left arm is a little shorter than the right, caused by having been broken at bend of arm; rather a lounging gait, carrying his hands in his pockets in a leisurely way.

"Usually wears dark clothes and woolen shirts, a No. 8 boot, but no jewelry. Does not use tobacco; drinks, but not to excess; does not gamble, but can play the game of seven-up; is somewhat of a country story teller, relating stories of snake, dog and cat fights, etc. . . ."

In 1890, Rube Burrow, alone, robbed another train. As he strolled away from the train to his horse, gingerly swinging a sackful of loot and whistling, a wily detective for the Southern Express Company blew off his head with a shotgun.

CASEY, JAMES P.
Murderer • (? -1856)

San Francisco was a rough town in the Nineteenth Century, even for civilized people. Though James Casey was the editor of the *Sunday Times*, his position did not prevent him from calling his enemies out into the street for fistfights or shootouts.

One arch-foe Casey found particularly intolerable was James King, who edited the rival *Evening Bulletin*. Spotting King on a San Francisco street May 14, 1856, Casey yanked out a revolver and shouted: "Draw and defend yourself!" But he gave King no time to do so (King was unarmed anyway) and immediately fired at him, killing him on the spot.

While Casey was awaiting trial, San Francisco's Vigilance Committee stormed the jail and dragged him outside, along with three other prisoners—Charles Cora, Philander Brace, and Joseph Heatherington. In a wild torchlight ceremony, all four men were pronounced guilty of various crimes—Casey's killing of King given prominence—and were then promptly hanged while 20,000 good citizens cheered.

CHADWICK, CASSIE L.
Swindler • (? -1907)

Her beginnings were indescribably poor, yet she would rise to the dizzy heights of millionaire's row through one of the most subtle swindles in American crime.

Born Elizabeth Bigley on a Canadian farm, Cassie moved alone to Toronto as a teenager. She ordered calling cards printed which read, "Miss Bigley—Heiress to $15,000" and handed these out at various department stores. Naive managers showered her with grand wardrobes, graciously accepting her worthless cards as promissory notes to pay.

Naturally, Cassie, bedecked in the latest fineries, skipped town. Crossing into the U.S., this auburn-haired, green-eyed seductress bilked, through fraud and blackmail, dozens of prosperous American businessmen. One historian estimated the young vamp made more than $1,000 a week from gullible Pullman car travelers.

Authorities finally overtook her; she was quickly tried and convicted of fraud, and sent to prison for three years. Upon her release, penniless, Cassie fielded about for more victims but her fleshy charm had dissipated. She turned to prostitution and, while working in a run-down whorehouse, met dim-witted Dr. Leroy Chadwick of Cleveland, Ohio.

The good doctor believed Cassie when she told him that she was merely on hand in the bordello to instruct the girls in courtly manners. He fell in love with the scheming trollop and married her.

Cassie, once established as Mrs. Leroy Chadwick, traveled to New York, taking a plush suite of rooms at the Holland House, a hostelry favored by socialites. In the lobby, she "accidentally" bumped into a prominent Ohio lawyer named Dillon. They knew each other slightly and Cassie asked if he would be good enough to escort her to the home of her father. Dillon agreed and an hour later sat stunned in an open carriage as Cassie Chadwick alighted and walked into the majestic Fifth Avenue mansion of Andrew Carnegie, the wealthiest man in the country.

Mrs. Chadwick stayed close to twenty-five minutes inside the Carnegie palace while Dillon waited and wondered. She had brazenly pushed aside the butler and, once past the front door, demanded to speak to the housekeeper. When the puzzled woman arrived, Cassie grilled her about the background of a domestic maid she was thinking of hiring.

Though the housekeeper denied that such a girl ever worked for Mr. Carnegie, Cassie kept chattering; her object was to consume time and she accomplished that feat quite neatly by slowly explaining how she must have been the victim of a hoax.

As she left the mansion, Dillon saw her wave to someone in the hallway; he assumed, Carnegie (it was the butler). Cassie had difficulty reentering the carriage and a slip of

Swindler Cassie Chadwick in 1894, the year she was caught after bilking millions from banks as the fake daughter of tycoon Andrew Carnegie. (UPI)

paper fell from her hand. When Dillon picked it up he was close to being struck dumb—it was a $2 million promissory note signed by the great Carnegie.

Apologetically, demurely, hesitantly, Mrs. Chadwick explained that she was really the multi-millionaire's illegitimate daughter and as such, Carnegie's guilt compelled him to foist huge sums of money upon her. Cassie stated that there was another $7 million in promissory notes from her "father" at home in Cleveland tucked away in a desk drawer. This was nothing, of course, said Mrs. Chadwick off-handedly, to the $400,000,000 she would inherit outright upon Carnegie's death.

Dillon, upon returning to Cleveland, and sworn to secrecy, immediately told everyone and anyone of importance about Cassie "Carnegie" Chadwick, as Cassie knew he would. At his insistence, Cassie took a sealed envelope to the biggest bank in town for safekeeping in a deposit box. Her scheme to swindle millions through this hoax was based heavily upon the fact that no one would dare embarrass tycoon Carnegie by asking that he verify the existence of an illegitimate daughter, namely Mrs. Chadwick. In this, Cassie was right.

The cashier at the bank, confident of Mr. Dillon's assurances, gave Mrs. Chadwick a receipt for $7 million without ever opening the envelope. In a short time, unscrupulous bankers all but forced her to take enormous loans against her notes. She pretended to be naive and accepted, correctly reasoning that the loans were attached with such illegally high interest rates that the bankers would never admit to making them. It was a high stakes flim-flam game that paid Cassie Chadwick off in millions.

She became the empress of Ohio as the duped bankers showered her with over $1,000,000 a year, never bothering to call the loans—delightedly watching the interest grow to staggering sums. When Carnegie died, they reasoned, Cassie Chadwick would pay . . . and pay handsomely.

Mrs. Chadwick thoroughly enjoyed her millions, reportedly spending $100,000 on a single dinner party; she bought diamond necklaces for the same amount, carriages, golden organs, thirty wardrobe closets full of the finest gowns in America. But never once did Cassie attempt to capitalize on her crooked fortune by investing. She got what she wanted—the money. To her it was to be spent.

Banks in New York and Cleveland never dared to question her loans, but after she applied for and received a $190,000 loan from a Boston bank, its meticulous New England president looked into Mrs. Chadwick's background.

He was aghast at the gigantic loans other banks had made to her and called his loan in. Cassie couldn't pay. The press blared the news and an Oberlin, Ohio bank which had given her $800,000 suffered a run so drastic that it closed its door forever.

Carnegie, the eternal bachelor (he had promised his mother, the story goes, that he would never marry while she lived), issued a statement through one of his aides when he heard of Mrs. Chadwick's preposterous swindle. "Mr. Carnegie does not know Mrs. Chadwick of Cleveland," the statement read. "Mr. Carnegie has not signed a note for more than thirty years."

It was the end of the golden dream. Cassie was arrested in 1904 and was convicted of swindling millions. She was sentenced to ten years in prison, where she died three years later as she had begun, forgotten and impoverished.

CHRISTIE, NED
Bandit • (? -1892)

An Oklahoma bandit, rumrunner, and horsethief, Christie began his criminal career in 1885 and was the terror of the Oklahoma territory. Seven years later, the renowned marshal Heck Thomas laid siege to an ancient but sturdy wooden fort near Tahlequah in which the outlaw and his gang had taken refuge.

Ned Christie, Oklahoma bandit, fought it out with lawmen and lost; he is shown here, propped up with a rifle in his hands, after having been killed in a gun battle. (Western History Collections, U. of Okla. Library)

Thomas brought in an army cannon and fired dozens of shells into the fort, but its double-wall construction prevented any damage. Next, Thomas ordered his sharpshooters to open up. After 2,000 bullets had whanged into the wooden edifice, the marshal resorted to dynamite. When a breach was finally made, Christie rode out through a cloud of smoke firing his rifle. Fifty guns wielded by possemen were trained on him; he was blasted dead from the saddle.

COPELAND, JAMES
Murderer • (? –1857)

Known in the 1840s as the "great Southern land pirate," James Copeland was an early outlaw in Mississippi whose gun could be purchased by the highest bidder. Copeland worked for the wealthy and corrupt Wages family who owned vast tracts of land around Augusta, Mississippi.

Copeland generally operated as a common highwayman, but he also murdered for profit. When two of his own band, Gale H. Wages and Charles McGrath, were shot and killed by James A. Harvey, Copeland received $1,000 from Old Man Wages to murder his son's killer. Copeland accepted this assignment with alacrity and dispatched Harvey on July 15, 1848, shooting him in the head.

Though apprehended, found guilty, and sentenced to death, Copeland remained alive for almost ten years, such was the influence of the Wages clan in Mississippi. He was finally hanged October 30, 1857.

CUNNINGHAM, CHARLES
Murderer • (1787-1805)

BACKGROUND: BORN IN YORK, PA., PLACED IN A POORHOUSE AS A SMALL CHILD; MADE A "BOUND" SERVANT TO AN INNKEEPER NAMED EICHELBERGER AT AGE 12 IN 1799. NO FORMAL EDUCATION. DESCRIPTION: TALL, DARK, THIN. ALIASES: NONE. RECORD: STRANGLED A YOUTH, JOSEPH ROTHROCK, TO DEATH, 5/16/1805; ARRESTED AND CONFESSED TO THE MURDER; EXECUTED 9/19/05.

Charles Cunningham's life had been anything but pleasant. Born into poverty, he was soon deserted by his mother and placed in a poorhouse—where he was fed one skimpy meal a day and made to slave from dawn till dusk. By the time he was twelve, Cunningham had become an unthinking, insensitive animal. He was sent to an inn in York, Pa. as a "bound" servant, his master being a certain Mr. Eichelberger. The innkeeper did not improve Cunningham's lot.

The youth, at eighteen, had taken to drinking large quantities of the inn's whiskey. Much of the time Cunningham gambled with neighborhood boys in the inn's kitchen. On May 16, 1805, he began a game of hustlecap with two teenage boys—John Heckendorn and Joseph Rothrock. (Hustlecap was a common street game which consisted of shaking and tossing coins into a cap.)

Cunningham and his friends soon left Eichelberger's and walked to another tavern where they continued to gamble, drinking whiskey and cideroyal. Cunningham won Rothrock's money, plus a box, handkerchief, and silver brooch.

Tiring of the game, the boys began to shoot dice. This time Rothrock began to win. Heckendorn said that he wanted to check the dice. The apparent distrust made Cunningham angry. Thinking he was being cheated, the eighteen-year-old shouted at his companions.

Though he had been drinking heavily, Cunningham later swore: "I was in liquor, though as well as in my senses as I am now."

His claimed sobriety, however, did not prevent him from leading his friend Joseph Rothrock into a dark alley and then drawing forth a knife. He intended to slit Joseph's throat. The knife slipped from his hands.

As Rothrock looked at him in horror, Charles jumped forward. In a later confession, the youthful killer admitted: "I sprung upon him, and grasped him by the neck with both my hands, placing both my thumbs in his throat, and squeezing with all my might until he fell down and appeared to be dead."

But Joseph soon revived. Cunningham produced a piece of rough twine and, placing it about Joseph's neck, used it to strangle him to death. "I then committed a most horrid indignity on the dead body, for which I cannot otherwise account than that it was done by the immediate instigation of the Devil," Cunningham later stated.

He grabbed the dead boy's face and slammed it to the cobblestones, face down, until Joseph's features were obliterated.

Swiftly apprehended, Charles Cunningham confessed and was hanged September 19, 1805.

CZOLGOSZ, LEON
Assassin • (1873-1901)

A 28-year-old laborer, Czolgosz (pronounced *Chol-gosh*) was a confirmed anarchist who was impressed with the rash of assassinations sweeping Europe at the turn of the century, particularly the killing of King Humbert of Italy who had been slain by a laborer from New Jersey.

Czolgosz, traveled from the Midwest to the Pan-American Exposition in Buffalo, N. Y. in early September, 1901, with a single thought in mind—to kill the much-loved William McKinley, twenty-fifth President of the United States.

McKinley, an affable hand-shaker, greeted the assembled crowds at the Exposition on September 6, 1901, and stood inside the main temple as lines of citizens pressed forward to clasp his hand. While fifty guards lounged near the President, Czolgosz got in line and slowly inched forward. A white handkerchief was wrapped around his hand but the guards took no notice of it; it was assumed that he had been injured in an accident.

Anarchist Leon Czolgosz "thought it would be a good thing" to kill President McKinley and did so in 1901. (UPI)

The assassin was not a suspicious-looking person. A guard later stated: "He was the last man in the crowd we would have picked out as dangerous."

Czolgosz reached McKinley at 4:07 p.m. The President, thinking the young man had been injured, reached for the anarchist's left hand. The assassin pushed it aside and dropped the handkerchief wrapped around his right hand to reveal a .32-caliber pistol. Before anyone could react, Czolgosz shoved the barrel to within inches of the President and fired two shots. One ploughed through McKinley's abdomen, a fatal wound.

"I done my duty!" the illiterate killer screamed as guards wrestled him to the floor. The President, swooning in the arms of his aides, gave his killer a painful glance and then quietly and magnanimously said: "Be easy with him, boys." He was rushed to a hospital but died eight days later of gangrenous poisoning, a condition brought about through inept medical attention.

Czolgosz was tight-lipped, a prisoner whose only statement on the shooting was, "I thought it would be a good thing for this country to kill the President."

He offered no defense at his trial, sitting mutely in court with a blank expression on his face. In seventeen days he was found guilty and sentenced to death. On October 29, 1901, Leon Czolgosz—wearing a neatly pressed suit, wing-collar, and highly shined shoes sat down in the electric chair in New York's Auburn Prison.

"Anything to say?" the warden asked.

"I am not sorry," Czolgosz muttered as the switch was thrown.

DALTON BROTHERS

DALTON, EMMETT
Bankrobber, Trainrobber • (1871-1937)

BACKGROUND: BORN TO LOUIS AND ADELINE (YOUNGER) DAL-
TON IN A FARMHOUSE IN CASS COUNTY, MO., ONE OF FIFTEEN
CHILDREN. MINOR EDUCATION. MARRIED JULIA JOHNSON IN
1907. BEGAN A REAL ESTATE BUSINESS IN LOS ANGELES, 1920.
WROTE SEVERAL SCENARIOS FOR SILENT MOVIES. AUTHOR:
"WHEN THE DALTONS RODE," 1931. DESCRIPTION: 6', BROWN
EYES, BROWN HAIR, SOLID BUILD. ALIASES: UNKNOWN. REC-
ORD: STUCK UP A FARO GAME IN NEW MEXICO, 1890, WITH HIS
BROTHER BOB: ROBBED THE SANTE FE'S TEXAS EXPRESS WITH
BROTHERS BOB AND GRAT, GEORGE "BITTER CREEK" NEW-
COMB, CHARLEY "BLACK FACE" BRYANT, NEAR WHARTON,
OKLA., 5/9/91 ($14,000); ROBBED A MISSOURI-KANSAS & TEXAS
EXPRESS TRAIN NEAR LELIETTA, OKLA. IN THE SUMMER OF 1891
WITH BROTHERS BOB AND GRAT, NEWCOMB, BILL POWERS,
CHARLEY PIERCE, WILL MCELHANIE, DICK BROADWELL, AND
BILL DOOLIN ($19,000); ROBBED A SANTE FE TRAIN NEAR RED
ROCK ON THE CHEROKEE STRIP WEEKS LATER WITH SAME
GANG ($11,000); ROBBED AN EXPRESS TRAIN WITH THE SAME
BAND NEAR ADAIR, OKLA., 7/14/92, WOUNDING GUARD SID
JOHNSON ($17,000); ATTEMPTED TO ROB WITH BROTHERS BOB
AND GRAT, DICK BROADWELL, AND BILL POWERS TWO

BANKS—THE FIRST NATIONAL AND CONDON BANKS—IN COF-
FEYVILLE, KAN., 10/5/92, BROTHERS BOB AND GRAT, POWERS
AND BROADWELL KILLED BY ARMED CITIZENS, EMMETT SE-
VERELY WOUNDED AND CAPTURED; TRIED FOR KILLING TWO
COFFEYVILLE CITIZENS, GEORGE CUBINE AND LUCIUS BALDWIN
(MAINTAINED THEY WERE SHOT BY HIS BROTHER BOB) DURING
THE RAID AND FOUND GUILTY; SENTENCED TO LIFE IMPRIS-
ONMENT IN THE KANSAS STATE PENITENTIARY IN LANSING,
KAN., IN MARCH, 1893; PARDONED BY KANSAS GOVERNOR E.
W. HOCH IN 1907; COMPLETELY REFORMED AND BECAME A
LEADING BUSINESSMAN IN THE LOS ANGELES COMMUNITY,
DYING OF OLD AGE 7/13/37.

DALTON, GRATTON (GRAT)
Trainrobber, Bankrobber • (1862–1892)

BACKGROUND: BORN IN CASS COUNTY, MO. MINOR PUBLIC
EDUCATION. SERVED BRIEFLY AS A MARSHAL IN FORT SMITH,
ARK., AND LATER WITH THE INDIAN POLICE ON THE OSAGE
RESERVATION. DESCRIPTION: 5'9", BROWN EYES, BROWN HAIR,
SLENDER BUILD, MUSTACHE. ALIASES: UNKNOWN. RECORD:
ATTEMPTED TO ROB TRAIN NO. 17 OF THE SOUTHERN PACIFIC
WITH BROTHERS BILL AND BOB, 2/6/91 (DRIVEN OFF BY THE
EXPRESS GUARD), CAPTURED WITH BROTHER BILL AND TRIED,
SENTENCED TO 25 YEARS IN PRISON, BUT ESCAPED; $6,000
REWARD POSTED FOR GRAT AND BOB (FOR FURTHER INFORMA-
TION, SEE ABOVE); KILLED IN THE COFFEYVILLE RAID 10/5/92.

DALTON, ROBERT (BOB)
Trainrobber, Bankrobber • (1867–1892)

BACKGROUND: BORN IN CASS COUNTY, MO. MINOR PUBLIC
EDUCATION. SERVED AS A MARSHAL IN FORT SMITH, ARK. WITH
BROTHER GRAT FOR A BRIEF TIME. ALSO SERVED AS A LAWMAN
ON THE OSAGE INDIAN RESERVATION. ENGAGED TO EUGENIA
MOORE WHO DIED A FEW WEEKS BEFORE HIM. OF CANCER.

DALTON, WILLIAM (BILL)
Trainrobber, Bankrobber • (1873–1893)

BACKGROUND: BORN IN CASS COUNTY, MO. MINOR PUBLIC
EDUCATION. TRAVELED TO CALIFORNIA WITH ANOTHER DAL-
TON BROTHER, LITTLETON, MARRIED AND HOMESTEADED. DE-
SCRIPTION: 5'11", BROWN EYES, BROWN HAIR, SOLID BUILD.
ALIASES: UNKNOWN. RECORD: ROBBED A CALIFORNIA TRAIN
IN 1891 (SEE INFORMATION UNDER GRAT DALTON); ROBBED
SEVERAL SMALL TOWN BANKS AND SOME TRAINS WITH THE
DOOLIN GANG IN OKLAHOMA; KILLED BY LAWMEN ON HIS
FRONT PORCH.

As robbers, the Daltons had a perfect heritage. Their cousins, the Younger brothers, had ridden with Jesse and Frank James. Missouri, the place of their birth, was called "Mother of Bandits." Lower Kansas, around Coffeyville, where they once lived, had been torn apart by Civil War guerrillas and roving bands of thieves and cutthroats. The wild Oklahoma Indian Territory, where their parents finally settled, was overrun with train and bank robbers. The trouble was—the Daltons never realized it until a fateful day in Coffeyville, Kan.—that the border bandit days were gone and they had strapped on their guns too late.

Of the fifteen children Mother Dalton bore, only four turned bad and went against the law. Frank Dalton was a special exception. Frank pinned on a marshal's badge and served on Judge Isaac C. Parker's ("The Hanging Judge") police force in Fort Smith, Ark. He came upon three bandits running illegal whiskey one day and was killed by them.

The older Dalton brothers—Grat, Bob, and Emmett—became so enraged by their brother's murder they also put on stars, but they never caught Frank's killers. Life on the right side of the law was dull. The boys quit their Fort Smith posts and moved onto the Osage Indian Reservation to serve with the Indian Police. It was lazy duty and they soon turned to rustling a few head of cattle to pick up side money. Grat got tired of the penny-ante stealing, turned in his star, and rode to California to join his brothers Littleton and Bill who had moved there to homestead.

Bob and Emmett Dalton drifted south to New Mexico. The two got into a faro game in a small town there and, suspicious of being cheated, held up the game for a few dollars and raced for Oklahoma. "Wanted" posters were out on them for the first time in 1890.

Emmett returned to the family home in Kingfisher, Okla., but Bob, yearning for adventure, headed for California. There, he teamed up with his brothers Bill and Grat and on February 6, 1891, went after a big score. The boys stopped the Southern Pacific's Train No. 17 which was approaching Los Angeles.

Riding as passengers, they merely got up from their seats, adjusted large red handkerchiefs about their faces, and climbed into the locomotive cab from the tender. Before the train was brought to a halt fireman George Badcliff panicked. One of the bandits shot him in the stomach. He fell to the floor in agony and died hours later.

The brothers ran alongside the halted train to the express car.

Charles C. Haswell, the express guard, was terrified. He rashly pressed his face against the car's window to see the bandits flourishing guns outside.

Bob Dalton, the gang's natural leader, yelled to him: "Open up and be damned quick about it!"

Haswell stalled. One of the outlaws fired a shotgun at the window and buckshot tore across the guard's forehead. In a rage, Haswell grabbed his own shotgun and let the bandits have it. He claimed to have hit one of them before he drove them off.

The first Dalton holdup was a dismal failure. Not only was the gang driven off without getting a dollar but Bill and Grat were soon hunted down and arrested. Bob, racing back to Oklahoma, heard that Bill had been cleared but that Grat had drawn a twenty-year sentence for armed robbery. Then Grat escaped and headed back East to join his brothers.

The Southern Pacific offered $6,000 rewards for the two brothers. Bob later told Emmett that the robbery was a foolish act but that the railroad "put the running iron on our hides" when they posted the rewards. It was the same kind of claim made by the James boys, the Cassidy gang, and hundreds of other outlaws. Whether real or imagined, the old refrain of "they made me a criminal" did nothing to prevent the Daltons from living up to their unsavory publicity.

Bob, Grat, and Emmett rounded up one of the toughest bands of outlaws in Oklahoma's history for a terrifying robbery spree that was destined to last eighteen months and forever be remembered. The handsome and quickdraw gunman George "Bitter Creek" Newcomb joined them. So did "Black-Face" Charley Bryant. His odd monicker resulted after a gunfight when Bryant's face was scarred by powder burns. ("I want to get killed in one hell-firing minute of smoking action," Bryant allegedly stated.) Bill Doolin, who would have a gang of his own one day, Dick Broadwell, Bill Powers, Charley Pierce, and Bill McElhanie, all top gunmen, also joined up.

The first target was, naturally, a railroad. The band held up the Texas Express on the Santa Fe line near Wharton, Okla. in early 1891. They took $14,000 out of the express car without firing a shot. When "Black-Face" Bryant suggested they rob the passengers, the Dalton brothers turned as one and sneered no. In their strange code of honor, the brothers insisted on leaving the passengers alone (a trait not common to their cousins, the Youngers).

With his share of the loot, Bryant rode into the small town of Hennessey, Okla. and happily shot up the town.

He was promptly arrested by Marshal Ed Short, who accompanied him on the train to Wichita to stand trial before a federal judge. During the trip, Bryant, held captive in the baggage car, grabbed a gun and both he and Short fired at the same time, killing each other.

Bob Dalton was neither surprised or upset. Bryant asked for it. He was foolish, he told his brothers. But, a little over a year later, Bob would commit one of the most foolish mistakes ever made by a Western badman.

The gang struck again at Lelietta, Okla., smoothly relieving a Missouri-Kansas & Texas express of $19,000 in currency and silver.

Bob Dalton insisted that there be no letup. He figured every man in the gang would be wealthy enough to retire "inside of twelve months." Bob had a good reason. He was engaged to attractive Eugenia Moore who was no stranger to his robberies. Not until forty years later would it be learned that the reason the Daltons' struck with such accuracy, just when large shipments of money were being moved, was Eugenia. She worked for Bob (unknown to all except Dalton's brothers) as a sort of advance scout,

Bob Dalton, leader of the Dalton brothers, with his sweetheart, Eugenia Moore; she scouted for the gang, setting up robberies. (Western History Collections, U. of Okla. Library)

inquiring at waystations which train would be the best protected. She stated that she wanted to ship some of her own money. Naturally, she was told, the best trains by which to ship her money were those carrying large bank note shipments; they were always heavily protected. Eugenia obtained the proper schedules and passed these to Bob Dalton.

Emmett had a reason to retire, too. Her name was Julia Johnson, a childhood sweetheart. While on the run, Emmett secretly visited her while his brothers stood guard outside the Johnson house in the event a posse should arrive by night. Dalton wanted to marry her but felt it was impossible. "What had I to offer Julia," he wrote later, "a man with a price on his head and no clear way to extricate myself from the compounding results of crime? I rode away. An outlaw has no business having a girl, no business thinking of marriage."

The gang then stuck up a Santa Fe train near Red Rock, taking $11,000 without firing one bullet. The next strike was not so easy. Lawmen learned that the Daltons were going to stop a Texas train July 14, 1892, on its way to Kansas at Pryor Creek, Okla. Bob Dalton, through Eugenia, heard about the fifty-man posse and stopped the train at Adair before it got to the entrapment area. They had to wound Deputy Sid Johnson, an express guard, to get $17,000. Ironically, Johnson had served with the Daltons as a peace officer at Fort Smith.

Bob then planned the biggest raid of his life. Since childhood he had heard romantic stories about how the James and Younger boys tried to rob two banks at the same time in Northfield, Minn. They had failed and were shot to bits, but that didn't mean it couldn't be done, Dalton reasoned. He knew of a small town that had two ripe banks, a town where he and his brothers had briefly lived as small boys—Coffeyville, Kansas.

Eugenia Moore had no hand in casing this job, unfortunately for the Daltons. She was dead. Suddenly stricken with cancer, Bob's sweetheart died only weeks before the Coffeyville raid. Dalton threw her picture into a campfire. The next day Emmett, Grat, and Bob rode to Kingfisher to see their mother but were afraid to go near the farmhouse. Lawmen, they suspected, might be waiting in the shadows.

The outlaw brothers sat on their horses in the middle of the night and watched their mother move past the windows of their boyhood home. It was bitter nostalgia that moved Emmett to later write: "For a moment we saw her in the distant window, her flitting form, setting the house in order for the night. None of us dared look at each other. With one accord we spurred our horses. And at the sound, I saw her turn her face to the window, listening intently, as if she heard the passing hoofbeats. Such was Bob and Grat's last outspoken salute to the grand old lady who bore them."

Dick Broadwell, Bill Powers, and Bill Doolin made the journey northward the next day with the three Dalton Brothers, heading for Coffeyville, disaster, and eternal Western fame. Only Doolin was to escape that cauldron of death. His horse went lame a few miles from the town. He said he would go to a nearby ranch, steal a horse, and catch up. He didn't.

The other five men rode into Coffeyville on the morning of October 5, 1892, sauntering into the main plaza off Eighth Street at 9:30 a.m. Each outlaw carried single-action .45s, one on the hip and one in a shoulder holster. After dismounting in an alley behind the jail, the five took out their Winchester rifles and headed up the street.

Stable owner Aleck McKenna recognized the Daltons as they calmly walked past him, spurs jingling. The false beards Bob and Emmett wore didn't fool him; he had known them as boys. He watched, awe-struck, as Grat, Powers, and Broadwell entered the Condon Bank and Bob and Emmett Dalton quickly entered the First National Bank. Through the window of the Condon Bank he saw Grat Dalton raise his weapon and aim it at the cashier.

He let out a terrifying scream: "They're robbing the bank! The Daltons! They're robbing the bank!"

Inside the Condon Bank, Grat was having serious problems. Vice President Charles T. Carpenter, bookkeeper T. C. Babb, and cashier Charles Ball gaped at his leveled guns.

"Open the safe and be quick about it!" Grat ordered.

"It's a time lock. Won't open until 9:45." Ball was lying, playing for time.

102

Grat put his Winchester only inches from Ball's head. "Open it, or I'll kill you!"

Ball tried to placate the oldest Dalton brother by hauling out a sack containing $4,000 in silver. Grat knew that there was a lot more in the safe—there was, ten times that amount. He looked at his watch. It was 9:42. "That's only three minutes," Grat said. "I will wait."

Bob and Emmett in the First National held three bank officers and a customer at bay. Tom Ayres, the cashier, attempted to fill the grain sack Bob had tossed to him with coins.

Dalton smiled at Ayres' ploy. "Keep that silver out. It's too heavy to bother with. The vault! The big stuff!"

Quickly, the cashier emptied the vault of $21,000, dumping the cash into the grain sack. Bob and Emmett headed for the door. A slug smashed through a window. The street was crawling with citizens, armed to the teeth, firing on both banks. Dozens of shells crashed in about the two Dalton brothers. Bob slammed the bank's heavy front door closed. "The back way," he ordered and pushed W. H. Sheppard, a customer, in front of him.

In the alley, Bob and Emmett, walking behind Sheppard, saw a man approaching and holding a pistol.

"Look after the money sack," Bob said and tossed it to his younger brother. "I'll do the fighting. I have got to get that man." He raised his rifle and sent a slug into Lucius M. Baldwin, a clerk, who died instantly.

The battle of Coffeyville was on.

As Bob and Emmett raced down side streets to the alley—now known as *Death Alley*—where their horses waited, Grat Dalton, Powers, and Broadwell made a mad dash from the Condon Bank with only $1,500 in small bills. A withering fire from dozens of vigilantes chewed up the dusty street about them as they made for the alley.

Taking their various routes, the boys ran into armed citizens at every corner. Two bootmakers who had made shoes for the boys when they were children—George W. Cubine and Charles Brown—rounded an alley just as Grat came upon them. The bandit shot them both dead.

Bob Dalton, on the run, shot Tom Ayres through the head.

After Bob and Emmett left his bank, Ayres had rushed

across the street to a hardware store, grabbed a pistol, and chased after the outlaws. He died trying to recapture the money the bank entrusted to his care.

All five bandits met in the alley. Dozens of men converged on them from either end. The Daltons were doomed and knew it. Grat told them to retreat but there was nowhere to retreat to; everywhere they turned they met a wall of fire. Powers was shot down first. He got up firing his six-guns. Broadwell went down and got up again. He, too, kept firing his Winchester into the advancing crowds. Bob was hit. Emmett was shot twice. During the battle, Bob turned suddenly and moaned. His brother Grat received a bullet in the chest. He was dead. Before Grat fell he advanced on Marshal Charles T. Connelly, who also stalked the outlaw. Both men's pistols roared as they approached each other and both fell dead.

The next to die was Bill Powers. He managed to mount his horse, but was shot off. His horse galloping madly down the street, Dick Broadwell sagged in his saddle, riddled. He was the only one to escape Death Alley, but fell dead from his horse a few miles outside of the Coffeyville city limits.

Only Bob and Emmett Dalton were left. Sorely wounded in the right arm and hip, Emmett climbed on his horse, still clutching the grain sack full of money. He was about to make his break when he looked back for his brother Bob. His intense loyalty would not allow him to leave the bandit leader.

Bob Dalton was shot to pieces. As Emmett rode back to help him, Bob weakly called up, "Don't mind me, boy. I'm done for. Don't surrender! Die game!"

Emmett reached his shattered arm down from the saddle. Bob shakily reached upward. Just as their hands touched, liveryman John J. Kloehr and the town barber, Carey Seaman, ran up with shotguns and fired a mighty volley at the two brothers. Emmett fell from the saddle. Bob Dalton died instantly.

For moments, as the gunsmoke drifted through the alley, there was an odd silence. Then a hollow-sounding voice called across the street to the main group of vigilantes: "They're all down!"

Emmett Dalton was the only one to survive, wounded

Bob and Grat Dalton minutes after their disastrous raid on two Coffeyville, Kan. banks, dead or dying, being held up by lawmen, 10/5/92. (Western History Collections, U. of Okla. Library)

more than twenty times. He was sent to prison for life for killing George Cubine and Lucius Baldwin, although Bob had done the shooting. Pardoned in 1907, Emmett led an exemplary life until his death in 1937, a strong testimony to personal reformation.

His younger brother Bill took up the outlaw trail after Coffeyville and rode with the Doolin gang. Emmett sadly related how lawmen crept up on Bill as he was playing with his young daughter on the front porch of his farm and shot him dead from behind.

The remaining Dalton brother, after completing his saga of the bandit brothers, *When the Daltons Rode*, revisited Coffeyville, Kansas in 1931. He stood at the foot of a common grave that held the bodies of Bill Powers and Grat and Bob Dalton. He pointed solemnly to the grave and stated: "I challenge the world to produce the history of an outlaw who ever got anything out of it but that or else be huddled in a prison cell . . . The biggest fool on earth is the one who thinks he can beat the law, that crime can be made to pay. It never paid and it never will and that was the one big lesson of the Coffeyville raid."

[ALSO SEE Bill Doolin, Jesse James]

DEAD RABBITS GANG

The Dead Rabbits were an early (circa 1850) New York gang of thugs with criminal activities centered in the Lower East Side. Their battle flag when openly warring with other gangs and police was a dead rabbit mounted high on a spear. Members were made up of Irish and Welsh immigrants who specialized in muggings, pickpocketing, and robbery.

In the criminal argot of the day a "dead rabbit" was a fearless and strong hooligan who could not be tamed. The Dead Rabbits gave way to succeeding gangs within two decades.

DOANE GANG

Led by rail-thin Moses Doane and his five brothers, the Doanes were the first important outlaw band in the country, rising from the turmoil of the Revolutionary War. The Doanes, mounted on fast horses, raided the Bucks County, Pa. area and sometimes roamed as far east as New Jersey, operating at their peak around 1780.

The gang numbered anywhere from sixteen to twenty men, big, raw-boned highwaymen all. The Doanes specialized in robbery, their biggest strike being the raid on Newton, Pa. in October, 1781, when they forced county treasurer John Hart to turn over close to $2,000 to them. (The robbers stopped at the schoolhouse in the center of town and by lantern light counted their loot, giggling like small boys.)

Moses, Abe, and Levy Doane (also spelled Doan) were Tories and worked for the British cause when the mood suited them; they struck down colonial tax collectors in the name of England but kept the proceeds for themselves. This gang's reign of terror ended in the late 1780s when several members were apprehended and hanged. Abraham and Levy Doane were hanged at Philadelphia Commons in 1788, Moses shortly thereafter.

The most dashing member of the band, James Fitzpatrick, known as "Sandy Flash," eluded several manhunts but was taken in 1787 and hanged.

DONNELLY, EDWARD
Murderer • (? -1808)

A habitual wife-beater, Donnelly went too far one night in early February, 1808, killing his wife Catherine. Though the poor woman let out piercing screams, the neighbors living in Carlisle, Pa. thought little of it. "There's Ned licking his wife again," one resident was reported to have said.

Donnelly, upon discovering he had murdered his wife, then dissected the body and burned it piece by piece for two days. Teeth and jawbone were discovered in the ashes of his fireplace and this led to his downfall. He confessed at his trial and was hanged February 8, 1808 in Carlisle before a throng of four thousand—who were in a disagreeable temper due to inclement weather.

DOOLIN, WILLIAM ("BILL")
Trainrobber, Bankrobber • (1863–1896)

Either luck or apprehension caused Bill Doolin's horse to pull up "lame" before he followed the Dalton brothers into the death trap at Coffeyville, Kan. in 1892. He was the only regular member of the Dalton gang to survive that bandit massacre and, upon hearing of the gang's extermination, rode furiously back to Oklahoma where he put together another band of outlaws, the last significant bandit gang in the Southwest.

His riders were the last elements of other gangs which had been systematically destroyed by an increasingly vigilant citizenry, relentless detective agencies, and modernized law enforcement organizations.

Bill Dalton, last of the outlaw brothers, forsaking his family in California, journeyed East and joined Doolin. Train robber Dan Clifton, known as "Dynamite Dick" came in; so did George "Bitter Creek" Newcomb, George "Red Buck" Weightman, Jack Blake (alias Tulsa Jack), Charley Pierce, "Little Bill" Raidler, Roy Daughtery (alias Arkansas Tom), and Dick West (alias Little Dick).

For more than three years this formidable band swept through the Oklahoma territory robbing stages, banks, and trains. They headquartered in the small town of Ingalls, Okla., where the residents protected them from the prying eyes of Pinkertons, Rangers, and marshals (and where they spent their loot).

On September 1, 1893, a dozen marshals, hidden in a wagon, entered Ingalls for a showdown with the gang. Bitter Creek Newcomb spotted the wagon, called to Doolin and the others, and the battle of Ingalls was on. After several hours of trading lead, the outlaw band moved out, Newcomb and Red Buck wounded and riding double on the horses of their friends. Three marshals had been killed.

Doolin, a good-natured bandit who once prevented the

murderous Red Buck from shooting Marshal Bill Tilghman from ambush, hit some big strikes in 1894, his largest haul—$40,000—taken from a bank in East Texas.

A super posse headed by lawmen Chris Madsen, Heck Thomas, and Tilghman went after the gang in a chase that stretched through three states. The Doolins never rested, knowing that the posse, financed by the railroads and banks they had robbed, was always behind them.

Tilghman was so close once that Doolin and his boys barely finished breakfast before an informer rushed into a farm house to announce that the lawmen were thundering toward them, only a few miles distant. Doolin told the farmer, who thought his outlaws part of a posse, that "the other boys" coming up the road would be hungry, too, and that they would pay for the meals.

When Tilghman, Madsen and Thomas appeared on lathered mounts, the farmer greeted them with an affable smile and said: "The others said you'd be along. We got dinner ready." The lawmen ate the dinner and reluctantly paid the price for both meals—their own and what the Doolin gang had eaten before them.

In 1895, the gang separated. Tilghman tracked down Little Bill Raidler in October on a ranch near the Osage Indian territory and brought him in after a wild gun duel in which Raidler was severely wounded. He was given a ten-year prison sentence but was paroled on Tilghman's recommendation when he developed an incurable disease.

Red Buck was next, killed while attempting to rob a bank. Doolin, who had married in 1894, first hid out with his wife and baby, but felt moving about with his family was too risky. He rode alone to Eureka Springs, Ark. Tilghman found him there and, in a slugfest inside of a public bathhouse, subdued the outlaw and brought him back to Guthrie, Okla. to stand trial.

Doolin's reputation was such that when Tilghman arrived with the bandit, 5,000 residents at the train depot cheered wildly—not for the marshal, but the outlaw. The federal jail couldn't hold Bill Doolin; he broke out weeks later and thirty-seven prisoners escaped with him.

His freedom was brief. Doolin joined his wife, bought a small farm and hoped he could live out his life in obscurity. Then Marshal Heck Thomas found him walking down a dirt road one night in 1896 and killed him with a single blast from his shotgun.

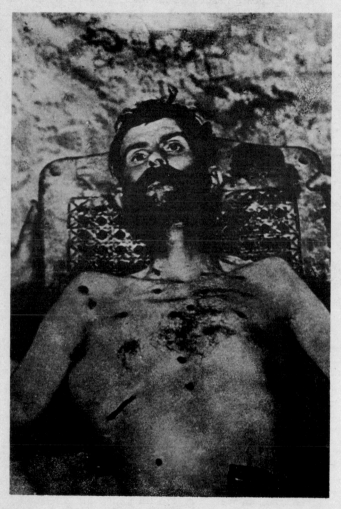

Oklahoma trainrobber Bill Doolin, shown dead after being gunned down by Marshal Heck Thomas in 1896. (Western History Collection, U. of Okla. Library)

DUNBAR, REUBEN A.
Murderer, Robber • (1829-1850)

The Lester family in Albany, N.Y., was quite well-to-do, their estate including large farmlands and many other holdings. When the widowed Mr. Lester died, his stepson, Reuben A. Dunbar, 21, sought to gain control of the entire estate by killing his two young nephews Stephen V. Lester, 8, and David L. Lester, 10.

Dunbar killed little Stephen with a club and hanged David from a tree. With his relatives out of the way Dunbar filed a claim on the Lester property, but his victims' bodies were quickly discovered. Dunbar was tried and convicted after writing out a confession.

The would-be landowner was hanged September 28, 1850.

DURRANT, WILLIAM HENRY THEODORE ("THEO")
Murderer • (1874-1898)

BACKGROUND: BORN AND RAISED IN SAN FRANCISCO. A SENIOR MEDICAL STUDENT AT COOPER MEDICAL COLLEGE. WORKED AS AN ASSISTANT SUNDAY SCHOOL SUPERINTENDENT AT THE EMANUEL BAPTIST CHURCH IN SAN FRANCISCO. DESCRIPTION: 5'5", BLUE EYES, BLACK HAIR, HEAVY MUSTACHE, SLENDER BUILD. ALIASES: NONE. RECORD: STRANGLED BLANCHE LAMONT TO DEATH 4/3/1895; KILLED AND MUTILATED MINNIE

Nothing about Theo Durrant suggested impropriety,
let alone the compulsion to murder. He was an
excellent medical student at San Francisco's reputa-
ble Cooper Medical College. He was also a staunch pillar
of his local church, Emanuel Baptist.

As an assistant Sunday-school superintendent, Theo was
also appointed church librarian, was an usher at masses,
and secretary to the church's youth group, Christian En-
deavor. Minor duties about the church, located at 22nd
and Bartlett Streets, included fixing pews and sealing leaky
pipes. To perform these chores, Durrant was given the
master key to the church.

Though Theo was the image of virtue to his fellow
parishioners, something dark and sinister lurked beneath
his religious veneer. The first evidence that all was not
right with Theo came to light in early 1895. A young woman
of the congregation, at Theo's request, entered the church
library after services. He asked her to wait for a moment
while he checked on a few things. She waited. Moments
later, Theo reappeared before her stark naked, grinning.
The woman ran screaming from the church.

The woman's charges of indecency were whispered to
her friends but nothing was done. Theo Durrant's reputation with the church congregation was impeccable. Even
the gossip that he attempted to kiss young ladies at church
socials was pooh-poohed.

On April 3, 1895, at about 4 p.m., several members of
the congregation saw Durrant alight from a cable car near
the church. One of the prettiest girls in the neighborhood,
buxom Blanche Lamont, was with Theo, walking arm-in-
arm. Blanche was a senior high school student. As the
pair walked into the wooden church, Blanche talked of
her dream to become a teacher.

Durrant led Blanche into the library. There, to the young
girl's amazement, he stripped. She screamed, but unlike

her predecessor, she did not run. Blanche's screams only served to incite Theo's anger—he dove for her neck, his powerful hands squeezing the life from her.

When her limp body fell forward, Theo grabbed Blanche by the waist and, as one would carry a cord of wood, carted her into an ante-room where he dressed. He then carried Blanche's body slowly up the steep stairs leading to the church belfry. He had to make the final ascent with a ladder, hauling Blanche up after him by her waist-length hair.

There, Durrant stripped the body and sexually assaulted it. After indulging himself, Theo put a wooden block under the dead girl's head—a makeshift pillow—folded her arms, and calmly climbed down. Downstairs, an organist, who had arrived early for practice, became alarmed at Durrant's appearance.

"I was fixing a gas jet and inhaled some fumes by mistake," he explained.

When Blanche's disappearance was noted the following day, authorities came to Theo. He had been seen with the girl. Did he know her whereabouts?

Durrant denied any such knowledge and then theorized for police that it was quite possible that poor Blanche had been seized by one of the roving gangs of white slavers then plaguing San Francisco and sold to a brothel in a foreign city.

Implausible as this idea seems today, such events were common in the 1890s, particularly in the still unsettled West Coast. The police were satisfied with Durrant's explanation and the church-going Theo became, for a while, a local celebrity. Young girls excited with the thought of being shanghaied approached Durrant, enamored with his white slaver theories.

One girl was petite Minnie Williams, 21, an attractive blonde. Theo made the same advances toward her as he had toward Blanche but Minnie happily responded. Later evidence revealed that the two met many times in the church library and had intercourse. The odd thing was that Theo Durrant still killed Minnie.

The reason for his second murder was never given but one report has it that Theo had admitted his murder of Blanche to Minnie and she threatened to tell the police.

Minnie's death was painful. While making love to her, Theo suddenly tore part of her dress away and jammed it violently down the girl's throat, asphyxiating her. Durrant then produced a knife and slashed Minnie's throat, forehead, and wrists. Following this orgy of bloodletting, Theo mutilated the body for over an hour with his knife. He was not satiated until he threw himself upon the corpse and had intercourse.

It was not until the next morning that some of the congregation, entering the library, discovered the gory scene. The walls and floor of the library were crusted with blotches of Minnie's blood.

Answering the screams of the church women, police quickly discovered Minnie's body in a closet. One of the detectives followed a hunch and climbed to the belfry where he saw the naked body of Blanche Lamont. "The body was white," he remarked later, "like a piece of marble."

Theo was brought in for questioning. He denied any knowledge of the two hideous murders. Police, however, found Minnie's purse in his closet, stuffed into a suitcoat.

Over one hundred witnesses testified at Durrant's trial. The accused himself testified, still claiming innocence, but the jury quickly condemned him. Appeals dragged on for three years and on January 7, 1898, Durrant's time ran out.

He mounted the scaffold in a dignified manner. As the sheriff approached him, Durrant aloofly stated: "Don't put that rope on, my boy, until I talk." His remark was ignored (and future historians were left to guess what mad Theo might have said). The sheriff ordered the hangman to continue and Durrant was abruptly sent through the trapdoor.

Theo Durrant's strange behavior was matched by that of his parents, who attended the hanging and watched their son die without comment. "They seemed proud of the whole thing," the prison warden commented.

As the Durrants waited for their son's body, the warden asked if they were hungry. They said they were. He had a small dinner brought to them and they calmly sat down, devouring slabs of roast beef and boiled potatoes. The two did not look up as Theo's body was brought into the same room and placed in an open coffin, not more than five feet from the table where they sat eating.

Their son's face was wreathed in a horrible grimace. It was black, the eyes bulged terribly. Durrant's swollen tongue jutted from his mouth, half bitten through.

Mrs. Durrant glanced only once in the direction of the coffin, then turned to her husband and said, "Papa, I'd like some more of that roast."

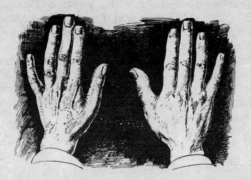

Apprentice newspaper czar William Randolph Hearst touted the gruesome murders of Theo Durrant in his **San Francisco Examiner** by showing the killer's hands on the front page. (N.Y. Historical Society)

DUTARTRE, PETER
Murderer • (? –1724)

Dutartre was a gullible soul with an equally naive wife. When Christian George, a Swiss religious fanatic, began to preach free love to the residents of Charlestown, S.C., Peter and Judith Dutartre became his followers.

They, along with about a dozen others, joined George in the Orange Quarter of South Carolina, setting up a love commune. Judith Dutartre often slept with George and became pregnant.

When Justice Symmons heard of the coming of "the Devil's child," he rose in anger and, leading a mob of irate and pious citizens, marched on George's barricaded camp. The love group refused to be arrested. Peter Dutartre picked up a musket and fired a shot, killing Justice Symmons. The mob stormed the fort and captured the congregation of lovers.

Following a two-day trial, Dutartre was convicted of murder along with Christian George and Peter Rombert. All three were hanged the following day. The good people of Charlestown returned to their churches, praying for Divine guidance.

FAIRBANKS, JASON
Murderer • (1780-1801)

Fairbanks was a 21-year-old rejected suitor, who, after failing to get permission from the parents of Elizabeth Fales to marry her, sought revenge. He led Miss Fales, 19, of Dedham, Mass. to a meadow near her home and slashed her throat, killing her. He then attempted to commit suicide but his efforts were clumsy.

Taken into custody, Fairbanks was quickly tried and convicted. He escaped; he was tracked through New England, and was overtaken in Whitehall, Vermont just as he was preparing to enter Canada. Fairbanks was immediately hanged.

FARRINGTON BROTHERS

Ex-guerillas who fought with Quantrill during the Civil War and had taken part in the bloody raids at Lawrence, Kan. and Centralia, Mo., the Farrington brothers, Levi and Hilary, were brutish bandits with murderous natures and short-lived careers as outlaws.

Following the Civil War, the Farringtons moved back to their native Mississippi, terrorizing the small towns in the swamp country and committing blood-soaked robberies. In 1870, the brothers, accompanied by William Barton and Bill Taylor, stopped the Mobile and Ohio flyer at Union City, Tenn. and stole more than $20,000 from the express car.

The Southern Express Company hired the Pinkerton

Pinkerton detectives battling the Farrington gang at Lester's Landing. (Pinkerton, Inc.)

Detective Agency to recover their money and capture the outlaws. William Pinkerton and train detectives caught up with Hilary Farrington in Verona, Mo. weeks later. The outlaw was holed up in a deserted farmhouse with several rifles. A day-long siege concluded when possemen rushed the place, pistols barking. Farrington was taken alive but, in an effort to escape his captors while being extradited to Tenn. on the steamboat *Illinois*, he struggled with the guards and was knocked overboard. He was crushed to death by the ship's stern paddle.

Levi Farrington was located the following year in the small town of Farmington, Ill. Drunk, Levi shot up the town square, challenging one and all to a duel. A lawman named Brown, affiliated with the Pinkertons, dashed into the square and wrestled the giant outlaw to the ground.

Levi was lynched by the irate citizens of Union City weeks later.

FOOY, SAM
Murderer, Robber • (1844–1875)

A half-breed Indian, Fooy went on a week-long rampage in the Oklahoma territory in 1875, ending with the brutal murder of a school teacher who was reluctant to give up $500 in savings.

Sentenced to death by Judge Isaac Parker in Fort Smith, Ark., Fooy, hours before he died on the gallows, told a reporter he had made peace with God.

"I dreamed I was on the gallows before a great crowd of people," Fooy said, "I was sick and weak and felt like fainting, and thought I could not face death.

"Just then a man stepped up from the crowd, came right up to me and said, 'Look, Sam, don't you be afraid to let them jump you. Jesus is standing under the floor and He will catch you in His arms.'

"That made me feel strong, when the drop came, and I felt no pain. I just fell asleep and woke up in the beautiful garden. It had running waters and stars were dancing on the waves."

Sam Fooy went through the trap on September 3, 1875, sent to his Maker, along with five others that day, by Fort Smith's dreaded executioner, hangman George Maldeon. A meticulous man, Maldeon made his own hanging ropes from Kentucky hemp and kept them well oiled at all times, using them over and over again on the sixty men he sent to death on the gallows (at $100 per man). He was as cold-blooded as they came. "I never hanged a man," Maldeon once said, "who came back to have the job done over."

FORTY THIEVES GANG

A group of professional muggers and pickpockets, this gang operated in the Lower East Side of Manhattan as early as 1820. Its immigrant members were often used as political sluggers who destroyed polling places during elections.

Like many another gang succeeding them, the Forty Thieves encouraged a sub-mob made up of juvenile delinquents dubbed the Forty Little Thieves Gang (from which new talent was recruited). The gang disappeared from view shortly before the Civil War.

GARCIA, MANUEL PHILIP
Murderer, Thief • (? -1821)

Garcia was a roughneck and thief who, with Jose Demas Garcia Castillano, operated in the Norfolk, Va. area as a burglar and highwayman. When another of his band, Peter Lagoardette, began courting a local girl, Castillano became incensed. The girl was his he told Garcia, and the two plotted murder.

Enticing Lagoardette to a deserted house in Norfolk March 20, 1820, Garcia and Castillano fell upon him with cutlasses, killing him. They dissected the body but authorities, inspecting the premises after neighbors reported smoke coming from the empty house, discovered Lagoardette's head, feet and hands half burned in the fireplace.

Garcia and Castillano, tracked down through laundry marks on clothes left in the deserted house (one of the first instances where such clues were used by police), were tried and hanged in Norfolk June 1, 1821.

GIBBS, CHARLES
Murderer, Pirate • (? -1831)

A native of Rhode Island, Charles Gibbs went to sea as a youth and soon fell into evil ways, first pilfering supplies on board ships and then participating in several mutinies and murders (he confessed to killing over 400 men before his execution, although this figure is in doubt and probably exaggerated by the melodramatic reports of the day).

Gibbs' final mutiny took place on board the *Vineyard*, which sailed from New Orleans for Philadelphia November 1, 1830. After spotting $50,000 in precious cargo, Gibbs, joined by a Negro cook, Thomas G. Wansley, killed Captain William Thornby and his mate, William Roberts, throwing them overboard off Hatteras.

Abandoning the ship at Long Island, Gibbs, Wansley and three others made their way ashore in a long boat. Gibbs' shipmates informed authorities of the mutiny and murders and Gibbs and Wansley were arrested, tried and convicted. The two were hanged after a large ceremony on Ellis Island, April 22, 1831.

GILLETTE, CHESTER
Murderer • (1884-1908)

At age twenty-two, Chester Gillette saw a new life dawning for himself. He had risen from poverty, orphaned at fourteen by parents who deserted him to spread the word of the Salvation Army throughout the land. Chester never harbored hatred for his religious-zealot parents. Their absence made him free of a home, schooling, and authority; he bummed his way through the country, hopping freights into strange towns and working at odd jobs.

Gillette became so familiar with the rails that he took a job as a railroad brakeman when a yard detective, who had collared him, kindly suggested it. A dull, routine-ridden job, it turned Gillette inward upon his own forgotten loneliness. At twenty, Chester was stirred with ambition and, remembering his uncle, a factory-owner in Courtland, N. Y., he wrote, asking for work. A task-master, the uncle agreed to hire his itinerant nephew if he was willing to begin at the bottom. The boy agreed and soon won promotion to shop foreman of the Gillette skirt factory at a salary of $10 per week.

As a distant member of the well-to-do Gillette family, Chester attended local society functions. At one ball, he met a socially prominent girl and fell in love with her, planning marriage as soon as his fortunes improved.

Petite Grace "Billie" Brown, an eighteen-year-old secretary who worked at the factory, brought Gillette's dreams to doom. Normally a reserved, calculating young man, Chester disregarded his rigid moral code (imbued in him since childhood by his fanatical parents) and seduced Grace.

Gillette forgot about her weeks later. She was a mere farm girl who had traveled to Courtland to earn a miserable $6 a week. He dismissed Grace as an unimportant flirtation, his eyes still focused upon his High Society girl. It was the spring of 1906. He had worked industriously for his uncle for two years. He would better his status by demanding and getting a junior partnership in the Gillette firm, he reasoned, and then be free to marry the girl he loved.

Billie Brown came to him in May and informed him that she was pregnant. She was in tears. He would marry her, wouldn't he? It was the decent, honorable, Christian

123

thing to do. The code of the Edwardian era demanded it or scandal and ruination was assured.

Chester Gillette stalled. Billie was not part of his plans. He was a gentleman now, elegantly attired in a wing collar and expensive suit, a young man on the rise. He couldn't be held back by a milkmaid of a girl, settling for a dowdy, inconspicuous, and socially vacuous marriage.

He convinced Billie to return to her father's farm and be patient. He would work something out very soon and come to her. The girl waited. When he failed to appear, Billie began to write imploring, tear-soaked letters. None were answered. Gillette finally received a letter from Billie in which she threatened to inform his uncle of his careless love-making.

Clutching the letter, Gillette panicked. He informed his uncle in July that he needed a vacation; he was worked out and needed rest, he explained. With $25 of borrowed money in his pocket, Chester journeyed to Utica, N. Y. on July 8, 1906, where he met Billie. They stayed at a hotel overnight as man and wife and then, at Gillette's suggestion, traveled southward into Herkimer County in the Adirondacks. Chester acted aimless. He was unresponsive to Billie's questions about marriage. But he had a plan and it was murder.

First, Gillette took the girl to Tupper Lake where they stayed at a lodge. The lake was crowded; Gillette required isolation. Chester carefully inquired if there was "any old hotel where they have boats to rent." He and Billie moved to the gabled, ramshackled Glenmore Hotel on Big Moose Lake.

The couple did not pretend marriage, oddly enough, when registering at the Glenmore. Gillette wrote down a false name. Billie wrote her real name and address. The management was not shocked since they took separate rooms. On the morning of the next day, July 11, 1906, Chester rented a boat. He placed a suitcase containing a large picnic lunch and a tennis racket in the craft, and he and Billie shoved off into the water at noon.

It was the last time Billie Brown was seen alive.

At about 8 p.m. that night, Gillette, lugging the suitcase, his clothes soaking, was spotted as he walked solemnly through the woods stretching from Big Moose Lake. An

Chester Gillette, who murdered Grace Brown on 7/11/06 on Big Moose Lake in upstate New York, sold this photo of himself to admiring women and used the money for catered meals in his cell. (UPI)

hour later he registered at the Arrowhead Inn on Eagle Bay. Still wet, Gillette strolled out to the beach and sat next to a bonfire to dry off. He lifted his melodic voice in song with a group of vacationers.

The desk clerk at the Arrowhead became suspicious of Gillette after the young man approached him and asked: "Has there been a drowning reported on Big Moose Lake?"

"No," came the reply.

Billie Brown's battered body floated to the surface of the lake that day and a coroner ruled her death a homicide. Her face and body had been battered. The suspicious clerk at the Arrowhead Inn called police when he heard of the killing, and Gillette was arrested.

The murder weapon was soon discovered. Searchers found the tennis racket Chester had hastily buried next to the shore of Big Moose Lake. At his sensational trial, Gillette shouted his innocence. Billie committed suicide by leaping into the water, he first claimed. Then he said he had accidentally capsized the boat and Billie, hit on the head by the hull, was drowned. Then he said that, perhaps, she was not unconscious but that she couldn't swim anyway and died in the water.

"But you can swim?" he was asked.

"Yes."

"Well?"

"Yes."

"And yet you made no effort to save her?"

Chester Gillette only shrugged on the stand.

For twenty-two days, the prosecution battled to prove murder. Gillette, to earn money to pay for specially catered dinners, sold autographed pictures of himself from his cell to the curious at $5 each. He cut out pictures of attractive women from newspapers and plastered the walls of his cell with these. Always at ease, he acted like a man still on vacation.

The jury heard more than 100 witnesses testify and finally, on December 4, 1906, found Chester Gillette guilty of murder. He was sentenced to death in the electric chair. He fought off execution through legal appeals for more than a year from his cell in Auburn Prison.

His time ran out on March 30, 1908. Refusing to confess to Billie's murder to the last, Gillette was led silently to the electric chair and executed.

Novelist Theodore Dreiser, basing his classic *An American Tragedy* upon the Gillette case, aptly described the boy's last moments: "And his feet were walking, but automatically, it seemed. And he was conscious of that familiar shuffle—shuffle—as they pushed him on and on toward that door. Now it was here; now it was being opened. There it was—at last—the chair he had so often seen in his dreams—that he so dreaded—to which he was now compelled to go. He was being pushed toward that—into that—on—on—through the door which was now open—to receive him—but which was as quickly closed again on all the earthly life he had ever known."

GOLDSBOROUGH, FITZHUGH COYLE
Murderer • (1880-1911)

Goldsborough fit the image of the eccentric young man born into wealth during the lazy, fat-cat years at the turn of the century. He was a workless, listless neurotic who squandered time in opulent surroundings. A Philadelphian, he had been trained for leisure. Thin-faced and pale, Fitzhugh kept mostly to himself, spending whole weeks in bed, devouring by the dozens mawkish, maudlin novels of the era.

His socially active sister, a spinster, was Goldsborough's only joy; he doted on her whims and fancies and would tolerate no criticism of her scatterbrain ways, not even from his parents. When the elder Goldsborough mildly chided his daughter, Fitzhugh would explode. He would rage and shout fist-shaking threats at his father. The son's conduct was excused following these rows. He was merely overprotective and sensitive about his sister, the family reasoned. Such affection was touching no matter how volatile its display.

In one reading orgy, Fitzhugh came across a novel written by David Graham Phillips, one of the most popular writers of the day. The novel, *The Fashionable Adventures of Joshua Craig*, dealt with a frivolous, selfish young lady placed well in American High Society. Goldsborough immediately assumed that Phillips' portrait of the spoiled girl was based upon his sister and became incensed.

He made no attempt to learn whether or not Phillips had ever met his sister (he had not). Fitzhugh wrathfully decided the popular novelist had wronged his sister and set out to make amends through murder.

Handsome well-dressed David Graham Phillips was the very essence of the popular man of letters in that Gibson Girl day. Indiana-born, he had gone to Princeton and worked for the *New York World* (once quoted as saying he would "rather be a reporter than president"). His eleven-year career as a novelist produced immensely lucrative best sellers such as *The Great God Success.* At forty-three, Phillips had finished his latest work, a book he considered his best writing to date, *Susan Lenox: Her Fall and Rise* (published in 1917 and thought for years by critics to be a minor masterpiece).

He would never live to see this book published. On January 23, 1911, the writer stepped from his fashionable Gramercy Park apartment for his morning stroll, an important walk this day in that he was on his way to mail a short story to the *Saturday Evening Post*.

As he slowly walked through the park, a well-cut, expensive overcoat shielding him from the brisk, clear day, his path was barred by an ashen-faced, hand-twitching man. For a moment, Phillips thought he was a panhandler, judging from his shabby clothes, unkempt hair and wild, blinking eyes. Just as he was about to reach into his pocket for change, Fitzhugh Coyle Goldsborough pulled forth a pistol.

"Here you go!" Goldsborough screamed and, at close range, shakily shot Phillips, his arm describing a purposely made circle in the air, a self-designed technique to assure several fatal wounds in the victim's head and torso.

Never glancing at Phillips, who had fallen to the sidewalk writhing in pain, Goldsborough shouted for horrified spectators to hear: "Here I go!" He placed the pistol next to his temple and blew away the front of his head. Phillips died days later in the hospital.

Police solved the mystery when Goldsborough's grieving parents came forward, explaining their son's error in thinking Phillips had maligned his sister. It was a thoroughly unromantic end for both men, an end not in keeping with that gentle epoch of hoop skirts and horse-drawn cabs. A sullen and sinister intruder into the world of New York Society, this murder.

GOLDSBY, CRAWFORD ("CHEROKEE BILL") Murderer, Robber • (1876-1896)

Goldsby, known in the Oklahoma territory as "Cherokee Bill," was the killer of thirteen men before his death on the gallows at age twenty.

His bloody career began in 1894 when he shot Negro Jake Lewis at a barn dance in Fort Gibson, Okla. He fled, wandering through the Creek and Seminole reservations. There he met and joined the outlaw gang led by Bill and Jim Cook. In June, after several small robberies, the gang rested in Tahlequah, Okla. A posse roared into town seeking the Cook brothers, but they escaped. As they fled from town, Cherokee Bill whipped about in his saddle and threw a shot at the pursuing lawmen. Deputy Sequoyah Houston dropped dead from his horse.

Bill, hiding out, went to stay with his sister Maude. Her husband, George Brown, was not the gentle sort and when Bill came upon him whipping his sister with a leather strap, he shot him. He next killed a railroad agent named Dick Richards who tried to argue him out of robbing a train station. That same day, Bill attempted to rob a train stopped at the station and shot a conductor, Sam Collins, for trying to push him away from the express car.

Cherokee next robbed a general store in Lenepah, Okla. When a local man, Ernest Melton, walked through the door, Bill sent a bullet into his head.

Judge Isaac Parker of Fort Smith offered $1,300 for Bill dead or alive, preferably dead. Two farmers, Clint Scales and Ike Rogers, overpowered the boy bandit in their house on January 29, 1895. He was taken to Fort Smith where he attempted numerous escapes. In one attempt, on June 26, 1896, he shot and killed guard Lawrence Keating, the father of four children.

Cherokee Bill was dragged from his cell weeks later and led to the gallows. He noted the hundreds of spectators gathered about the open yard and commented: "Hell, look at all the people. Something must be going to happen."

On the gallows he looked sharply about and then at the clear blue sky. "This is about as good a day as any to die," he said.

Cherokee's mother, at the bottom of the gallows, began to weep.

"Mother," the killer said, "you ought not to have come."
"I can go anywhere you go," she sobbed back.
"You got anything to say?" a guard said to Bill.
"No. I came here to die, not make a speech."
He swung off moments later.

Twenty-year-old Crawford Golds-by, called Cherokee Bill, murdered thirteen men before being hanged in 1896. (Western History Collection, U. of Okla. Library)

GRAVES, THOMAS THATCHER
Murderer, Thief • (1843-1893)

The killing of wealthy Josephine Barnaby by Dr. Graves in 1891 became one of America's classic murder mysteries. Mrs. Barnaby was the wife of a wealthy clothing store owner in Providence, R.I. When he died, Mrs. Barnaby, who had been estranged from her husband for a number of years, inherited only $2,500 annually.

Dr. Graves, who had treated Mrs. Barnaby for minor illnesses, learned of her husband's vindictive will. He advised Mrs. Barnaby to contest it, particularly the major parts of the estate left to the two Barnaby daughters. Graves became more than an adviser. Mrs. Barnaby gave him power of attorney over her holdings. When the will was successfully reversed, Graves began to systematically steal Mrs. Barnaby's assets.

To manipulate the estate, Dr. Graves insisted that Mrs. Barnaby travel for her health. He arranged one long trip after another for her. When the old woman grew suspicious, Graves told her that she was not able to handle her own business affairs and that if she attempted to do so, she would be declared incompetent and might be placed in an old people's home.

At one point, Graves boldly wrote to Mrs. Barnaby (while she was away on one of her extended vacations): "I wish to explain what being placed under guardianship means. You could not sign a paper legally, you could not borrow money, you could not have nothing [sic] charged more than a five-year-old, you could never step foot again in the Adirondacks for you could not even leave town, as you could not raise funds; you would have to live in your old home."

Mrs. Barnaby became alarmed by Graves' letter; this was an out-and-out threat. She was determined to return from

California and get rid of the bounder. On her return trip, Mrs. Barnaby stopped in Denver to visit a friend, a Mrs. Worrell.

Awaiting her in Denver was a package mailed to the Worrell home from the East. Pasted to the bottle of whiskey in the package was the note: "Wish you a Happy New Year's. Please accept this fine old whiskey from your friend in the woods."

Mrs. Barnaby and Mrs. Worrell mixed drinks from the bottle. Mrs. Worrell sipped her drink. "This is vile stuff," she said but drank down the whiskey as did Mrs. Barnaby.

Following a violent sickness which lasted for six days, both women died April 19, 1891. One of Mrs. Barnaby's daughters, Mrs. Mabel Conrad, when learning of the gift of whiskey, paid $1,000 to have her mother examined. The autopsy proved the old woman had been poisoned. Dr. Graves was immediately suspected and arrested.

While Graves went free on a $30,000 bond, authorities unearthed evidence to convict him of murder. At his trial, the prosecution surprised Graves when they produced a startling witness, one Joseph M. Breslyn. The witness, a young man, stated that Dr. Graves had approached him in November, 1890 (fully five months before the poisonous whiskey was delivered to Mrs. Barnaby in Denver) in the Boston train station and asked him to pen a note, claiming he could not write.

Breslyn agreed and Graves dictated: "Wish you a Happy New Year's. Please accept this fine old whiskey from your friend in the woods." Obviously, Graves did not intend to have his handwriting traced, the prosecution insisted, and the jury agreed. The Doctor was sentenced to die.

While awaiting a new trial in April, 1893, Graves was found dead in his cell. He had committed suicide by taking a heavy dose of poison.

GREEN, EDWARD W.
Murderer, Bankrobber • (1833-1866)

Though many historians insist that the first bank robbers in America were Frank James, the Youngers, and six other Missouri outlaws, this odd distinction belongs to Eddie Green, the postmaster of Malden, Mass. Green, who had been crippled in an accident as a youth, fell heavily into debt and began to drink.

The idea of robbing a bank was a spur-of-the-moment action. When Green walked into the Malden bank on December 15, 1863, he noticed that only Frank E. Converse, seventeen, the bank president's son, was on the premises.

Green returned to his home and got a pistol. Quickly, he went back to the bank and shot Converse twice in the head, killing him. He then helped himself to $5,000 of the bank's cash and fled.

Police received reports that Green was suddenly spending a lot of money and picked him up for questioning. He confessed and was sentenced to die. Execution took place February 27, 1866.

GREEN, HENRY G.
Murderer • (1823-1845)

A reformed drunk, Green became a temperance advocate. During one high-spirited meeting held to lay "Demon Rum" low, he chanced to meet eighteen-year-old Mary Ann Wyatt, whom he later married in Berlin, N.Y.

Soon after, Green began to have marital problems. His mother hated his wife, telling him that Mary Ann was not a fit life-mate. Apparently Green agreed with his mother, for he shortly gave Mary Ann a fatal dose of arsenic.

He was quickly taken, tried, and convicted. The execution was at Troy, N.Y. September 10, 1845.

GRINDER, MARTHA
Murderer • (1815–1866)

Mrs. Grinder, a resident of Pittsburgh, Pa., was a mental case. A raving sadist, she enjoyed any form of punishment and pain endured by others. In her confessions, Mrs. Grinder admitted: "I loved to see death in all its forms and phases, and left no opportunity unimproved to gratify my taste for such sights. Could I have had my own way, probably I should have done more [murder]."

To this end, Mrs. Grinder poisoned her neighbor, a Mrs. Carothers, with arsenic and then "nursed" the poor woman to her death.

She was tried and condemned to death, being executed January 19, 1866.

GUITEAU, CHARLES JULIUS
Assassin • (1844-1882)

BACKGROUND: BORN AND RAISED IN RURAL ILLINOIS. A SELF-TAUGHT, SELF-APPOINTED LAWYER. MARRIED BRIEFLY TO A SIXTEEN-YEAR-OLD GIRL WHOM HE ABANDONED. DESCRIPTION: APPROXIMATELY 5'9", BROWN EYES, BLACK HAIR, SLIGHT. ALIASES: NONE. RECORD: SHOT AND FATALLY WOUNDED PRESIDENT JAMES A. GARFIELD, 7/1/1881 (GARFIELD DIED 9/18/81); AFTER A LENGTHY TRIAL WHERE HE SERVED AS HIS OWN LAWYER, GUITEAU WAS HANGED 6/30/1882.

Guiteau was the classic political malcontent who would also, by today's standards, certainly be judged insane. A drifter and deadbeat, Guiteau practiced a weird brand of law. He took on small claims cases which gave him the opportunity to vent his hysterical tirades in court. The defendants of these cases rarely saw any compensation. Guiteau kept three-quarters of all settlements. He never paid any of his own bills and was, therefore, being constantly sued.

When hauled into court for his own debts, Guiteau, who fancied himself a powerful evangelist, called upon the Lord to aid him against heathen creditors. Somewhere in the midst of all his hopeless legal battles, dodging landladies, and preaching the true word of God, Guiteau married a sixteen-year-old street waif. He soon abandoned her, moving to Washington, D.C. There the self-styled lawyer patronized street prostitutes, caught syphilis, and decided he had earned an ambassador's appointment to Paris.

Politics interested Guiteau, and in 1880 he ran errands for the Republican group headed by Roscoe Conkling which was working for Grant's nomination at the convention. James A. Garfield finally got the nod and Guiteau switched sides, feverishly writing out a long-winded, erratic speech for Garfield to use in his campaign. After mailing his speech to Garfield, Guiteau had copies printed and these he passed out at meetings.

Garfield never used Guiteau's speech but, after the presidential election, the lawyer concluded that his words alone had swayed the voting public. He went to the White House and demanded his appointment to Paris in return for his unwanted literary efforts.

Though Lincoln had been murdered a scant sixteen years before, no security men, other than a few unarmed male secretaries, were in evidence at the White House. Guiteau entered and left the building at will. The President did see Guiteau once but, when the lawyer pressed for his appointment to Paris, Garfield put him off.

Guiteau then began to harass Secretary of State Blaine. The little man with the high-pitched voice accosted Blaine

Assassin Charles Guiteau was placed under arrest moments after fatally shooting President Garfield. (N.Y. Historical Society)

in White House corridors almost every day. Blaine lost patience and finally shouted: "Never speak to me about the Paris embassy as long as you live!"

According to his irrational thinking, there was nothing left for the political petitioner to do but to seek vengeance by killing the President. Guiteau purchased a .44-caliber pistol and began target practice on the trees lining the Potomac River. When he felt that he had become an accomplished marksman, he began to dog the President's movements.

Through the local newspapers which printed the President's daily schedule, Guiteau learned that Garfield would be taking the train to his alma mater, Williams College, to deliver an address on July 1, 1881. He hid in the Baltimore & Potomac train station and when Garfield, accompanied by Blaine, entered the terminal at 9:20 a.m., Guiteau rushed up and fired a bullet into the President.

Aides grabbed Guiteau and in a matter of seconds he was on his way to jail. Garfield's wound (he had been hit in the back, the bullet lodging behind the pancreas) proved fatal and the President died a little more than two months later.

Guiteau's trial in November of 1881 was a sensation. The prosecution quickly proved his premeditation. Wardens testified that Guiteau had inspected the District of Coumbia jail before the assassination, stating that it was "an excellent jail." Guiteau endorsed these statements by remarking that he wanted to see what his future home would be like.

The madman also stated that he had kept Garfield in his gun sights for weeks before he killed him. From a bench in a nearby park, he had watched the President leave the White House every day. He had stood behind Garfield in church once ready to kill him there, but had decided against it because the President's wife was with him. (Guiteau called her "that dear soul.")

With bursts of venomous outrage, Guiteau conducted his own defense for more than ten weeks, yelling, screaming, dancing ludicrously about the courtroom floor. His conduct went unchecked. He interrupted prosecution witnesses by calling them "dirty liars." Other times he would run in front of the prosecutor's table yelling that he was "a low-livered whelp," and "an old hog."

At other times, Guiteau appeared to be rational. "I had a very happy holiday," he told the judge after Christmas and New Year's, comments unsolicited by the bench.

Guiteau seemed to enjoy his imprisonment. So did the thrill-seeking people of Washington. He walked peacock-proud back and forth behind the bars while crowds (encouraged by the authorities) gaped at him.

The summation Guiteau delivered at the end of his trial was nothing short of spectacular. He told his jury that God had divined the assassination of President Garfield. When questioned about how God let him know this, Guiteau responded with: "God told me to kill." In a shrieking voice the assassin rose from his chair and said: "Let your verdict be, it was the Deity's act, not mine!"

Charles-Julius Guiteau acted as his own attorney at his trial; he mocked the judge and called the prosecutor names. (N.Y. Historical Society)

When he heard the jury's death verdict, Guiteau wagged his bony finger at each jurist, growling, "You are all low, consummate jackasses!"

At dawn, June 30, 1882, the day of his execution, Guiteau rolled back the blankets from his face (he suffered fitful nightmares and slept fully covered). Hurriedly, he dressed and then carefully trimmed his scraggly beard. He asked for bootblack and shined his shoes to a high gloss, humming and whistling his satisfaction at their appearance.

All through a mammoth meal, Guiteau carried on a one-sided conversation with God. When jailers came for him, he coolly adjusted his clothes and calmly walked from his cell to the gallows without comment. Once on the scaffold, he began to whimper and sob.

Seeing the rope awaiting him, he suddenly brushed away his tears, smiled, and produced a poem he had written for the occasion. As the executioner moved forward, Charles Julius Guiteau began to recite in a clear, high voice: "I am going to the Lordy. . . ."

GUNNESS, BELLE
Murderer, Robber • (1860–1908?)

BACKGROUND: BORN IN INDIANA IN 1860. MINOR PUBLIC EDUCATION. MARRIED PETER GUNNESS, SETTLED IN LAPORTE, INDIANA, BORE THREE CHILDREN, DISAPPEARED IN A FIRE IN HER FARMHOUSE 4/28/08. DESCRIPTION: 5'5", BLUE EYES, BROWN HAIR, CORPULENT. ALIASES: NONE. RECORD: POISONED ANDREW HELGELIEN AND THIRTEEN OTHER SUITORS IN THEIR SLEEP, STOLE THE MONEY THESE MEN POSSESSED AND DISAPPEARED IN 1908; HER CONFEDERATE, RAY LAMPHERE, WAS SENTENCED TO TWO TO TWENTY-ONE YEARS IN THE INDIANA STATE PENITENTIARY WHERE HE DIED.

The advertising departments of Chicago newspapers loved her. She regularly placed personal ads with them for a husband. She paid on time and her appeals made for interesting reading. But no one seemed to answer Mrs. Belle Gunness' ads.

No one the newspapers ever knew. Belle and her lover, handyman Ray Lamphere, knew a lot. almost all of Belle's lovelorn ads hit paydirt and her marriage-seeking correspondents hit only dirt.

All of Belle's matrimonial ads ended with the same essence-of-propriety warning, "triflers need not apply."

To the unsuspecting, Belle Gunness was a good, hard-working widow woman who supported her three fatherless children. Their father, Peter Gunness, had died in an accident.

Well, his death was finally ruled an accident after Belle faced an angry coroner and a curious jury. It seems that Peter Gunness, who ran a small hog farm and butchering shop, had been killed by a blow from the meat grinder which had toppled from a shelf. That was Belle's story.

The coroner of LaPorte, Indiana, didn't believe it. "This is murder!" he said and drew up a special jury to sift the evidence.

One of the Gunness children told a schoolmate: "My mamma killed my poppa. She hit him with a cleaver."

Even this hearsay didn't cause a ruffle in Belle's composure. She stuck to her story, and the coroner's jury freed her.

Just after her husband's untimely death, Belle took up with a handyman, Ray Lamphere, who helped out with the family business. He also shared the grieving widow's bed.

About this time, Belle hit upon her highly-successful scheme to bilk lovelorn suitors.

Several men from distant states answered Belle's carefully-worded ads. Some were seen escorting her briefly in the Laporte area; then they disappeared.

The last suitor to appear was Andrew Helgelien who answered Belle's ad in a Norwegian-language newspaper. The thrifty, love-seeking bachelor received a honey-kissed letter from Belle who promised true love and a long life of wedded bliss. She also casually mentioned that she needed $1,000 to pay off a pressing mortgage.

She ended her letter with: "My heart beats in wild rapture for you, come prepared to stay forever." Her words were prophetic to say the least.

Helgelien traveled from South Dakota with his wallet full of money and his heart aching for Belle. Before his arrival, Belle changed from her usual attire of overalls in which she butchered hogs to a flouncy dress. This in itself was a hardship since Belle enjoyed wearing men's clothing.

Helgelien showed up and was immediately introduced to Lamphere as the hard-working widow's next husband.

Suddenly Helgelien disappeared.

Nothing more would have been said about the amazing vanishing acts performed by Belle's suitors except that a roaring fire occurred on the night of April 28, 1908 and Belle's farmhouse went up in smoke.

The Gunness place was entirely gutted and the good citizens of LaPorte rocked with tragedy. Belle had been found with her three children, ages eleven, nine, and five.

Upon further investigation, Sheriff Smutzer became puzzled. The body of the woman, burned to a crisp, was oddly shriveled. Belle, who stood 5'5", tipped the scales at 280 pounds. Yet the dead woman found in the Gunness ruins was only 150 pounds.

Smutzer found it impossible to believe that the fire, irrespective of its heat, could have reduced Belle by 130 pounds. What made the job of identification even more difficult was that the dead woman's head was missing!

At first, the coroner had speculated that a falling beam had decapitated the helpless victim. A closer look favored the fact that a murderer had severed the head and set fire to the entire building.

But who?

Ray Lamphere was drinking heavily after the burning of Belle's house. Sheriff Smutzer picked him up. Lamphere bragged to him how he had slept with Belle. Then Smutzer charged him with killing Mrs. Gunness and setting fire to her house.

Lamphere screamed his innocence.

Smutzer knew that Belle had fired Lamphere after Helgelien arrived and that the handyman had repeatedly tried to force himself on her after that. The sheriff also knew that Belle had Lamphere arrested for trespassing on her property.

At that time Belle had told the arresting officer that "I'm afraid he'll set fire to the place." It was a meaningful statement coming from her.

Just as Sheriff Smutzer was trying to puzzle out the Gunness mystery fire, Helgelien's brother Asle arrived from

South Dakota. He insisted Belle had killed his brother Andrew for his life savings. His suspicions increased when diggers, looking for Belle's head in the ruins of her home, began to unearth shocking artifacts.

Found were eight men's watches; also in the rubble were bones and human teeth. Asle Helgelien helped the diggers search and intuitively pointed to Belle's hog pen. "Try here," he told the workmen, pointing to a pen surrounded by a six foot fence.

The diggers turned up four bodies expertly sliced up and wrapped in oil cloth. One of them was Andrew Helgelien . . . or what was left of him.

The following day three more dissected bodies were unearthed. Fourteen bodies in all were unearthed on Belle's property.

Smutzer pieced the story together this way: Belle had lured her lovesick suitors to LaPorte with promises of marriage and a happy home. Then she drugged them in their sleep, crushed their heads, and cut them up, just as she butchered her hogs.

The sheriff estimated that Belle had stolen over $30,000 from her hapless victims. This was an astronomical sum for the year 1908.

Yet the body of the headless, 150-pound woman remained a mystery to Smutzer. The sheriff figured that Belle must have been a heartless creature to kill her attractive children in the fire if she was responsible for it. There was a good chance that she was.

The woman found in the ashes, the sheriff reasoned, was not Belle. But he needed proof. Smutzer went to a man in LaPorte who had been a prospector in the great California gold rush of 1849.

Smutzer was interested in locating the false teeth Belle was known to have had. The prospector went to work building a sluice. The entire Gunness building, or what remained of it, would be sifted through the sluice in search of Belle's teeth.

Hundreds of LaPorte's citizens turned out for the sluicing operations. Very soon after the water began to flow, charred pages from books dealing with hypnotism and anatomy were identified.

More male teeth and watch parts and clothing were also

discovered. Then the prospector hit pay dirt. Belle's porcelain plate, attached to one of her real anchor teeth, turned up. This convinced the sheriff that the 150 pound body was Belle's. The mystery was solved.

Or was it?

Lamphere stood trial for the murder of his murderous lover. The jury exonerated him of the murder of Belle but convicted him of setting fire to the Gunness place. He was sentenced to two to twenty-one years in the state penitentiary.

He never saw freedom again. During his trial, Ray Lamphere developed tuberculosis, and he died in prison.

Before he died, Lamphere confessed the whole sordid story to his cellmate. He knew all about Belle's murders and had, in fact, helped her by burning the bodies of her victims, he said.

But as far as the headless woman found in the burned out ruins of the Gunness home, she definitely was not Belle. Lamphere stated that Belle had lured a drunken derelict from Chicago and killed her by slipping strychnine into her glass of whiskey. She then decapitated the hapless harlot and put her in bed with her pathetic children and burned the house down around them.

As a final touch, Belle had ripped out her own anchor tooth and false plate and tossed them into the burning house. Lamphere said she made off with a fortune stolen from the men she had killed. She was supposed to contact the moronic Lamphere later but never did.

"For all I know," Lamphere moaned, "she's living the high life in Chicago or New York or even San Francisco . . . what China blue eyes she had."

Incredible as it may seem, Ray Lamphere died in his cell still in love with this human monster.

And Belle? No one ever heard from or saw her again.

HALBERT, HENRY
Murderer • (1735–1765)

According to his own confession, Henry Halbert had led a life of sin which included "drinking, whoring, cursing, swearing, breaking the Sabbath, and keeping all manner of debauched company." To this he added the senseless murder of a Philadelphia youth, Jacob Woolman, by cutting his throat one night while drunk.

Halbert was hanged October 19, 1765, in Philadelphia.

HARDIN, JOHN WESLEY
Murderer • (1853–1895)

BACKGROUND: BORN IN BONHAM COUNTY, TEX., 5/26/1853, THE SECOND OF TWO SONS (JOSEPH WAS OLDER BY TWO

YEARS) TO ELIZABETH AND REV. J. G. HARDIN. MINOR PUBLIC EDUCATION. MARRIED JANE BOWEN IN 1872, WHO BORE HIM TWO GIRLS AND A BOY; JANE HARDIN DIED 11/6/92; REMARRIED TO CALLIE LEWIS 1/8/95. ORIGINAL OCCUPATION, RANCHER. DESCRIPTION: 5'11", BLACK EYES, BLACK HAIR, THIN. ALIASES: J. H. SWAIN. RECORD: KILLED A NEGRO NEAR BONHAM IN 1868 AT AGE 15; REPORTEDLY KILLED THREE SOLDIERS TRACKING HIM FOR THE MURDER WEEKS LATER; WITH SIMP DIXON KILLED TWO MORE SOLDIERS IN 1869; SHOT AND KILLED A CIRCUS HAND MONTHS LATER; KILLED GUNFIGHTER JIM BRADLEY IN 1870; KILLED AN UNKNOWN ROBBER IN KOSSE, TEX., 1871; ARRESTED IN LONGVIEW, TEX. AND CHARGED WITH MURDER (DISCLAIMED BY THE DEFENDANT); ESCAPED, KILLING A HALF-BREED GUARD IN EARLY SPRING, 1871 AND THREE SOLDIERS WHO TRACKED HIM DOWN; KILLED WITH HUGH ANDERSON GUNFIGHTER JUAN BIDENO, IN AUGUST, 1871 (BIDENO WAS WANTED FOR THE MURDER OF TEXAS CATTLEMAN WILLIAM C. COHRON); KILLED AN UNKNOWN GUNFIGHTER IN ABILENE, KAN. LATE 1871; KILLED GONZALES COUNTY POLICEMAN NEGRO GREEN PARAMOOR, AND WOUNDED HIS AIDE, JOHN LACKEY, LATE 1871; ALLEGEDLY KILLED THREE MORE NEGRO POLICEMEN WHO CAME TO ARREST HIM WEEKS LATER; KILLED DEPUTY SHERIFF J. B. MORGAN IN CUERO, TEX., 1873 WHILE INVOLVED IN THE SUTTON-TAYLOR RANGE WAR; KILLED WITH JIM TAYLOR SHERIFF JACK HELM IN DEWITT COUNTY, TEX. IN APRIL, 1873; KILLED BROWN COUNTY, TEX. SHERIFF CHARLES WEBB 5/26/74 IN A GUNFIGHT; CAPTURED BY TEXAS RANGER JOHN B. ARMSTRONG AND POSSE 8/23/77 IN THE PENSACOLA, FLA. TRAIN DEPOT; TRIED IN AUSTIN, TEX. FOR THE WEBB MURDER IN SEPTEMBER, 1877; FOUND GUILTY AND SENTENCED TO TWENTY-FIVE YEARS AT HARD LABOR AT RUSK PRISON IN HUNTSVILLE, TEX.; PARDONED IN 1894; SHOT IN THE BACK AND KILLED BY JOHN SELMAN, SENIOR 8/19/95 IN AN EL PASO, TEX. SALOON.

"I f you wish to be successful in life, be temperate and control your passions; if you don't, ruin and death is the inevitable result." This upstanding exhortation was penned by none other than the most notorious gunslinger of the Old West, a man straight out of fiction whose quick-draw duels in dusty Texas streets were real, the twenty-one men (or more) who fell before his guns authentic—the most notorious, whooping, leather-slapping gunfighter of them all—John Wesley Hardin.

a preacher, like Billy, he killed his first man as a young teenager. Hardin's bloody Texas trail is almost as hard to follow as Billy's, except that his infamous gun duels were reported (with all the literary embellishments indigenous to the era) in the press and in Hardin's own book, written in dime-novel style, a self-aggrandizing autobiography known more for its colorful flare than for its honesty.

Reportedly, John Wesley Hardin killed more than forty men, almost all in gunfights, but the actual count is somewhere in the twenties, an intimidating record which brands Hardin the most diligent killer of his day.

A product of the South, Hardin and his family felt the Confederate defeat deeply after the Civil War. John Wesley, named after the famous Methodist leader in England, hated all Negroes. At fifteen, while living with his family in Bonham, Tex., Hardin reported that a Negro bully "came at me with a big stick," and so he shot the fellow dead with an old Colt pistol.

Like Billy Bonney, this teenage murder caused him to flee a fugitive "not from justice," Hardin rationalized, "but from the injustice and misrule of the people who had subjugated the South."

The young firebrand made his way to Navarro County, after (again by his own report) shooting down three Union soldiers pursuing him for the Bonham killing. In Navarro, Hardin went to work for a ranch as a cowboy. About this time, Hardin, with his cousin Simp Dixon, shot down two more Union soldiers in a quarrel and followed up these killings with a gun duel with gunslinger Jim Bradley. Hardin had taken offense and stood up shooting after Bradley accused him of cheating at cards.

As a teenager, Hardin had developed a fast draw, one of the quickest in the West. He was a rare gunslinger in that he employed a cross-draw. His two holsters were sewn into a vest, the pistol butts pointing inward across his chest. When Hardin drew, he crossed his arms and pulled his guns forth in a wide arch, a one-motion movement, rather than reaching down to a hip holster and jerking the pistol upward and outward. He figured it saved him vital seconds and, many times, his life.

After settling an argument with a circus roustabout by

John Wesley Hardin of Texas, the top killer of the West. (Western History Collections, U. of Okla. Library)

shooting him through the head, Hardin headed for Kosse, Tex. where he knew a dance hall girl. When Hardin was in her room, the door burst open and an enraged man identified himself as the girl's lover. The unknown gunman held a pistol on Hardin and demanded $100 or he would kill him. Hardin explained that he possessed only $60 but the robber was welcome to that. The bandit agreed. Hardin clumsily handed the money over, most of the bills falling to the floor.

"When he stooped down to pick it up and as he was

straightening up," Hardin later related, "I pulled my pistol and fired. The ball struck him between the eyes and he fell over, a dead robber."

While being taken to Waco, Tex. to stand trial for a murder he emphatically denied committing, Hardin escaped from his guard, killing him. He explained that he had purchased a Colt pistol from a fellow prisoner in Longview where he was first arrested and had secreted the gun on his person before the journey.

Three Yankee soldiers sent to recapture the boy gunman, were slain by Hardin on the open prairie; he was on foot and the three were mounted when they rushed him. The youth made his way to a ranch where he took a job herding cows. The owner, William C. Cohron, was shot to death by Juan Bideno, a cattle rustler.

With another ranch hand, Hugh Anderson, Hardin tracked Bideno for weeks, finally catching up with him in early August, 1871. The two charged each other on ponies; Hardin won. Bideno received a bullet in the heart.

Though most of John Wesley Harden's wild exploits had taken place in small Texas tank towns, his reputation as a fast triggerman preceded him to Abilene, Kansas, where he showed up in 1871. Abilene was a wide-open cattle town with violent gun battles taking place every day on its wagon-rutted dirt streets. The only law came in the personage of 6'2", long-haired James Butler "Wild Bill" Hickok, town marshal and savage gunman.

Hours after Hardin hit town he began to drink, emerging from a saloon in festive spirits. He fired several shots into the air as a way of announcing his arrival, and then turned to face the tall Hickok who stood in his path.

"You can't hurrah me," Hickok said coldly. "I won't have it."

"I haven't come to hurrah you," Hardin replied just as coldly, "but I'm going to stay in Abilene."

Hickok studied the frail-looking poorly-dressed cowboy. "I'll have your guns first," the marshal said.

With that, John Wesley Hardin later claimed, Hickok became a victim of the celebrated "border roll" or gun-spin. Hardin wrote: "I said all right and pulled them out of the scabbard, but while he was reaching for them, I reversed them and whirled them over on him with the muzzles in

Wild Bill Hickok, "The Prince of Pistoleers"; some said Hardin backed Hickok down in Abilene in 1871 with a quick gun-spin. (The Kansas State Historical Society, Topeka)

his face, springing back at the same time. I told him to put his pistols up, which he did."

Facing down Hickok was a heady claim to make, and many Wild Bill enthusiasts refuse to believe Hardin ever performed this trick, but he did stay in Abilene. The fact that Hardin felt no animosity toward Hickok was evidenced one night in the Bull's Head Saloon and Gambling House, owned by Ben Thompson, the scourge of the plains. Thompson, who had had several run-ins with Hickok, reportedly asked Hardin to shoot the marshal down.

Hardin became indignant. He was no hired killer, he insisted. "If Bill needs killin', why don't you do it yourself?" he said. Thompson declined.

The boy gunslinger left Abilene abruptly weeks later. A ruffian who proclaimed his hatred for Texans to one and all in a saloon where Hardin was drinking was drilled on the spot. John Wesley, knowing Hickok would be on the prod for him after the shooting, jumped on his horse and dashed out of town.

He journeyed back to Texas, ranching a bit in Gonzales County. There, two Negro policemen, Green Paramoor and John Lackey, went hunting for him. Hardin shot Paramoor and ran Lackey off after wounding him several times.

In 1872, Hardin's luck came "with the bark on." First, he was wounded in a gunfight with Phil Sublet in a gambling disagreement. Sublet let Hardin have a load of buckshot. A posse came riding into Trinity City after him with a warrant for the Paramoor killing. Hardin, after a furious gun-blasting chase, escaped, but not before one of the pursuing lawmen had shot him in the leg.

Too much, John Wesley decided. The best way to continue living was to surrender, and that he did, turning over his guns to Sheriff Richard Reagan who escorted Hardin to the Gonzales jail. As he was being placed in his cell, a jittery deputy squeezed off a round, wounding the gunfighter again in the knee.

Hardin tired of jail and cut his way through the bars of his cell with a saw smuggled to him by a friend. He returned to his wife Jane, whom he had married only months before.

Connubial life couldn't hold John Wesley for long (although he did manage to sire three children during the lulls of his battles). He soon limped off to neighboring DeWitt County where his relations—the abundant Taylor family—were having trouble with the Suttons. It was a blood feud that dated back to 1868 when clan chieftain William Sutton had shot Buck Taylor from ambush.

Some claimed that the feud dated back two decades before the Civil War, moving with the two families as they settled first in South Carolina, then in Georgia, and finally in Texas, curiously always on neighboring lands. Leaders of the Taylor faction were Pitkin, Creed, Josiah, William, and Rufus Taylor. Against them were the volatile and vehement Suttons whose 200-man army all but dominated the territory and controlled the range. Backing them up were lawman Jack Helm, cattle baron Abel Head "Shanghai" Pierce, and Joe Tumilson.

Hardin first worked for the Clements family, also his cousins and stalwart Taylor supporters. In the small town of Cuero, wedged in the heart of the contested territory, Hardin ran into Sheriff J. B. Morgan, a Sutton man. Morgan, according to Hardin, passed several unkind remarks about his personality, parentage, and physical appearance, all of which caused Hardin to take stern umbrage. In no time, the two reached for their guns. Hardin wrote: "I pulled my pistol and fired, the ball striking him just above the left eye. He fell dead. I went to the stable, got my horse, and left town unmolested."

The war raged on through 1873. Two of Pitkin Taylor's cousins, Bill and Henry Kelly, were arrested by Jack Helm who looked the other way while his two deputies, Doc White and John Meador, shot the prisoners. Helm was booted out of the state police force but that didn't prevent Sutton men from shooting Pitkin Taylor weeks later on his front porch. His son, Hardin's best friend at the time (friendships with gunfighters were as transitory as their addresses), Jim Taylor, swore vengeance: "I will wash my hands in old Bill Sutton's blood!"

Taylor and Hardin set an ambush in Bank's Saloon but Bill Sutton and some of his boys got off with light flesh wounds. Hardin's aim was better a few weeks later when two Sutton partisans, Jake Chrisman and Jim Cox, were shot and killed.

Then, Jack Helm, a man "whose name was a horror to

all law-abiding citizens," according to Hardin, came up against Hardin in a blacksmith shop. When Helm jerked forth a knife and tried to plunge it into Jim Taylor's chest, Hardin let him have both barrels from a shotgun he was holding.

The war culminated in a full-scale week-long battle which raged through the town of Clinton, Tex. Both factions fought from the area of Tumilson House down into the town, some two miles distance. Waves of charge and countercharge finally ebbed at the Clinton Courthouse where a queasy truce was finally accepted by both sides, mediated by Judge Clay Pleasants.

Pot-shooting went on into 1874 but the war came to a blood-soaked end when Jim and Bill Taylor, on a tip from Hardin, located Bill Sutton, his chief aide, Gabe Slaughter, and Sutton's wife and baby, as they were about to board the New Orleans-bound steamer at Indianola. Jim Taylor completed his vow by sending a bullet into Bill Sutton's heart. Gabe Slaughter fell with a ball sent to the same spot by Jim's brother Bill.

The decades-old Sutton-Taylor feud was ended. John Wesley Hardin went home to his wife and children at Commanche, Tex.

But there would be no peace for the gunfighter now; he had killed too many men, one too many for Brown County Sheriff Charlie Webb, a brave lawman who learned Hardin and Jim Taylor were residing in Commanche. Both men, he knew, were wanted, especially Hardin. Almost every sheriff in Texas held warrants for his arrest except Commanche's John Karnes, a friendly marshal who enjoyed playing cards with Hardin in one of the town's six saloons.

It was Hardin's twenty-first birthday when Charlie Webb came to town. The one-street Commanche held races in Hardin's honor and his big bay swept the meets. He had pocketed more than $3,000 and enough cattle, horses, and equipment to outfit a large ranch.

In the midst of the celebration, Sheriff Webb rode up slowly to the saloon. Hardin was on the steps with a drink in his hand, his last of the day. His little brother Jeff sat in a buckboard, waiting to take the outlaw to his ranch and family.

Webb tethered his horse to a hitching post fifteen feet away as Hardin eyed him. The sheriff walked to within five feet of the gunfighter, staring at him, his hands folded behind his back. Hardin spread his coat, revealing his gun butts jutting outward, vest-high. He kept his hands poised outward, limp, bent, as if he were about to drop them lightly upon piano keys and play.

"Have you any papers for my arrest?" Hardin asked Webb.

"I don't know you," the sheriff replied.

"My name is John Wesley Hardin," the outlaw said.

"Now I know you, but I have no papers for your arrest."

Hardin then ceremoniously invited Webb into the saloon for a drink and the lawman accepted with alacrity. Hardin led the way. After taking a step toward the saloon's swinging doors, a friend, Bud Dixon, called to Hardin: "Look out!"

The gunfighter jumped to one side, yanking out his deadly pistols with his turn-about and firing in the same motion. Webb, who had half-drawn his pistol behind Hardin's back (proving him to be one of the slowest guns in the West), was caught flat-footed, and Hardin's first bullet wickedly tore into his left cheek, killing him. Though dead on his feet, the sheriff, before he collapsed, got off a spasmodic shot which wounded Hardin in the side. According to Hardin's count, Webb was his fortieth victim.

It was nothing but running after that. Hardin bade a quick farewell to his small family and, leading a string of mounts, headed East with a posse behind him. A lynch mob caught up with his brother Joe and hanged him. The Dixon brothers, Tom and Bud, were hanged days later. Hardin's friends Ham Anderson and Alex Barrickman were hunted down and shot to death. The name of John Wesley Hardin had become anathema in Texas. A $4,000 reward was placed on his head.

The Pinkertons took up his trail. So did the Texas Rangers. Dozens of apprentice fast-draw artists were also searching for him. One could make a reputation for one's self by putting a bullet into John Wesley Hardin. But he was nowhere to be found. He had vanished. Lawmen staking out his ranch gave up in disgust after several months. Vague reports drifted in from Georgia, Florida, Louisiana, and Alabama. He had been seen there, robbing trains.

After three years of search and surveillance, the Rangers were rewarded. They determined Hardin would be in Pensacola, Fla. after intercepting a letter he had sent to his wife.

The Pensacola station was jammed to every platform board with Rangers on August 23, 1877, when the train came in. Texas Ranger Lieutenant John B. Armstrong first spotted Hardin sitting at a window, his elbow bent on the sill, his cupped hand cradling a placid, unsuspecting face. The Rangers boarded the car from both ends and converged on Hardin; he struggled fiercely in the narrow train aisle with a dozen lawmen before he was subdued and knocked to the floor.

When he looked up, Armstrong's pistol was aimed at his forehead. Hardin's heroic account has him uttering: "Blow away! You will never blow a more innocent man's brains out, or one that will care less!"

The outlaw then wrote that Armstrong stopped one of his deputies from clubbing him, majestically saying: "Men, we have him now; don't hurt him; he is too brave to kill and the first man that shoots him I'll kill him."

Uninspired reality flagged down such roaring rhetoric. When Armstrong walked down the train's aisle toward Hardin, the outlaw spotted the lawman's raised 7½" barrel Peacemaker, the type of weapon commonly used by the Rangers.

"Texas, by God!" Hardin yelled and yanked for his high-riding pistols while attempting to stand up. He was a ridiculous sight. His guns snagged in his suspenders. "He almost pulled his breeches over his head," Armstrong reported.

While Hardin was trying to untangle himself, one of his companions jumped into the aisle and fired a wild shot at Armstrong which coursed through his wide-brimmed hat. Armstrong aimed carefully and plugged the man square in the chest. He grunted and then dove through a window, got up from the platform and staggered a few feet, dropping dead at the feet of James Duncan, another lawman.

John Gipson "Gyp" Clements.
(N.H. Rose Collection)

Frustrated, Hardin still hadn't freed his guns. As he stood struggling and cursing, Armstrong reached over and hit him alongside the head, knocking him unconscious. The other three outlaws meekly surrendered their sixguns to the fearless Ranger and were escorted from the train. Hardin had to be carried; he was unconscious for two hours.

John Wesley insisted that he was J. H. Swain all the way back to Texas. He had come to Pensacola to buy timber, he claimed. Who was John Wesley Hardin? By the time he crossed the border into the Lone Star State, Hardin admitted his identity. Taken to the jail in Austin, Hardin passed his idle moments with some infamous fellow prisoners—Johnny Ringo, Manning Clements (who with Joe and John Gipson "Gyp" Clements had fought on the Taylor side in the DeWitt County War), and Bill Taylor.

The courthouse in Gonzales was packed when Hardin was moved there for the murder trial of Sheriff Webb. The eloquent outlaw rose in his own defense on the stand, pleading his case with the sweep and flower of a Shakespearian actor.

155

"Gentlemen," he began, "I swear before God that I never shot a man except in self-defense. Sheriff Webb came to Commanche for the purpose of arresting me, and I knew it. I met him and defied him to arrest me, but I did not threaten him . . . I knew it was in his mind to kill me, not arrest me. Everybody knows he was a dangerous man with a pistol." He looked about the courtroom with pleading eyes. "I know I don't have any friends here but I don't blame them for being afraid to come out for me. My father is a good man, and my brother who was lynched never harmed a man in his life."

He became solemn, his resonant voice carrying throughout the stilled courtroom, a tall, thin young man dressed all in black like his preacher-father. "People will call me a killer, but I swear to you gentlemen [fixing his wide-set eyes upon the jury], that I have shot only in defense of myself. And when Sheriff Webb drew his pistol I had to draw mine. Anybody else would have done the same thing. Sheriff Webb had shot a lot of men. That's all, gentlemen." He eased himself into his chair and waited.

The jury shuffled from the box and returned in an hour and a half. He was found guilty of second-degree murder. Hardin's flamboyant ability with words had saved his life. He was sentenced to serve twenty-five years of hard labor at Rusk Prison in Huntsville, Tex.

John Wesley Hardin went into the Huntsville prison a boy gunman and was released sixteen years later, reformed, he claimed, in February, 1894. The reformation was painful. Hardin rebelled against the prison authorities for close to ten years. He tried to escape several times, was caught, and whipped. He led revolts and was thrown into solitary confinement, given no food or water for days. Then he conformed, quieted, and began to study law in his cell for hours on end.

He was forty-one when he was set free and he immediately threw himself into law studies. His wife Jane had died while he was in prison; his children had grown up and moved off. Alone, he traveled to El Paso where he worked as a lawyer. Citizens of the modern frontier hailed his rehabilitation with cheers. The El Paso Times praised his good citizenship and community leadership.

But there was an unrelenting wild streak in John Wesley Hardin and he was soon back in the saloons gambling and ofttimes wearing his irons. He took a pretty new wife, Callie Lewis, a girl who became infatuated with his legendary exploits. The marriage was a bad one. Callie, only eighteen, soon tired of her carousing husband and left him. Hardin began to drink all the more. He lost his ability to hold liquor and was often found, dead drunk, in the gutters that fronted on the sleazier El Paso dives.

His nerve seemed to flee, too. He became enamored with a fun-loving married woman, heavyset Mrs. Martin McRose. Her husband, a wanted cattle rustler, was hiding out across the border in Mexico. When McRose, Vic Queen, Tom Finnessy, and other members of this outlaw band crossed into the U.S., they were shot down by Ranger Jeff Milton and U.S. Marshals George Scarborough and Frank McMahon. Hardin, upon hearing of the incident, boasted in the bars that he had hired the lawmen to shoot McRose so he could have Mrs. McRose to himself.

Milton flew into a wild rage when he heard of this and tracked Hardin down in a bar where he demanded an apology. Hardin said he was not wearing his guns or the Ranger wouldn't speak so to him.

"You're lying again," Milton stormed. "You're always armed. And you can go for your gun right now or tell all these men here and out loud that you lied."

Without hesitation, Hardin turned to the soggy faces in the saloon and swept an encompassing hand before them. "Gentlemen," he intoned, "when I said that about Captain Milton, I lied."

Worse came to Hardin days later. Beyond public humiliation, he endured one of the most inglorious ends to ever befall a feared Texas outlaw.

Following an argument with lawman John Selman, who had the effrontery to throw Mrs. McRose in jail for rowdy conduct, Hardin passed several unpleasant comments about Selman's heritage, calling the policeman's father an assortment of vile names.

Old John Selman's hatred for Hardin went back for years. When he heard that Hardin had stated, "Old John better go fixed at all times," Old John, town constable, picked

Hardin's killer, John Selman, Senior. (N.H. Rose Collection)

up his pistol and headed for the Acme Saloon on July 19, 1895. He found Hardin there as he knew he would, and quickly walked up behind him.

Hardin was at the bar, shooting dice with the bartender. "Four sixes to beat," John Wesley said after a roll and at that moment he looked up into a mirror and saw Selman's pistol pointed at him. He never had a chance to move.

The first bullet killed him, splitting open the back of his head. Wordless, the great gunfighter toppled to the floor, dead. Selman was acquitted of murder; his lawyer, Albert Fall (of the future Teapot Dome scandal), successfully pleaded his client innocent, stating he had acted in self-defense. Hardin was going for a gun in a shoulder-holster, Fall maintained.

The death of John Wesley Hardin was ignominious, a weird slur upon his personal credo of honor that demanded gunfighters face each other in fair draw, life awarded to the man with the fastest hands and the sharpest eyes.

He did, however, die with his boots on.

[ALSO SEE Clay Allison, Ben Thompson.]

HARE, JOSEPH THOMPSON
Highwayman • (? -1818)

A freebooter born in Chester, Pa., Hare, at an early age, gathered a band of cutthroats and preyed upon the stages running between Nashville, Tenn. and Natchez, Miss. He was a legend for a dozen years, totally unknown to lawmen of the day. He was caught in 1813 and sent to prison for five years. Upon his release, Hare immediately resumed his old ways, stopping the Baltimore night coach near Havre de Grace.

The coach was carrying a special bank shipment and Hare made off with more than $15,000, his biggest haul and an enormous prize for those days.

Unfortunately for the bandit, he never lived to spend it. Apprehended only days after the robbery, he promptly was hanged on the yard gallows of the old Baltimore Jail on September 10, 1818.

HARPE BROTHERS

William Micajah "Big" Harpe (born 1768) and his brother, Wiley "Little" Harpe (born 1770), alias Roberts, were the scourge of the Wilderness Trail leading from Knoxville, Tennessee to the unchartered West.

The brothers were tories in North Carolina, their birthplace, and, following the surrender of the British, fled to

Tennessee, robbing and killing the Westward-moving settlers working their way along the Wilderness Trail. The two giant, bearded, wild-eyed men were captured time and again but always managed to free themselves from the flimsy frontier jails.

Five particularly vicious murders were attributed to the Harpes in the early 1790s; the brothers attempted to hide the bodies of their victims by disemboweling them, filling them with rocks, and throwing them into the Barren River.

A kingly sum of $300 was offered for their capture in Tennessee but the Harpes, restless robbers, moved on to the Ohio country and made their headquarters at a place called Cave-in-the-Rock, a natural fortress honeycombed with subterranean passages so large that the Harpes hid herds of cattle and horses in them.

Sixty-odd miles south of this hideout, pirates openly freebooted on the Ohio River. The buckskinned brothers, heavily armed and carrying the scalps of Whites and Indians in their belts were described by the Ohio pirates at this time as "men turned into wild wolves."

Dozens of settlers were murdered in their beds by the "Terrible Harpes," one man merely because he snored too loudly. In 1799, a large group of frontiersmen trapped the Harpes in the wilds of Ohio. Wiley escaped but Micajah was blown from his horse by a well-directed volley. Such was the fear of the blood-lusting Harpes that the possemen set upon Micajah with long knives and attempted to cut off his head. As they were sawing, the mammoth killer bellowed at one of the executioners: "You are a Goddamned rough butcher but cut on and be damned!"

Harpe's head bounced along in a saddle bag on horseback as the pioneers made their way back to camp. Lack of provisions caused them to boil "Big" Harpe's head for supper one night; the skull was nailed to a tree and remained there, looming white in the wilderness clearing for years, an ominous warning to those who would take up the highwayman's life.

Wiley Harpe disappeared into the woods, reappearing along the trails to kill and loot. He disappeared some time after 1800, some said as the victim of a wild wolf pack. Ironic justice, settlers grimly joked. The wolves had claimed one of their own.

HART, PEARL
Stagerobber • (? –1925)

Pearl was a young hellion living in the Globe, Ariz. area in the late 1890s. She had become enamored of the Wild West after reading thrilling tales of Jesse James and Butch Cassidy and moved to Arizona from the East where she had been a student.

Pearl Hart, the last bandit to rob a stage in Arizona. (Arizona Historical Society Library)

Miss Hart, in her twenties, adorned her curvacious body with two giant six-guns at the hips and several more stuck into ammunition belts. Carrying a rifle almost as long as she was tall, she convinced a town drunk, Joe Boot, to help her rob the local stage.

The two unlikely outlaws, days later, stopped the Globe stage and took about $450 from the passengers—Wells Fargo had discontinued the shipping of money in strong boxes at that late date.

The pair subsequently got lost in their getaway and were quickly arrested and tried. Pearl got five years in the Yuma Territorial Prison for her prank robbery. Upon her release, she disappeared for two decades, returning to the scene of her crime decades later on a nostalgic visit.

Pearl Hart would be forgotten today if it were not for the fact that she pulled off the last stagecoach robbery in the history of the West, an impulsive and foolish crime that nevertheless earned for her an odd if not enviable distinction.

HAYWARD, HARRY T.
Murderer, Swindler • (1864-1894)

Hayward was content to be a common swindler in the Minneapolis, Minn. area during the Gay Nineties; the prospect of $10,000 in one lump sum led him to murder. After his engagement to Catherine M. Ging, Hayward convinced the gullible girl to take out $10,000 in insurance policies, and to make him the beneficiary.

Next, Hayward went to Claus Blixt, a janitor who had collaborated with him on previous swindles, and asked him to shoot Catherine for the insurance while pretending to rob her. Murder was too much for Blixt, who begged off.

Determined to realize his scheme, Hayward then went to his brother Adry and asked him to kill Catherine. He, too, refused. Adry Hayward reported the conversation with his brother to an attorney but Harry's reputation as a notorious liar prevented the lawyer from acting.

Hayward carried out his murder plan himself and was soon apprehended. Blixt and Adry Hayward testified against him.

Harry Hayward's dying request was probably the most unusual in criminal records. He asked that the rope and the gallows upon which he would be hanged be painted red, his favorite color. The Minneapolis sheriff complied, at least partially. When Hayward ascended the gallows stairs, he was fairly beaming with delight. The scaffold had been painted a bright fire engine red. The rope, however, had not.

HEDGEPETH, MARION
Trainrobber, Bankrobber • (? -1910)

His name was slightly effeminate and he looked like nothing of the Wild West, but Marion Hedgepeth was one of the most raw-boned, gutful gunfighters and bandits of his era, a quick-draw expert so fast, some reports said, that he could outpull and drill a man whose pistol had already cleared the holster. This horse-faced six-footer dressed in all black with a large wing collar, cravat spliced by a diamond stickpin, and a derby hat precariously balanced on his head.

Hedgepeth ran away from his birthplace in Cooper.

County, Mo. at age fifteen and moved West, becoming a cowboy for brief spells in Wyoming and Colorado.

In 1890 he turned to crime, robbing trains with a ruthless band of outlaws dubbed by lawmen as the "Hedgepeth Four"—Marion, Albert "Bertie" Sly, James "Illinois Jimmy" Francis, and Charles F. "Dink" Burke. The gang first held up a passenger train of the Missouri Pacific near Omaha, Neb. on November 4, 1890, taking a mere $1,000 from the express car. On November 12, 1890 the fast-moving gang hit the Chicago, Milwaukee & St. Paul line. They didn't wait for the express guard to surrender. They placed dynamite beneath the express car. Its walls and roof were blown away in a single blast (the guard somehow survived). Hedgepeth got $5,000 this time.

Weeks later, the four men boarded a St. Louis train, stopped it near Glendale, Mo. and took $50,000 from the express car safe without firing a pistol. Traveling to St. Louis, the gang settled into rented rooms, buried their weapons in a shed and waited for the hard-riding posses to burn out following their purposely misleading trails. A child, however, was their undoing.

Playing in the shed, a small girl dug up the gang's weapons and found the envelopes used to hold the money taken from the Glendale strike.

The discovery led authorities to Marion Hedgepeth's room, where he was staying with a mistress. He was placed under heavy guard and his sensational trial was held in 1892. The dapper bandit was the toast of St. Louis. Droves of women sent him so many flowers that he was almost crowded from his cell by the posies.

It was while awaiting judgment in St. Louis that Hedgepeth met a man named H. H. Holmes from Chicago. Holmes, whose real name was Herman Webster Mudgett, was the then-unknown slayer of more than two hundred gullible females, all butchered for their insurance and doweries in his claptrap Chicago dwelling, later called "Murder Palace."

Holmes, arrested for fraud, asked Hedgepeth if he could suggest a shrewd attorney to get him out of jail. The bankrobber, for an agreed-upon price, did, and Holmes was set free. Hedgepeth, who was later to reveal Holmes' murderous activities to astounded authorities, never collected his payoff and was sent to the state prison at Jefferson City for twelve years.

"That's what a life of graft got me," he lamented at the prison gates, a false signal of reform in Hedgepeth who, when released at the end of his sentence, quickly went to Omaha, Neb. where he was caught redhanded while breaking into a company safe. He went back to jail for two more years.

In 1908, Hedgepeth reappeared in small Western towns with a new gang of thieves. After several small robberies, he traveled to Chicago. There, while drinking in a saloon on January 1, 1910, Marion decided to rob again. He slipped behind the bar, warded off the bartender with an ugly-looking six-gun, and filled his pockets with money from the cash register.

At that moment, a policeman, seeing the robbery from a street window, rushed into the bar with his pistol drawn. "Surrender," the lawman ordered.

Hedgepeth, thin and weak now from TB contacted in prison, coughed just once and then roared a defiant "Never!"

Both men shot at the same time. Hedgepeth's usually deadly aim had been spoiled by years of prison, sickness, and dissipation. He missed. The policeman's aim was true, his shot hitting Hedgepeth squarely in the chest. The outlaw, firing all the rounds of his gun wildly into the sawdust floor, died on his knees.

[ALSO SEE Herman Webster Mudgett.]

HELLIER, THOMAS
Murderer, Thief • (? -1678)

Life for Thomas Hellier became unbearable after he was sentenced to bondage on a Virginia plantation following a number of thefts. The master to which he was bound sold him to another gentleman farmer, one Cutbeard Williamson, who owned the ominously-named estate called Hard Labour.

Resenting his intolerable slavery, Hellier waited until the Williamson family was asleep one night and then entered the mansion where, with an axe, he slew Williamson, his wife, and the maid.

Following his hanging, August 5, 1678 at Westover, Va., Hellier was lashed with chains to a tall tree overlooking the James River, a gruesome exhibit for other rebellious bound servants to view as they were carried up the river in barges. The body remained on the tree for several years until it rotted away.

HENDRICKSON, JOHN JR.
Murderer • (1833-1853)

Shortly after marrying his nineteen-year-old fiancee Maria, Hendrickson decided on murder. Living with seven members of his family in Bethlehem, N.Y., the newlyweds were subjected to constant bickering and arguments.

Hendrickson's relatives stated that it was all caused by Maria, who was possessive and strong-willed. A dim-witted youth, Hendrickson gave his wife a heavy dose of aconite poison (the first known case of such poisoning in the U.S.) to eliminate the family problem.

The family attempted to cover up the murder but local police examined the body and determined Hendrickson's guilt. He was hanged March 6, 1853.

HORN, THOMAS
Murderer • (1861-1903)

Horn was a man completely turned around in life—from lawman to murderer. His is the story of simple corruption. In his twenties, Horn was one of the most fearless men in the Arizona Territory, working scrupulously and doggedly for the Army and later as an agent for the Pinkertons.

Born and raised in Memphis, Mo., Horn thrilled to tales of the border bandit, Jesse James. At age fourteen he ran off to Arizona, working for the pony express, and then traveled to California to try his hand at gold mining. There he met Indian scout Al Sieber in the fields and the two, realizing that myriad prospectors before them had panned out the streams, gave up and rode back to Arizona where they became scouts for Army General Nelson A. Miles, who was then conducting a campaign against the Apaches under Geronimo.

In August, 1886, the Geronimo campaign ended; more than any other man, Tom Horn was responsible for its conclusion. He had tracked the wily Geronimo to his lair high in the Sierra Gordo in Sonora, Mexico. As Chief of Scouts, Horn went in alone to Geronimo's camp and negotiated a surrender to U.S. troops across the border.

Following Geronimo's momentous surrender and subsequent acceptance of peace terms (at which Horn acted as interpreter, the only man the Apache chief would trust), Al Sieber and Horn drifted back to gold digging. Young Tom soon tired of this and went to work as a ranch hand. His prowess as a cowboy was displayed in the Globe, Ariz. rodeo where, in 1888, he captured the world's championship for steer roping.

He was in Wyoming shortly after that, working as a Pinkerton operative. In one spectacular encounter with outlaws in the notorious Hole-in-the-Wall bastion, Horn single-handedly captured a notorious bandit known as Peg Leg Watson (alias McCoy).

Watson had robbed a mail train with his gang and Horn discovered him living in a lonely cabin high in the hills. After exchanging random shots with the outlaw, Horn called out, telling Peg Leg he was coming for him. He gingerly stepped out from behind a rock and crossed a large, open field, his Winchester pointed toward the ground. Peg Leg only stared in awe at the lone lawman. "He didn't give me much trouble," Horn prosaically stated later, but it was considered one of the most heroic feats in Western law enforcement.

In the early 1890s, Horn quit the detective agency by informing his employers that he "had no more stomach for it." At this time, he moved to Cheyenne, Wyo., and went to work for cattle barons who wanted to settle old scores with their range-war enemies. Horn changed completely from the respected lawman and scout to a hired killer. He grew avaricious. There wasn't anyone he wouldn't kill for the right price.

Dozens of men fell before his guns, victims of his clever bushwackings. Horn preferred stealth in these later years to brazen face-to-face encounters. His reputation as a bloody-handed murderer grew. Ranchers, farmers, and townspeople about Cheyenne knew that Tom Horn would wait weeks or months to get his man. He left an odd trademark in his grisly business—a rock placed beneath each dead man's head.

Not until 1902 did the law catch up with Tom Horn. Late that year, Horn shot and killed fourteen-year-old Willie Nickell while lying in wait for the boy's father, a sheep raiser whose death was desired by several local cattlemen.

Though the murder was commonly attributed to Horn in Cheyenne, proof was lacking. Then Joe Lefors, a U.S. Marshal, (the man who had led the super posse in dogged pursuit of Butch Cassidy and the Sundance Kid) got Horn drunk one night and coaxed a confession from him while witnesses jotted down every word.

Horn was quickly convicted of killing the Nickell youth and sentenced to hang. While in jail he shaved off his elegant mustache and hurriedly penned his memoirs; he mounted the gallows and died November 20, 1903.

Lawman turned killer, Tom Horn, with a rope he made in jail and by which he was hanged. (Denver Public Library)

HUTTON, PEREGRINE
Murderer, Highwayman • (? -1820)

Peregrine Hutton was a highwayman without luck. Along with his fellow thief, Morris N. B. Hull, he attempted to rob the Baltimore mail coach twice but was driven off by shots from the driver.

But Hutton was a determined fellow. He exacted his partner's promise that on their third attempt they would kill the coach driver if they thought he recognized them. They did stop the Baltimore mail coach in their third try and Hutton shot the driver to death.

"He recognized me," was his laconic statement before he was hanged with Hull, July 14, 1820 in Baltimore.

IRVING, JOHN
Pickpocket, Gangleader • (? -1883)

The once-feared Dutch Mob operating east of the Bowery during the 1870s was the invention of a professional sneak thief and pickpocket, Johnny Irving. The Dutch Mob, which at one time counted three hundred professional pickpockets in its ranks, was ultimately broken up by police in 1877. That year a newly appointed police captain, Anthony Allaire, developed a new approach to breaking up gangs. He sent flying squads into the gang-infested area from Houston to Fifth streets, the police members of which clubbed anything in their path resembling a crook.

Irving took the hint and became a freelance crook once more. In 1883, accompanied by friend and fellow thief, Billy Porter, Irving entered the infamous Sixth Avenue saloon owned by bankrobber Shang Draper (he had been implicated in the robbery of the Manhattan Savings Institution). A rival gangleader, Johnny Walsh ("Johnny the Mick") was at the bar.

The two men exchanged glances and then went for their pistols. Walsh was faster and killed Irving on the spot.

Billy Porter then drew his gun and killed Walsh. Draper pulled his gun out from behind the bar and shot Porter, who, though severely wounded, escaped.

Irving's sister, Babe, later became a mistress of the notorious bankrobber, George Leslie.

[ALSO SEE George Leslie.]

JAMES, JESSE WOODSON
Murderer, Bankrobber, Trainrobber •
(1847-1882)

BACKGROUND: BORN 9/5/47 IN KEARNEY, CLAY COUNTY, MO.
TO ROBERT AND ZERELDA COLE JAMES (BOTH FROM KEN-
TUCKY). MINOR PUBLIC EDUCATION. ONE BROTHER, ALEX-
ANDER FRANKLIN JAMES, BORN 1/10/43. SERVED IN QUAN-
TRILL'S GUERILLAS WITH "BLOODY BILL" ANDERSON DURING
THE CIVIL WAR (1864–1865). MARRIED FIRST COUSIN ZERELDA
MIMMS 4/23/74; TWO CHILDREN, JESSE JR., MARY. ORIGINAL
OCCUPATION, FARMER. DESCRIPTION: 5'11", BLUE EYES, LIGHT
BROWN HAIR, MUSCULAR, MISSING TIP OF MIDDLE FINGER ON
LEFT HAND (SHOT OFF WHILE CLEANING PISTOL). ALIASES:
HOWARD, WOODSON, DINGUS. RECORD: REPORTEDLY ROBBED
WITH BROTHER FRANK AND OTHERS THE CLAY COUNTY SAV-
INGS AND LOAN ASSOCIATION BANK IN LIBERTY, MO., AT WHICH
TIME A BYSTANDER, GEORGE WYMORE, WAS KILLED, 2/13/66
($15,000 IN GOLD, $45,000 IN NON-NEGOTIABLE SECURITIES),
INCORRECTLY SAID TO BE THE FIRST DAYLIGHT BANK ROBBERY
IN AMERICAN HISTORY; ROBBED WITH HIS BROTHER FRANK AND
THE YOUNGER BROTHERS THE ALEXANDER MITCHELL BANK
IN LEXINGTON, MO., ON 10/30/66 ($2011.50); ATTEMPTED TO
ROB WITH FIVE OTHER RIDERS MCCLAIN'S BANK IN SAVANNAH,
MO.. 3/2/67. JUDGE WILLIAM MCCLAIN WOUNDED BY THE BAN-
DITS; ROBBED WITH HIS BROTHER FRANK, COLE, BOB AND
JAMES YOUNGER, JAMES WHITE, JOHN WHITE, PAYNE JONES,
RICHARD BURNS, ISAAC FLANNERY, ANDREW MAGUIRE.

THOMAS LITTLE. THE HUGHES & MASON BANK IN RICHMOND, MO., MAYOR SHAW, B.G. & FRANK GRIFFIN KILLED BY THE BANDITS, 5/22/67 ($4,000 IN GOLD); ROBBED WITH HIS BROTHER FRANK, THE YOUNGER BROTHERS, AND TWO OTHERS THE BANK IN RUSSELVILLE, KEN., 3/20/68 ($14,000); ROBBED WITH BROTHER FRANK AND COLE YOUNGER THE DAVIES COUNTY SAVINGS BANK IN GALLATIN, MO., 12/7/69, BANK CASHIER JOHN W. SHEETS KILLED BY JESSE ($500); ROBBED WITH BROTHER FRANK, COLE, JIM AND JOHN YOUNGER, JIM CUMMINS, CHARLIE PITTS (NEE SAMUEL WELLS), AND ED MILLER THE OCOBOCK BANK IN CORYDON, IOWA, 6/3/71 ($45,000); ROBBED WITH FRANK, COLE YOUNGER, AND CLELL MILLER THE DEPOSIT BANK, COLUMBIA, KY., KILLING R.A.C. MARTIN, BANK CASHIER, 4/29/72 ($600); ROBBED WITH COLE AND BOB YOUNGER, WILLIAM CHADWELL ALIAS BILL STILES THE SAVINGS ASSOCIATION BANK IN STE. GENEVIEVE, MO., 5/23/72 ($4,000); ROBBED WITH BROTHER FRANK AND COLE YOUNGER THE KANSAS CITY FAIR GATE RECEIPTS IN KANSAS CITY, MO., 9/23/72 ($978); ROBBED WITH BROTHER FRANK, COLE & JIM YOUNGER, CLELL MILLER, BOB MOORE, AND COMANCHE TONY AN EXPRESS TRAIN NEAR ADAIR, IOWA, WITH ENGINEER JOHN RAFFERTY KILLED WHEN THE TRAIN WAS DERAILED, 7/21/73 ($2,000); ROBBED WITH BROTHER FRANK, COLE, JIM YOUNGER, CLELL MILLER THE CONCORD STAGE NEAR MALVERN, ARK., 1/15/74 ($4,000 IN CASH AND JEWELRY); ROBBED WITH BROTHER FRANK, COLE, BOB AND JIM YOUNGER, JIM CUMMINS, CLELL AND ED MILLER, SAM HILDEBRAND, ARTHUR MCCOY, AND JIM REED THE LITTLE ROCK EXPRESS TRAIN AT GADSHILL, MO., 1/31/74 ($22,000) (TWO MONTHS LATER, ON 3/16/74, JOHN AND JIM YOUNGER SHOT AND KILLED TWO PINKERTON OPERATIVES, LOUIS J. LULL AND E. B. DANIELS, NEAR OSCEOLA, MO.; JOHN YOUNGER KILLED ON THE SPOT); MURDERED PINKERTON AGENT JOHN W. WHICHER NEAR KEARNEY, MO., IN EARLY 1874 WITH JAMES LATCHE AND CLELL MILLER; ROBBED WITH BROTHER FRANK, COLE, BOB, JIM YOUNGER, CLELL MILLER, AND BUD MCDANIELS THE EXPRESS TRAIN AT MUNCIE, KAN., 12/12/74 ($25,000 IN CASH, GOLD AND JEWELRY); PINKERTON AND RAILROAD OPERATIVES ATTACKED THE FARMHOUSE OWNED BY JESSE'S PARENTS ON THE NIGHT OF 1/26/75, THROWING A BOMB THROUGH A WINDOW WHICH KILLED ARCHIE SAMUEL, JESSE'S EIGHT-YEAR-OLD HALF-BROTHER AND TORE THE ARM FROM HIS MOTHER; ROBBED WITH BROTHER FRANK, COLE, JIM AND BOB YOUNGER THE SAN ANTONIO STAGE NEAR AUSTIN, TEX., 5/12/75 ($3,000); ROBBED WITH BROTHER FRANK, COLE, BOB AND JIM YOUNGER, CLELL MILLER, CHARLIE PITTS, BILL CHADWELL, AND HOBBS KERRY THE MISSOURI-PACIFIC EXPRESS TRAIN NEAR OTTERVILLE, MO., 7/7/75 ($75,000); ATTEMPTED TO ROB WITH HIS BROTHER FRANK, COLE, JIM, AND BOB YOUNGER, CLELL MILLER, CHARLIE PITTS, AND BILL CHADWELL

THE FIRST NATIONAL BANK OF NORTHFIELD, MINN., 8/7/76, WHEREUPON THE CITIZENS OF NORTHFIELD TRAPPED THE GANG AND SHOT SEVERAL MEMBERS (FRANK AND JESSE ESCAPED, CHADWELL AND MILLER KILLED DURING THE GUN BATTLE, CHARLIE PITTS KILLED DAYS LATER IN A FIGHT WITH A POSSE, THE YOUNGER BROTHERS ALL CAPTURED AFTER BEING WOUNDED, AND GIVEN LIFE SENTENCES IN THE MINNESOTA STATE PENITENTIARY); J. L. HEYWOOD AND NICHOLAS GUSTAVSON, NORTHFIELD RESIDENTS, KILLED IN THE ROBBERY ATTEMPT BY OUTLAWS; ROBBED WITH BROTHER FRANK, BILL RYAN ALIAS TOM HILL, DICK LIDDELL ALIAS CHARLES UNDERWOOD, TUCKER BASHAM, ED MILLER, AND WOOD HITE THE CHICAGO & ALTON EXPRESS NEAR GLENDALE, MO., 10/7/79 ($35,000); ROBBED WITH BROTHER FRANK, DICK LIDDELL, BILL RYAN, AND ED MILLER THE STAGE NEAR MUSCLE SHOALS, ALA., IN MARCH, 1881 ($1,400); ROBBED WITH THE SAME GANG THE DAVIS & SEXTON BANK IN RIVERTON, IOWA, 7/10/81 ($5,000); ROBBED WITH THE SAME GANG THE CHICAGO & ROCK ISLAND & PACIFIC RAILROAD EXPRESS OUTSIDE OF WINSTON, MO., 7/15/81, KILLING FRANK MCMILLAN, A PASSENGER, AND ENGINEER WILLIAM WESTPHAL ($600); MISSOURI GOVERNOR THOMAS T. CRITTENDEN PLACED A $10,000 REWARD FOR THE CAPTURE AND CONVICTION OF FRANK AND JESSE JAMES 7/28/81; ROBBED WITH BROTHER FRANK, WOOD AND CLARENCE HITE, DICK LIDDELL, CHARLES FORD THE CHICAGO-ALTON EXPRESS TRAIN NEAR GLENDALE, MO., 8/7/81 ($1,500 IN CURRENCY AND JEWELS); KILLED BY CHARLES AND BOB FORD, 4/3/82 IN HIS HOME IN ST. JOSEPH, MO. (FRANK JAMES PERSONALLY SURRENDERED TO GOVERNOR CRITTENDEN 10/5/82, WAS TRIED FOR A NUMBER OF CRIMES BUT ACQUITTED; HE LIVED OUT AN INCONSPICUOUS LIFE UNTIL HIS DEATH ON 2/18/1915 AT THE SAMUEL FARM. COLE YOUNGER, WHO WAS PAROLED ON 7/11/01 FROM THE MINNESOTA STATE PRISON AT STILLWATER ALONG WITH HIS BROTHER JIM, DIED 3/21/16. JAMES YOUNGER COMMITTED SUICIDE IN 1902; BOB YOUNGER DIED IN PRISON, 8/16/89 OF TUBERCULOSIS).

No other American criminal has so deeply etched his imprint upon our culture as has Jesse Woodson James. Today he is folklore, a sweeping, rustic image of Americana, a Robin Hood about whom sagas have been spun so thickly that the man within is all but obscured. If there can exist such a person as a "great" criminal, then Jesse James was the greatest criminal in America.

Jesse James at seventeen, wearing three guns; this photo was taken in 1864 when Jesse was riding with Bloody Bill Anderson. (Western History Collection, U. of Okla. Library)

Yet, behind the legend, an unimpassioned study reveals Jesse James to be a glinty-eyed murderer, flaunting a boastful, callous, and totally unsympathetic nature: a man whose bark grew to the very center of his being.

Landowners on the Missouri-Kansas border harbored Jesse and his roving outlaws, worshipping them as heroes for close to two decades following the Civil War. The farmers in this area were fiercely loyal to anyone who had served the Southern Cause and, in their down-home way, thought the James boys victimized by Yankee authorities who had taken over control of the railroads, the banks, the very land itself upon which they grew their meager crops. Jesse himself often repeated the tired line, "We were driven to it."

The claim was partly true but wore thin and then disappeared into the haze of sixteen years of robbing and murder, a systematic, dedicated career of crime no rationalization could excuse. Bob Younger, the baby of the clan known as the Younger Brothers who so faithfully followed Jesse in one raid after another, explained the genesis and rationale of this most famous of outlaw gangs when he told a reporter (following his capture after the Northfield raid): "We are rough men and used to rough ways."

Prosaic, yes. But the statement reveals the phlegmatic attitude of Jesse and his boys. They were born and lived and robbed inside a tunnel of time that had not yet broken through to their intimately known and loved wilderness; the sites of their homes, the places of their daring robberies, the areas through which they made their unbelievable escapes represented America's first frontier in the middle of the Nineteenth Century.

While this Middle Frontier stubbornly and shakily resisted the progress of the East, Jesse James and those like him could flourish.

Dime novelists penned the tarnished exploits of the James gang, making them lurid and colorful. New York detective magazines churned out dozens of pamphlet-sized novellas in which Jesse and his men appeared as simple farmers driven to the gun by unscrupulous, vindictive and often sadistic lawmen. Words such as gallant, noble, honorable, so embedded in the nation's mores of this period, quickly came to typify Jesse James in these dime novels.

The railroads and banks became the culprits, not poor plagued Jesse, the humble man born in a log cabin. A spellbound country accepted and embraced the image of Jesse as a man fighting all odds.

This national reaction grew to an emotional heritage which exists in many quarters today, a feeling of deep reluctance to damn Jesse, let alone indict him, for his many crimes. Following Jesse's early death at age thirty-four, in 1882, R. T. Bradley aptly summed up the country's overall empathy for the James boys:

> "In men whom men condemn as ill
> I find so much of goodness still;
> In men whom men deem half divine
> I find so much of sin and blot;
> I hesitate to draw the line
> Between the two—where God has not."

The myth of Jesse James grew while the outlaw rode and robbed, years before he met his ignoble end at the hands of a treacherous "friend," Robert Ford and the James legend was nurtured by the outlaw himself in his last years. The claim that he "robbed from the rich and gave to the poor" was embellished by the James gang whenever they visited neighbors and relatives in the western wilds of Missouri while on the run from lawmen. They paid handsomely for their keep and meals. One story, more than any other, epitomizes the heroic legend of Jesse James.

Returning from one of his hold-ups (the locale changes from the Ozarks to the plains in different versions of this story), Jesse and his gang rest at a lonely widow-woman's cabin. Though impoverished, the widow feeds the outlaw band. Jesse notices tears welling up in the woman's eyes. He asks about her sorrow, and she tells him of her dead husband and the threadbare life she has led. She then explains that even the rickety cabin in which she lives is about to be taken from her. There is a final note on her mortgage due in the amount of $3,000 and an indifferent banker is to arrive that day to collect either the money or foreclose on the small farm.

Jesse smiles and withdraws the amount from his pocket, foisting it upon the stunned widow. She gratefully accepts

Jesse James at the height of his criminal career. (State Historical Society of Missouri)

and the band departs. A few hours later the banker arrives and is astounded when he receives the amount due him. The widow woman demands her note and mortgage (re-membering Jesse's warning to do exactly that) and these are handed over to her by the startled banker. Fondling his money, the greedy banker leaves in his buckboard.

Three miles from the cabin, Jesse James emerges from the brush, pistol in hand and leveled at the banker. He recoups his $3,000, plus the banker's watch for his trouble, and rides away chuckling.

This story has been told not only of Jesse James but of almost every important outlaw of the Old West. Yet most historians attribute the act to Jesse (Butch Cassidy told it of himself once), even the noteworthy James biographer, Robertus Love, who was once moved to say: "I for one shall continue to applaud his achievement. There was pathos in it, there was chivalric sentiment, there was simple human tenderness . . . and there was humor."

There were other stories, countless tales of Jesse the Brave, Jesse the Kind. This most desperate of men is said to have taken his best riding coat from his own back, to give it to an old man freezing alongside a deserted, wind-swept Missouri road. This killer of a dozen men is said to have alighted from his favorite race horse, Red Fox, to reduce to a bloody pulp a bully who had beaten a young Easterner half to death. He is said to have delivered his share of the proceeds of a train robbery to an orphanage so that the "little ones will have vittles through the winter." The youth of America, cluttered with ageless sagas of such feats, has always insisted on the truth of these tales. Well, he was Jesse James of the alliterative name, the bravest, boldest bandit ever seen in America. Was he not?

The parents of Frank and Jesse James went West into the frontier to homestead in the early 1840s, settling in untamed Clay County, Mo. near the small and struggling community of Kearney. Robert James a Baptist missionary, and his sturdy wife Zerelda (she married at seventeen), built a small log cabin and began to carve from the wilderness a modest farm.

The couple's first child, Alexander Franklin James, was born January 10, 1843. They were blessed by a second son four years later, September 5, 1847, whom they named Jesse Woodson James. The boys' father dreamed of wealth and soon set aside his religious work, leaving the hard-pressed family to fend alone as he made his way to California to labor in the teeming gold fields where he died of pneumonia. Mrs. James remarried. Her second husband, a man named Simms, could not get along with his rambunctious stepsons and this soon brought about a divorce.

Zerelda James Simms was determined that her sons would have some kind of father. She found another man, Dr. Reuben Samuel, a general practitioner and farmer. The marriage worked, basically because Dr. Samuel, a closed-lip type, kept to his work and allowed his wife to raise the James boys.

A few miles from the James homestead, at Lee's Summit, lived their cousins, the Younger brothers, Coleman, James, John, and Robert (the only four of fourteen children to

Frank James, an artist's rendering. (State Historical Society of Missouri)

turn to crime), wild hellions who raided many an apple orchard with Frank and Jesse.

The coming of the Civil War disrupted the peaceful farming life in Missouri. Frank James and Cole Younger rode off to join William Clarke Quantrill, the Southern guerrilla leader, and they subsequently participated in the bloody raid on Lawrence, Kan. Jesse joined one of Quantrill's lieutenants, "Bloody Bill" Anderson, when he was old enough, and in 1864, helped to massacre seventy-five unarmed Union soldiers at Centralia. It was his first taste of blood.

The seventeen-year-old Jesse became a wonder to his campmates. He rode a horse better than most men and his marksmanship was uncanny. His hatred for federal troops was unbounding; one story quietly repeated by his comrades was that Union troopers, searching for his brother Frank, had tied him to a tree on the Samuel farm and horsewhipped him in hopes of getting information. Jesse did not talk about this incident, but seethed with anger only abated by the deaths of Yankee soldiers shot down by his own hand.

Hours after the Centralia raid, a Major Johnson led a troop of Union soldiers against the retreating rebel guerrillas. Anderson's irregulars turned on the federals and charged into their midst, slaughtering them. Jesse James, his horse's reins in his teeth, rode furiously into the fleeing Yankee command, firing two pistols. He was credited with shooting down six men, killing three.

The youth made no comment about the battle that night. He sat silently at a campfire cleaning his pistol. Its hair trigger was accidentally bumped by Jesse and a shot was fired that blew away the tip of his left middle finger. The young guerrilla let out a painful cry and said as he stared at his wound: "If that ain't the dingus-dangast thing!" The name "Dingus" stuck but only his closest friends and Civil War comrades called him that. (Frank James was referred to as "Buck" by his fellow guerrillas.)

The war along the Middle Border between Kansas and Missouri was bloody and embittered. Regular troops fought pitched battles with farmers and irregulars. Homesteaders loyal to both sides were burned out, their families shot and bayoneted to death. The James boys' reputation under

Quantrill and Anderson grew to such proportions that Dr. Samuel and his wife were forced by Union soldiers to abandon their farm and were banished to Nebraska. At the close of the war, Frank and Jesse returned to their home to find it vacant. They lived in terror as federal troops searched for them. Regular Southern troops had been pardoned, but guerrillas were considered outlaws and were hunted down and shot.

A general amnesty for guerrillas was issued in early 1865 and Jesse James, leading a band of irregulars, including his brother Frank and Cole Younger, rode toward the small town of Lexington, Mo. under a white flag to surrender. A company of federal troops intercepted them and opened fire on the ex-guerrillas. Jesse was wounded in the chest but managed to take cover in the thick brush. Two Union soldiers pursued him but quickly backed off when he fired a single shot that killed one of their horses.

A farmer found the boy soldier lying in a creek bed soothing his wounds the next day and helped him travel to his family in Nebraska, where he recuperated slowly. At first, Jesse seemed as if he would die of the wound and begged his mother to take him back to Missouri. "I don't want to die in a Northern state," he reportedly said. Mrs. Samuel complied and moved her son to Harlem, Mo., where he was sheltered in a boardinghouse owned by his uncle, John Mimms. His cousin Zerelda (named after his mother), called Zee, nursed Jesse back to health. Before he left for the family farm in Kearney, the two became betrothed, but would not marry for a full nine years.

While the echoes of the war died, Frank and Jesse James peacefully farmed their land, living with guns on their hips. What changed them into the most feared outlwas of their day is uncertain. The war had already begun to change them—the battles, blood, and death made simple farm life boring and uneventful. Whatever the reason, they followed the path many irregulars chose—robbery and murder.

On February 13, 1866, ten men rode into the town of Liberty, Mo. and headed for the Clay County Savings Bank. One bandit approached cashiers Greenup and William Bird, holding pistols. "If you make any noise, you will be shot," the bandit told them (many reported this man later to be Frank James).

The bandit then ordered Greenup Bird into the vault and told him to hand over the money. "I hesitated and began to parley," Bird nervously stated later. "He told me that if I did not go in instantly, he would shoot me down. I went in."

Within minutes the two bandits inside the bank walked casually to the street with a wheat sack crammed with $60,000 of currency and non-negotiable bonds. The pair motioned to the other men standing in strategic positions along the street and the band mounted their horses and began to ride from town.

George "Jolly" Wymore, a student, was just then walking across the town square en route to classes at nearby William Jewell College. The ten men rode solemnly past him. One stared curiously at Wymore and, perhaps suspecting the youth of raising an alarm, drew his pistol and fired several shots into him. Wymore died instantly. With this, the band began whooping and firing their pistols into the air as they rode madly from town.

The horsemen crossed the Missouri River on the ferry and by the time a posse arrived in pursuit, the outlaws had disappeared in a blinding snowstorm. The Liberty daylight raid was the first bank robbery in America performed by an organized gang (the first daylight robbery of a bank occurred in Massachusetts in 1863—See Edward W. Green).

All evidence points to the fact that Jesse was not in this band but that it probably included his brother Frank and Cole Younger.

The next bank to fall was in Lexington, Mo., on October 30, 1866. A pattern emerged at the robbing of this bank which was to become all too familiar to law enforcement officers seeking Jesse James. A young man entered the Alexander Mitchell and Company banking house early in the morning. Another young man stationed himself at the entrance.

"Can you change this for me," the tall young man asked cashier J. L. Thomas. He held out a $50 bill.

Thomas was suspicious. The Liberty bank raid was still current and terrible news. "No," the cashier said. As he looked about, two more men entered the bank, drew their pistols and aimed them at his heart.

"You've got one hundred thousand dollars in this bank," the tall young robber said quietly. "Unless you turn it over, you'll be killed."

"That's not true," Thomas said.

"Let's have the key to the vault."

"I don't have it."

The robbers searched his pockets and found nothing. Disgusted they scooped up what cash there was in the drawers and left. One of the bandits was definitely identified as young Jesse James "from up Kearney way."

It was almost five months later before the James gang struck again, this time in Savanna, Mo. Bank president Judge John McClain offered stiff resistance. He refused to give up the keys to his vault. One of the bandits swore and shot him in the chest before the gang rushed back to their horses. McClain survived his painful wound and the bandits tallied nothing from the raid.

The setback only made the James gang all the more determined. The small, solid Hughes and Mason Bank squatting in the center of Richmond, Mo. became the object of the band's next attack. There was no elaborate ceremony to the raid. Jesse and his men rode into Richmond on May 22, 1867, guerrilla style, racing down the main street, hollering and firing their pistols wildly in the air which soon had pedestrians scurrying for cover.

Six men—Jesse and Frank James, the Younger brothers, and James White—dismounted in front of the locked bank while their confederates continued to terrorize the town. The six battered down the bank's doors, entered, and lined up the quaking tellers. Opening their wheat sack, the outlaws scooped up more than $4,000 from the largest county bank in Missouri.

Mayor Shaw led a small group of armed citizens to the town square and began to battle the outlaws. A group of the bandits rushed Shaw on horseback and killed him in the street with seven bullets. The riders then turned about and headed for the jail where several ex-guerrillas were being detained. They tried to break into the jail, but the solid oak door held. Jailer B. G. Griffin and his fifteen-year-old son, Frank, had taken up positions behind a tree nearby and began exchanging shots with the outlaws. The robbers swept past the pair riddling them. Both were killed by one volley.

Only one of this raiding party was ever tracked down: Payne Jones. His farmhouse was surrounded by lawmen, but Jones dashed directly into the group with two six-guns roaring. A posseman fell from his saddle, dead before he hit the ground. A young girl who had guided the posse to the Jones farm was also hit and died several hours later. The Richmond raid and its aftermath claimed the lives of five innocent persons.

Jones was later shot dead in a gun duel. Richard Burns, another member of the raiding party, who resided near Richmond, was taken in his farmhouse and led to a wooded area, where he was tried by torchlight and then hanged. The same fate befell Andy Maguire and Tom Little, who were apprehended and lynched a few miles outside of Warrensburg, Mo.

Incensed citizens thought of doing the same to Frank and Jesse but were dissuaded by "alibi cards" distributed by their friends—cards upon which Frank and Jesse had scribbled claims that they in no way had been part of the bank raids. These, incredibly, were accepted by local lawmen, who saw no reason to doubt the word of the James brothers.

Though Frank and Jesse James and the Younger brothers were suspected of being in these raids, investigation proved nothing. Their excuse was always the same. They were at home, tending to chores. Townspeople who identified them during the bank raids suddenly lost their memory when questioned later by the authorities. Nowhere in Western Missouri was it possible for a person to threaten the ex-guerrillas, such was the local sympathy for them. If a merchant or farmer did speak the truth he stood to be boycotted by his own neighbors or worse, shot some evening while traveling a lonely road. This silent conspiracy became a way of life in Clay and Ray Counties and lasted until Jesse's assassination.

The James gang, in these early years, really included almost any farmer who wanted to ride along with its hardcore elements—the James boys and the Younger brothers—to pick up a few dollars in a yearly bank raid to obtain seed money for next season's planting. Jesse and his kins-men were becoming professional robbers but prudently paced themselves, usually performing one or two robberies each year. The desperate robberies in later years came about only when the pressure from lawmen became un-bearable and the gang's thrust was aimed at a "big strike" to provide them with enough cash to allow them to escape permanently.

What made the gang's immunity from prosecution steadfast was the facelessness of its members. No pictures existed of the outlaws. The only photo of Jesse James was secreted in a gold locket his mother kept on her person. Identification became almost impossible. The gang would employ its anonymity well.

A year after the Richmond raid, on March 20, 1868, a man who had been using the name Colburn (Frank James) and for several days had pretended to be a cattle dealer from Louisville, entered the bank operated by Nimrod Long and George Norton in Russelville, Ky. He offered Long a $100 note and asked the banker to cash it. Long became suspicious.

"Colburn" jerked a thumb in the direction of the door where a tall, blue-eyed man stood. "I've got to pay off one of my hired hands."

Long examined the note carefully and stated: "This bill is counterfeit, Mr. Colburn."

"I reckon it is," the would-be cattle buyer chuckled after looking at the note. He tucked the bill into a vest pocket and then pulled out a Colt pistol. "But this isn't, Mr. Long. Open the vault!"

Long glanced to the young man in the doorway. He, too, was holding a pistol. The banker suddenly bolted for a rear door. The man in the doorway, Jesse, cursed loudly and sent a bullet in his direction that creased his scalp and dropped him to the floor. The bandit ran to him and began to strike Long on the head with his gun butt. Long, a well-built fellow, spun about and grabbed the bandit's hands. As they rolled about the foor, Frank James moved wildly around them, trying to squeeze off a shot at the banker, yelling to his brother to finish him.

With a burst of strength, the intrepid Long tossed the bandit aside, jumped to his feet, and raced to the door of the bank. Two bullets sent after him lodged in the door but the banker escaped, running down the alley next to the bank and shouting: "They're robbing my bank!"

Outside, three men waiting on horseback—the Younger brothers—calmly watched the terrified banker flee. Frank and Jesse James, within minutes, came from the bank dragging two large wheatsacks full of gold and cash, about $14,000. This they laboriously lifted onto their horses while Russelville citizens dashed about madly looking for water buckets, thinking the bank was on fire.

A wizened old man, confused rather than drunk, staggered blindly down the street between the dashing horses of the bankrobbers. Cole Younger rode up to him and shouted: "Old man, we're having a little serenade here and there's danger of you getting hurt. Just get behind my horse here and you'll be out of the way." With that, Younger edged the old man out of the road using his horse's flanks to push him along.

When Jesse and Frank joined their hooting companions, the outlaw band formed a single line and dashed down the main street as if carrying out a cavalry charge. An hour after they had disappeared, a fifty-man posse was on their trail into Allan County, a James-Younger stronghold.

Pinkerton detectives searched frantically for the James gang without success. They did interview George Hite, whose family was close to the outlaw clans and whose sons often rode with Jesse. Hite operated a store in Adairville and was reported to be one of Jesse's best friends. Hite knew nothing of the Russelville strike, he said, but his memory suddenly erupted fourteen years later following Jesse's death when he wrote how the outlaws worked out their raids: "They'd decide on going somewhere, and then they'd send word to all the others—they always knew where they were, and then went and done it [the robbery]. That's all there was of it."

Hite's statement was only one of many that supported the idea that Jesse was not the actual leader; neither was Frank James. The James boys and the Youngers, with several hand-picked henchmen would gather secretly at a deserted farmhouse or barn and, under the yellow, flickering glow of lantern lights, discuss each proposed robbery, arguing safety and escape factors. It was quite democratic. Jesse was always the most daring of the original gang, and therefore identified as the leader, though it was a nominal role. His willingness to murder, no doubt, inched him above the others as the most ferocious in their ranks. Later, after the Northfield disaster, Jesse would, indeed, come to be the absolute leader of his band, threatening his own brother Frank with death when he dared to criticize him.

Frank James was never the staunch savant-as-older-brother to Jesse that has been often pictured. He was a tight-lipped, sanctimonious sermonizer who spouted Shakespeare and the Bible whenever the whim urged him, much to the annoyance of his fellow outlaws. But none dared tell him to be still. Frank "Buck" James, though cautious and tedious in his manner, was almost as deadly with a gun as his younger brother.

Jesse's calculating ability to kill was never more pronounced than on December 7, 1869, when he, Frank, and Cole Younger rode into the small town of Gallatin, Mo., heading straight for the Davies County Savings Bank. Frank went inside first. He stopped at the teller's cage and offered cashier John W. Sheets a $100 bill to change. Sheets took the bill and turned to his desk.

Jesse then entered the bank as Cole Younger watched the horses outside. Jesse walked up to Sheets and said lightly, "If you will write out a receipt, I will pay you that bill." The banker began to reach for his receipt book and Jesse pulled out his pistol and shot Sheets twice, once through the head and once square in the heart; he was dead before he hit the floor.

Frank James ran behind the counter and threw all the bank's available cash into a sack. A bank clerk, William A. McDowell, bolted for the door and Jesse fired a shot at him that tore through his arm. McDowell managed to stagger into the street and alarm the town.

Jesse and Frank ran from the bank and jumped to their horses. Jesse missed, his foot caught in the stirrup while his horse raced down the street. The struggling outlaw was dragged almost forty feet before he managed to free himself. Frank James, seeing his brother's plight, wheeled his horse about and pulled Jesse up behind him. Hundreds of bullets smacked at their horse's hooves from weapons wielded by the enraged Gallatin townsmen, but the robbers again made a successful escape.

The take from the bloody Gallatin robbery was small, about $500, but Jesse's near-fatal experience unnerved the bandit so much that he and his brother stayed close to the Samuel farm for almost two years without plans for any future raids. There was something else which disturbed Jesse. His horse, an expensive, well-groomed animal, had been found by the good citizens of Gallatin and Jesse had been tentatively identified as one of the robbers. He countered that his animal had been stolen and lived on quietly at his farm, unmolested, planning his next move, his loot buried in a nearby meadow.

Jesse had further covered himself in obscurity following the Gallatin raid. Minutes after the outlaws rode from town, they encountered a Methodist minister named Helm whom they forced at gun point to guide them around an unfamiliar community nearby. Jesse told Helm: "I'm Bill Anderson's brother. I killed S. P. Cox who works in the bank back there in Gallatin. He killed my brother in the war and I got him at last." Thus, Jesse James wrongly identified himself and his victim, John Sheets, whom he knew had been a major in the Union army, to excuse murder.

The James gang remained in hiding for almost two years before riding out again to rob. Jesse and Frank James, Cole, Jim, and John Younger, Jim Cummins, Charlie Pitts, and Ed Miller rode slowly from Missouri into the peaceful town of Corydon, Ia. arriving on June 3, 1871. It was one of the easiest holdups of their careers.

The Ocobock Brothers' Bank off the main square was fairly bursting with money, a little more than $45,000 in gold and cash nestled in its safe. Jesse and Frank James, along with Cole Younger, entered the bank and found only one clerk on duty. The others waited outside, curiously noting the empty streets.

"Where's everybody at?" Frank James asked the clerk.

"Over to the Church," he answered, "listenin' to Mr. Dean." The clerk went on to explain that the famous orator Henry Clay Dean was lecturing at the Methodist Church and the entire town had turned out to hear him.

"All the better," Jesse said and pulled his pistol. In a matter of minutes the bank had been cleaned out and the outlaws sauntered their horses lazily up the street. As they came abreast of the church, Jesse flashed his now famous icy, thin smile. He told the outlaws to stop, dismounted and casually walked into the church. Standing in the middle of the aisle, Jesse raised his hand and the golden-throated Dean paused in the middle of his speech.

"What is it, young man?"

"Well, sir," Jesse said slowly, drawing out his words for effect, "some riders were just down to the bank and tied up the cashier. All the drawers are cleaned out. You folks best get down there in a hurry."

The crowd stared at the bandit who blinked back at them with chilling blue eyes. Jesse's mouth crinkled and his head lifted. A short laugh lengthened into a roar like a train getting up steam. He spun on the heels of his shiny boots and walked outside to his horse, mounted, and rode away with his men, all ripping with laughter.

For several seconds, the stunned townspeople merely looked out of the church's door. The silence was finally splintered by a man in their midst who shouted: "For God's sake! It's the James gang! They've just robbed the bank!"

The Corydon residents rushed to the bank, and then quickly organized a posse. The lawmen chased the James band back into Missouri but lost all traces of the outlaws near Clay County.

Though Jesse was again identified as the outlaw leader who led the Corydon robbery, witnesses either disappeared or refused to confront the bandit.

Another year eased into history before the gang struck again, this time at the bank in Columbia, Ky. on April 29, 1872. Jesse and Frank entered while Cole Younger and Clell Miller waited outside with the horses. When cashier R. A. C. Martin became reluctant to turn over the keys to the safe, Jesse shot him three times, killing him where he stood.

Frank cleaned out the cash drawers which only yielded $600 and the gang raced from town. More than one hundred men followed them but the outlaws outfoxed their pursuers by doubling back on their own trail, circling the town twice, and then riding off toward Missouri.

The gang next hit the Savings Association of Ste. Genevieve, Mo. on May 23, 1872. Riding at Jesse's stirrups were

Cole and Bob Younger (Bob's first robbery), Clell Miller, and Bill Chadwell (also a new recruit). It was a bloodless raid. Cashier O. D. Harris wisely gave the bandits no arguments when they ordered him to fill their wheat sack with money. The take was $4,000 and the outlaws rode quietly out of town.

Near a small farm, Jesse dismounted to adjust the heavy sack filled with gold hanging from his saddle. Suddenly, his horse dashed away, leaving the bandit standing in the middle of the road and looking quite foolish. A passing farmer was ordered to retrieve the horse by the gang. When he refused, several pistols were aimed in his direction.

The farmer chased the frightened animal through a field, caught it, and returned it to its owner. He smiled toothlessly up at Jesse and then said in a heavy accent: "I catch der horse. Vot do I get for dot, yah?"

Jesse gave him back his own thin smile. "Your life, Dutchy. Vot do you tink, yah?"

This oft-repeated story may be apocryphal, yet it becomes consistent with Jesse's sense of humor and his increasing consciousness of his own exploited myth. As his career spun forward he grew careless in protecting his own identity until he became indifferent, then strangely proud of his role as America's Robin Hood.

On September 26, 1872, Jesse, Frank, and Cole Younger rode leisurely into the giant fairgrounds of Kansas City, Mo. while more than ten thousand people milled about. They approached the main gate. Jesse dismounted and walked up to the cashier.

"What if I was to say I was Jesse James," he said to the cashier, "and told you to hand out that tin box of money—what would you say?"

The cashier, Ben Wallace, spat back: "I'd say I'd see you in hell first."

"Well, that's just who I am, Jesse James, and you had better hand it out pretty damned quick or—" Jesse brought his pistol to aim at Wallace's head.

The tin box, containing $978, was emptied into the traditional wheat sack. Jesse cursed at having gotten so little. Frank, who had scouted the fair for days before the raid, had reported that at least $10,000 would be on hand. He had been right, but only minutes before the outlaws struck thousands of dollars had been taken to a local bank for safe-keeping.

As the bandits threaded their horses through the throng, Wallace jumped from his booth and raced after them, clutching Jesse's leg in the stirrup and shouting: "It's the James gang!" The outlaw drew his pistol and sent a bullet toward Wallace which missed him and hit a small girl in the leg. The shot caused the fair-goers to run pell-mell in all directions and open a large space through which the thieves galloped to freedom.

The miserable proceeds from the fair made Jesse all the more determined to snare a large amount of money. Banks were hit-and-miss propositions. Trains, on the other hand, carried enormous amounts of cash, gold, and silver. The act of robbing trains was not new and certainly, contrary to popular belief, not invented by Jesse James. The first train robbery had been committed by the Reno brothers of Indiana in 1868. Seven years later Jesse and Frank James decided to go into the train-robbing business.

The brothers—Frank found time to put aside a copy of *Pilgrim's Progress* which he was reading—gathered up Cole and Jim Younger, Clell Miller, Bob Moore, and a half-breed outlaw from Texas named Commanche Tony and headed for Adair, Iowa in late July, 1873.

Frank and Cole had scouted as far as Omaha, Nebraska weeks before and had learned that the Chicago, Rock Island, and Pacific Express racing through Adair on July 21, 1873 would be carrying more than $100,000 in gold for Eastern banks. At dusk on that day, the gang loosened a rail in the tracks just outside of Adair. When the train came around a curve, engineer John Rafferty spotted the disjointed piece of track and threw his engine into reverse. It was too late; the engine soared through the break and crunched over on its side, killing Rafferty.

The seven bandits plunged from a wooded area and two of them—Frank and Jesse James—jumped into the baggage car and ordered the clerks to open the safe under gunpoint. There was no $100,000 inside, only a few thousand dollars in federal notes. The bandits rode away swearing. Jesse learned that the gold shipment train had been rescheduled for just such an emergency and had gone through Adair four hours before the robbery.

Though Jesse was reported to be the leader of the gang, no action was taken against him. Again, the James-Younger clan waited till the turn of the year before pulling another job. On January 15, 1874 the band traveled to Arkansas and held up the Concord Stage a few miles outside of Malvern, taking $4,000 in cash and jewels from the wealthy passengers.

During this robbery, Cole Younger proved that he, too, could practice that special flamboyance peculiar to this outlaw band. One passenger turned over his gold watch while protesting with a strong Southern accent.

Younger looked him over as he dangled the gold watch from his hamhock hand. "Are you a Southerner?"

"Yes, suh."

"Were you in the Confederate Army?"

"I had that distinction, suh."

"State your rank, regiment, and commanding officer."

The startled passenger did and was then shocked to see the giant bandit hand him back his watch.

"We are all Confederate soldiers," Younger said, garnishing his beau geste, "We don't rob Southerners, especially Confederate soldiers." He wagged a finger of warning at the rest of the passengers cringing in their seats. "But Yankees and detectives are not exempt."

Fifteen days later, on January 31, 1874, the James gang showed up in tiny Gadshill, Mo., a flag station for the Iron Mountain Railroad. Jesse, Frank, the Youngers, and five others took over the depot and flagged down the Little Rock Express train. The train's safe yielded a great haul—$22,000 in cash and gold.

As Jesse rode alongside the train after he and the others had pilfered the passenger cars, he shouted to Cole Younger who had the engineer under guard: "Give her a toot, Cole!" Younger yanked the whistle chord several times.

Before the gang departed, one story has it that Jesse threw a piece of paper wrapped about a stick to the engineer. "Give this to the newspapers," he shouted. "We like to do things in style."

The paper contained the bandit's own press release of the robbery, written carefully by Jesse only hours before the outlaws had struck. Jesse had penned:

"THE MOST DARING TRAIN ROBBERY ON RECORD!"

"The southbound train of the Iron Mountain Railroad was stopped here this evening by five [there were ten] heavily armed men and robbed of _____ dollars. The robbers arrived at the station a few minutes before the arrival of the train and arrested the agent and put him under guard and then threw the train on the switch. The robbers were all large men, all being slightly under six feet. After robbing the train they started in a southerly direction. They were all mounted on handsome horses. PS: There [sic] a h_____ of an excitement in this part of the country."

The robberies ceased. Jesse had decided to marry his cousin Zee after nine years of clandestine meetings in woods and lonely cabins. A reporter for the *St. Louis Dispatch* interviewed the bandit in Galveston, Texas where he and his bride allegedly awaited a steamer to take them to Vera Cruz where they planned to settle. The first-hand report stated:

"On the 23rd of April, 1874, I was married to Miss Zee Mimms, of Kansas City, and at the house of a friend there. About fifty of our mutual friends were present on the occasion and quite a noted Methodist minister [Reverend William James, an uncle] performed the ceremonies. We had been engaged for nine years, and through good and evil report, and not withstanding the lies that had been told upon me and the crimes laid at my door, her devotion to me has never wavered for a moment. You can say that both of us married for love, and that there cannot be any sort of doubt about our marriage being a happy one."

The *Dispatch* ran this improbable account under the subhead of, "All the World Loves a Lover."

But Jesse and Zee did not depart for Vera Cruz. Instead, they made their way back to Missouri, settling in a small cabin near Kearney, Mo. Jesse was tied to the roots of his birthplace and bound by habit to a life of crime. Married or not, the outlaw was by then dedicated to his ill-chosen career. No record today indicates his wife's attitude concerning his thieving, but several intimates later stated that she "looked the other way . . . out of love."

Wood Hite, when asked by a reporter in later years if

Jesse loved his wife, thought a moment and then said, "Yes, I believe he did . . ." The couple produced two children, Jesse Jr. and Mary, and Jesse doted upon them.

Frank James also married, eloping with a Jackson County farmer's daughter, seventeen-year-old Annie Ralston. The farmer first disowned his child but later accepted the couple whose marriage produced one son, Robert James, named after the outlaw brothers' father.

The Pinkertons and local law enforcement officers in Western Missouri were by then hot on Jesse's trail. They stalked him everywhere, lying in wait about his favorite haunts, surrounding his mother's farm.

On January 26, 1875, acting on a tip that the James boys were visiting the Samuel place, several Pinkerton detectives and local lawmen tossed a bomb through the window of the cabin. The explosion tore away most of Mrs. Samuel's right arm and a fragment embedded itself in the side of eight-year-old Archie Peyton Samuel, Jesse's half brother. The boy died in writhing agony inside of an hour.

The vicious bombing instigated a national hatred for the Pinkertons and the detective agency was vilified by the press as perpetrating an "inexcusable and cowardly deed." Jesse went further. He planned his revenge carefully, traveling to Chicago where he shadowed the head of the detective agency, Allan Pinkerton (who repeatedly denied that his men had thrown a bomb into the Samuel's place). Jesse's friend George Hite told reporters after the outlaw's death that James "went to Chicago to kill Allan Pinkerton and stayed there for four months but he never had a chance to do it like he wanted to. That was after the Pinkertons made a raid on his mother's house, blew off her arm and killed his step brother. He said he could have killed the younger one [one of Pinkerton's sons, William or Robert] but didn't care to. 'I want him to know who did it,' he said. 'It wouldn't do me no good if I couldn't tell him about it before he died. I had a dozen chances to kill him when he didn't know it. I wanted to give him a fair chance but the opportunity never came.' Jesse left Chicago without doing it but I heard him often say: 'I know that God will some day deliver Allan Pinkerton into my hands.'"

Later that year, Frank James, who had been brooding over events and a violent argument he had had with his

John Younger, killed in an 1874 gun duel with Pinkerton detectives. (State Historical Society of Missouri)

brother—some reported Frank had tried to convince Jesse of settling down and quitting crime—wrote a long letter to the editor of the *Pleasant Hill Missouri Review* disavowing his participation in the robberies attributed to him. He wrote that he and "Dingus" (his pet name for Jesse) "were not good friends at the time [of the K. C. fair grounds robbery] and have not been for several years."

Frank went on to complain about the Pinkertons hounding his family and shooting down John Younger the year before. (John and Jim Younger had shot it out with two Pinkerton operatives, Louis J. Lull and E. B. Daniels, in the woods near Osceola, Mo., on March 16, 1874; John had been killed. Frank did not mention the fact that his brother, along with Clell Miller and a local farmer, James Latche, had murdered Pinkerton detective John W. Whicher about a month later.)

Frank James concluded his self-alibis with ". . . the day is coming when the secrets of all hearts will be laid open before the All-Seeing Eye and every act of our lives will be scrutinized, then will his soul be white as the driven snow, while those of the accusers will be doubly dark."

Whatever the feud between the James brothers, it was apparently forgotten; the two were soon leading the Youngers and others in one robbery after another. While in Texas, the gang held up the San Antonio Stage, May 12, 1875, taking $3,000 in cash and jewelry from the passengers. Cole Younger had to be coaxed into this robbery, lured away from his amorous adventures with Belle Starr, a notorious bandit herself who lived in Collins County on a ranch owned by her father, John Shirley.

Cole, outgoing and friendly, even thought of settling down near Dallas and briefly became a census taker. But Jesse soon talked him out of such peaceful activities and he was off with his brothers riding behind Jesse and Frank back to Missouri. Word went out to Clell Miller, Charlie Pitts, and Bill Chadwell to meet at the Samuel place. There Jesse outlined his plans for stealing $100,000 from the Missouri Pacific Railroad.

He had gotten word from a bribed railroad employee that on July 7, 1875 the United Express Company was shipping a gigantic amount of gold East. When the train slowed down to cross a rickety bridge east of Otterville, Mo., Jesse explained, they would be waiting for it.

Everything went according to plan until Jesse, Cole, and Bob Younger approached the Adams Express safe inside the baggage car. Jesse ordered John Bushnell, the safe guard, to open it.

"It can't be done," he apologized. "I don't have the keys to it. It's locked all the way through and the keys are at the other end of the run."

Jesse turned to Bob Younger and told him to "get an axe." Within minutes Younger was wielding a fire axe which only succeeded in making tiny dents in the sturdy safe.

Burly Cole Younger stepped forward. "Let me have it," he said. Younger, a towering 200-lb. man, slammed the axe hard against the safe for a full ten minutes until a small hole was made in its top. Jesse, whose hands were smaller, reached inside and drew up a leather pouch which was slit. Bob Younger then worked stacks of money from the pouch until their wheat sack was bulging with $75,000.

The outlaws dragged the sack to the open door of the baggage car and lifted it onto a waiting horse, brought up by Frank and the others.

Before the band hurried off into the darkness, Jesse called up to the frightened baggage car guard: "If you see any of the Pinkertons, tell 'em to come and get us."

The success of the Otterville raid convinced Jesse that big money could be gotten if the gang planned its moves carefully and employed scouts to obtain intelligence about their strikes far in advance. Bill Chadwell acted as a scout in casing the Northfield, Minnesota First National Bank. Chadwell, a one-time Minnesota resident, insisted that it was the wealthiest bank in the Midwest. What further enticed the outlaws was the fact that its principal stock-holders were General William Butler and W. A. Ames, the most hated men in the South during the Civil War, Butler as a Union General who persecuted the hapless Confederates under his occupation of New Orleans and Ames who was thought to be the worst carpetbagger south of the Mason-Dixon Line.

The long trip from Missouri to Northfield began in August, 1876. Flush with money and confidence, the James-Younger gang set out on well-groomed, expensive horses with scabbards holding new carbines banging their flanks. Each man in the eight-man gang wore a pressed riding suit and new, shiny, black boots. They wore linen dusters to hide the deadly Colt pistols at their sides. Jesse wore extra pistols in shoulder holsters.

The eight outlaws—Jesse and Frank James, Cole, Jim, and Bob Younger, Charlie Pitts, Clell Miller, and the scout, Bill Chadwell—formed the hard core of the band that had existed for close to ten years, the most experienced bandits of their time. But the town they entered on August 7, 1876 was unlike any other they had ever raided.

Northfield was the center of a rich farming community and its citizens were of hardy pioneer stock. It was a trouble-free town where law and order prevailed, robberies were unknown, and the churchgoing populace zealously guarded their hard-earned savings. Unlike the residents of Missouri, that state aptly called "The Mother of Bandits," Minnesota's citizens were unused to daring bank raids and lawlessness in their streets, so unused to it that once such bedlam began the citizens turned out to defend what they owned with guns in hand rather than cower behind locked doors.

Just after two o'clock, Jesse James, followed by Bob Younger and Charlie Pitts, walked into the First National Bank. Clell Miller and Cole Younger waited outside the bank to watch for trouble and mind the horses. Frank James, Jim Younger and Bill Chadwell sat on their horses at the end of the street to guard the gang's escape route.

Trouble for the outlaws came instantly. Owner of a hardware store, J. A. Allen, noticed the activity around the bank and walked over to investigate. Clell Miller grabbed him by the arm as he was about to enter the bank and told him: "Keep your goddamned mouth shut!"

Allen broke away and began to scream: "Get your guns, boys! They're robbing the bank!"

Henry Wheeler, a university student home on vacation, lounging in a chair nearby, saw Allen and he, too, ran into the street yelling, "Robbery! Robbery! Robbery! They're at the bank!"

Cole Younger and Miller mounted their horses and were soon joined by Frank James, Jim Younger, and Chadwell. The five horsemen rode furiously up and down the street shouting to every one to "Get in! Get in!" But the citizens did not "get in." They came out of their homes, offices, and stores with pistols and shotguns.

Inside the bank Joseph Lee Heywood, acting bank cashier, was about to greet Jesse James when he noticed the pistol in the outlaw's hand. "Don't holler," Jesse told him. "There's forty men outside this bank."

Heywood nodded, stunned.

"Open the safe goddamned quick or I'll blow your head off," Jesse said.

"I can't do that," Heywood said. "There's a time lock on it."

Pitts raced up and sliced the cashier's throat with a hunting knife, inflicting a slight wound. Then he and Bob Younger took turns jamming their pistols into his stomach and ordering him to open the safe. Still Heywood refused, claiming he had no way of opening the safe. Oddly, the bankrobbers didn't bother checking the safe; it was already open.

199

The bandits were distracted when another clerk, A. E. Bunker, dashed through the director's room and out a back door. Pitts fired at him but missed. Bob Younger, cursing loudly, was able to find only a small amount of money in a cash drawer.

Charlie Pitts panicked. He ran to the front door and saw that citizens all along the street were shooting at their five companions outside. "The game's up," he shouted to Jesse. "Pull out or they'll be killing our men!" He ran outside.

Jesse and Bob Younger followed. One of them—it was never learned which—turned around at the door and, in an act of reckless vengeance, took deliberate aim at Heywood then attempting to stand up while holding his wounded throat, and sent a bullet into his head, killing him.

The street reeked of carnage. Elias Stacy, a resident, had shot Clell Miller full in the face with a load of buckshot. The outlaw was unrecognizable, his shirtfront sopped with blood. He rode crazily up and down the street moaning and shooting his six-gun blindly. One of his shots hit and killed a terrified immigrant, Nicholas Gustavson, who was trying to run for cover across the street.

Cole Younger took a bullet in the shoulder. Another citizen, named Manning, shot Bill Chadwell square in the heart and the outlaw toppled dead into the dust of the street. Miller, still blinded by his face wound, was next, shot to death by Henry Wheeler, the university student. Wheeler then saw Bob Younger stalking Manning and shot him in the right hand. Younger changed his gun to his left hand and kept firing.

Frank and Jesse James, Cole and Jim Younger, and Charlie Pitts were now charging up and down the main street with reins in their teeth and each firing two pistols at the townspeople. The cross-fire through which they rode was murderous. Pitts was wounded and then Jim Younger and then, again, Cole Younger.

Jesse surveyed the slaughter. "It's no use, men!" he shouted. "Let's go." Bob Younger, whose mount had been shot in front of the bank, climbed up behind his brother Cole and the gang thundered down the street as dozens of unarmed citizens ran forward stoning them with rocks.

A few miles from Northfield, Jesse examined Bob

Clell Miller, dead at Northfield. (State
Historical Society of Missouri)

Bob Younger, following his capture in 1876.
(State Historical Society of Missouri)

Bill Chadwell, dead at Northfield. (State
Historical Society of Missouri)

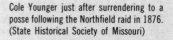

Cole Younger just after surrendering to a
posse following the Northfield raid in 1876.
(State Historical Society of Missouri)

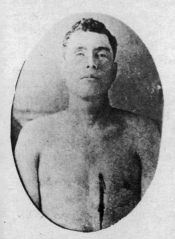

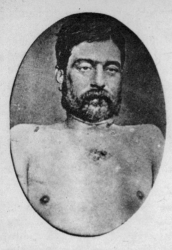 

Charlie Pitts, dead, killed by possemen. (State Historical Society of Missouri)

Jim Younger, bleeding from wound, after his capture. (State Historical Society of Missouri)

Younger's wound. The baby of the Younger clan was losing a lot of blood. Jesse turned to big brother Cole and told him that he thought it was best either to leave Bob behind or "put him out of his misery," much the way he would have killed a horse with a broken leg. For the first time in his life, Cole Younger blazed with anger at his cousin Jesse James. The two, hands fingering pistols, glared at each other. Younger then told Jesse that he would never desert his brother and suggested they split up.

Frank and Jesse went one way, the Youngers and Charlie Pitts another. The Youngers were slowed down by the conditions of their wounds and, fourteen days later outside the small town of Madelia, Minn., were surrounded by possemen. A full-scale battle ensued. After several hours of intense fighting, Sheriff Glispin, leader of the vigilantes, called out to the outlaws who were lying behind a log in a small swamp: "Do you men surrender?"

In the lull, nervous possemen reloaded and listened to the noises of the swamp birds and animals. Then a voice from behind the log was heard. "I surrender." Bob Younger, wounded five times, stood up shakily and raised his hands. "They're all down except me."

When the lawmen rushed up, they found Cole Younger with eleven bullets in him but still alive. Jim Younger had been wounded five times but he, too, still lived. Charlie Pitts, who had used up every bullet in his belt and in the pistol in his hand, lay still and quite dead with five bullets in his chest.

Taken into custody, the Younger brothers were given medical attention and survived to be sentenced to life imprisonment at the Minnesota State Penitentiary at Stillwater. Upon entering prison, Cole Younger told a reporter, "We were victims of circumstance. We were drove to it, sir."

Frank and Jesse James alone escaped the Northfield debacle. They rode southward for three weeks, stealing horses, living in barns, moving only at night, eating raw vegetables from the fields. Missouri was too hot for the James boys now. The entire nation had been alarmed at the Northfield raid and murders. The brothers decided to move to Tennessee and were driven by relatives in covered wagons to Nashville where they settled on small farms. For three years, the brothers tilled the land and lived quietly. Jesse, living under the name Howard, even entered his favorite horse, Red Fox, in local Nashville races, winning several events.

Then, in the fall of 1879, Jesse organized a new gang which included Frank, Bill Ryan, Dick Liddell, Tucker Basham, Ed Miller (Clell's brother), and Wood Hite. The gang roamed back through Missouri where they held up the Glendale train on October 7, 1879 for $35,000 and then as far south as Muscle Shoals, Ala., where they held up a stage for a paltry $1,400.

On July 10, 1881, Jesse led his men into Riverton, Iowa and held up the Davis and Sexton Bank, taking $5,000. Only five days later, Jesse struck the Chicago, Rock Island, and Pacific Railroad Express near Winston, Mo. Here, he killed a passenger, Frank McMillan, who attempted to interfere with the robbery, and Engineer William Westphal.

The brutality of the raid and the cold-blooded killing of McMillan and Westphal stirred Governor Thomas T. Crittenden to offer a $10,000 reward for the capture and conviction of Frank and Jesse James. It was an unheard-of-sum in those days and one to tempt even members of Jesse's own gang. The outlaw band Jesse and Frank had originally ridden with would never have dreamed of turning in either man. First, they had been protected by their cousins, the Youngers. Secondly, all the members of the gang were tied to Jesse and Frank through long years in the guerrilla service and were life-long residents of the farming community in which they lived, and living would no longer be possible should one betray the boys; Jesse's loyal kinsmen would see to that.

But after Northfield, Jesse was forced to go far afield to recruit new members for his gang. These new followers, especially the shifty brothers Ford, owed no particular allegiance to the outlaw. In fact, they openly criticized him and often came close to drawing their pistols against him. Crittenden's offer merely gave Robert and Charles Ford an additional reason to eliminate a man they personally disliked.

Robert Ford was never a full-fledged member of the second James gang. He moved within the periphery of associates who aided the outlaws in hiding out or escaping after a robbery. Charles Ford, however, did manage to be taken into the gang as a working member in time to participate in one of the strangest train robberies in American history.

On August 7, 1881 Jesse led his brother Frank, Wood and Clarence Hite, Dick Liddell, and Charles Ford to Blue Cut near Glendale, Mo., a few miles from his train robbery of 1879; the gang busied themselves with piling timber upon the tracks. At the sight of the obstruction, an engineer named Foote halted the Chicago, Alton Express.

A tall, bearded man with blinking blue eyes jumped into the locomotive's cab and formally introduced himself. "I'm Jesse James," he said. Then, motioning Foote down from the cab with his pistols, he ordered the engineer toward the express car.

Inside of the express car, Jesse, enjoying the popularity the dime novels had established for him, smiled widely and said, introducing the members of his gang, "This is Frank James, Wood Hite, Clarence Hite, Dick Liddell, and Charlie Ford." Each man smiled and gave a brief nod. The mood of the outlaws changed when they realized that their total take was slightly more than $1,500. They rode off grumbling. It was to be Jesse's last raid.

The Ford brothers had been secretly planning to kill him for months. They rode with him back to his mother's home while Frank stayed on at his Tennessee farm three miles from Nashville. Jesse, suspicious that Pinkertons might be watching the house, slept in the barn with his horse. The Fords stayed with him. The next morning, while Jesse ate breakfast at his mother's house for the last time, the Fords, according to Robert, "discussed the matter again and how we would kill him," for the reward.

That day Jesse left for St. Joseph, Mo. with the Ford brothers flanking him. Once in his small home, a quaint cottage on a hilltop overlooking St. Joseph, Jesse settled down for a while with his wife and children. The Fords stayed for several days and then went off on Jesse's orders to scout prospective robbery sites.

The second James gang, pressured by hundreds of lawmen and Pinkertons searching for them, became unnerved and finally began to dissolve. First Ed Miller's body was found on a lonely Missouri road. Jim Cummins, one-time James gang member, swore Jesse had killed him when Miller told him he wanted to surrender to the law. Next Wood Hite was killed by Dick Liddell and Bob Ford in an argument over $100 missing from the loot of the second Glendale train robbery. Dick Liddell then surrendered to lawmen on January 24, 1882. Liddell's confession implicated Clarence Hite, who was arrested, tried, and sentenced to prison for twenty-five years.

Only Jesse and Frank James and the Ford brothers were still at large. Jesse met the Fords in his home on the morning of April 3, 1882. He quietly outlined his plan for robbing the Platte County Bank. The three bandits ate breakfast prepared by Mrs. James as Jesse's children romped in the yard. Following breakfast, Jesse pulled out a newspaper and read about Dick Liddell's confession in which he implicated Jesse and Frank in several robberies. Though he spoke not a word, Bob Ford later stated that the look on Jesse's face was bone-chilling. Ford suddenly became terrified as he thought about what might happen to him if James learned how he and his brother Charlie had con-

Charlie Ford rode with Jesse, then betrayed him. (State Historical Society of Missouri)

Bob Ford shot Jesse James in the back and collected the reward. (State Historical Society of Missouri)

tacted Governor Crittenden and told him they would deliver Jesse James for amnesty and the reward money.

"I knew then I had placed my head in the lion's mouth," Bob Ford recalled at the inquest of Jesse James. "How could I safely remove it?"

His chance came minutes after Jesse tossed the paper aside. The bandit walked to the window, looked at his children playing and then turned around. He spotted a picture high on the wall which was tilted. He moved toward it. For a reason never explained, Jesse unbuckled his gun belts—he wore two, one about the hips and a shoulder holster, four guns in all—and placed them on a chair.

As he began to adjust the picture, Jesse's unprotected back offered a perfect target to the Fords. Robert Ford raised his pistol with a quaking hand and fired several times. The outlaw spun about with a wild look in his eyes and toppled forward. Mrs. James rushed into the room, fell to her knees and, weeping, cradled the head of her murdered husband in her arms.

Bob Ford stood in the middle of the room, holding his pistol up for examination. "The gun went off accidentally," he told Mrs. James.

Through tear-streaming eyes, Zerelda Mimms James looked up at her husband's murderer and said: "Yes, I guess it did go off on purpose."

The Ford brothers dashed from the house, Robert screaming at the top of his lungs, "I have killed Jesse James! I killed him! I killed him! I have killed Jesse James!"

The Fords got their reward, the newspapers their headlines, and Jesse Woodson James his immortality.

Newspapers from New York to Texas, from Missouri to California bannered the news. "Jesse by Jehovah," yelled the *St. Joseph Gazette.* "Good-Bye, Jesse!" lamented the *Kansas City Journal.*

Robert Ford and his brother Charles attended the coroner's inquest and gave unimpassioned testimony. Ford mounted the witness stand and calmly responded to the coroner's question "concerning the particulars of the killing."

"After breakfast, between eight and nine o'clock," Bob Ford stated, "he, my brother and myself were in the room. He pulled off his pistols and got up on a chair to dust off some picture frames and I drew my pistol and shot him."

"How close were you to him?"

"About six feet away."

"How close was the hand to him which held the pistol?"

"About four feet I should think."

"Did he say anything?"

Bob Ford paused and then said almost inaudibly, "He started to turn his head but didn't say a word."

"Was Jesse James unarmed when you killed him?"

"Yes, sir."

Hours later, aging Mrs. Zerelda Samuel entered the courtroom. She took the stand and said: "I live in Clay County, and am the mother of Jesse James." Then the mother who had protected her outlaw sons to the end, broke into deep moaning and sobs. "My poor boy . . . I have seen the body since my arrival and have recognized it as that of my son, Jesse . . . the lady by my side is my daughter-in-law and the children hers . . . he was a kind husband and son."

As the old woman was led from the courtroom in her grief, she saw Dick Liddell and the Fords sitting together. She stopped and in the hushed courtroom, her eyes fierce, steady, and fixed upon the three men, she raised the stump of her right arm and shouted in a half scream: "Traitors!"

The blood drained from the trio's faces and they hurried out of the courtroom via a side entrance. Jesse's mother and wife purchased a $500 coffin and took the outlaw home to Kearney where he was buried in a quiet field on the Samuel farm beneath a coffeebean tree.

A gleaming, white marble tombstone was placed above the grave which read:

> Jesse W. James
> Died April 3, 1882
> Aged 34 years, 6 months, 28 days
> Murdered by a traitor and a coward
> whose name is not worthy to
> appear here.

Five months later, the last of the infamous James gang, Alexander Franklin James, surrendered personally to Governor Crittenden in his Jefferson City office, October 5, 1882. He was then thirty-nine, a thin, tall man with a wispy mustache. He marched into the Governor's office and took off his gunbelt which held a single .44-caliber Colt pistol.

"Governor Crittenden," James said solemnly, "I want to hand over to you that which no other living man except myself has been permitted to touch since 1861." The outlaw pointed to the buckle on the belt which carried a U.S. stamp. "The cartridge belt has been mine for eighteen years. I got it in Centralia in 1861."

Crittenden promised James protection and a fair trial. As he was being led to jail, an enterprising reporter from the *Sedalia Dispatch* interviewed Frank James.

"Why did you surrender?" the reporter buzzed. "No one knew where you were in hiding, nor could anyone find out."

Frank shot back: "What of that? I was tired of an outlaw's life. I have been hunted for twenty-one years. I have literally lived in the saddle. I have never known a day of perfect peace. It was one long, anxious, inexorable, eternal vigil. When I slept it was literally in the midst of an arsenal. If I heard dogs bark more fiercely than usual, or the feet of horses in a greater volume of sound than usual, I stood to my arms. Have you any idea of what a man must endure who leads such a life? No, you cannot. No one can unless he lives it for himself."

The unscrupulous shooting of Jesse James so aroused the nation and, especially, the residents of Missouri that it improved Frank's chances of acquittal by a jury. After a series of trials, he was freed and returned to his farm. He lived without incident until February 18, 1915, when he died on the Samuel farm in the room where he had been born.

The Younger brothers were not freed until 1901. Bob Younger, who developed tuberculosis while in prison, died September 16, 1889 at age thirty-two. His sister, Retta, visited him at his deathbed in the Stillwater prison. His last whispered words were: "Don't weep for me." Cole and James Younger were paroled from the Minnesota State Penitentiary, July 10, 1901. Jim stayed in St. Paul, courting a young newswoman. When she rejected him, the ex-bandit committed suicide.

Cole Younger returned to Lee's Summit, Missouri to live out a quiet life. He and Frank James sometimes appeared at local fairs, running horse races and recalling the days of their youth. Younger lived the longest, dying from a heart attack March 21, 1916.

There was never any peace for the Ford brothers after the death of Jesse James. Charlie, plagued with the thought that he would be killed by one of Jesse's relatives, got drunk one night and blew away the top of his skull with his six-gun. Bob Ford drifted about the country, appearing in vaudeville shows and retelling the story of how he killed America's most famous bad man.

During the silver rush, Ford opened a saloon in Creede, Colo. One night, June 24, 1892, Ed. O. Kelly, a distant relative of the Younger brothers, walked into Ford's saloon and emptied his shotgun into the killer of Jesse James.

Almost from the moment Jesse was placed in his grave, claimants would come forward to state that another man had been killed and that they were, in reality, the bandit.

Jesse James in death, photo taken only minutes before burial. (Mercaldo Archives)

All were exposed as frauds, the latest pretender appearing in 1948 under the name of J. Frank Dalton, who insisted that he was 101 years old and the real Jesse James. He failed, however, to explain to skeptics how he had managed to grow a new tip to his left middle finger, the same finger which Jesse had blown off accidentally while cleaning his pistol when he rode with "Bloody Bill" Anderson.

These claims, however, were not unexpected, particularly when one realizes that almost every boy in America at one time or another wanted to be Jesse James, the strong, fearless bandit who came to symbolize the individuality of the American West (the murders he committed ignored as being unspeakable for a man of his courageous reputation). After generations, the man, Jesse James, has vanished and has been replaced by a dream image, rising from the blood-soaked earth of Missouri and towering with a long, nostalgic shadow that reaches into our considerably imperfect history as a nation.

And the history of that one man has become interminable and arcane, so hellishly involved with our collective emotions that his ghostly memory becomes something warm, delightfully indistinguishable and irretrievably rooted to a good past. In the end he becomes mistakenly worthy and honorable, this American killer.

A day after Jesse's death, a melodramatic ballad appeared as if by magic, attesting to the strange immortality gained by this strangest of outlaws:

Jesse James was a lad who killed many a man.
He robbed the Glendale train.
He stole from the rich and he gave to the poor,
He'd a hand and a heart and a brain.

(Chorus)
Jesse had a wife to mourn for his life,
Two children, they were brave,
But that dirty little coward that shot Mister Howard,
Has laid poor Jesse in his grave.

It was Robert Ford, that dirty little coward,
I wonder how does he feel,
For he ate of Jesse's bread and he slept in Jesse's bed,
Then he laid Jesse James in his grave.

Jesse was a man, a friend to the poor.
He'd never see a man suffer pain,
And with his brother Frank he robbed the Gallatin
   bank
And stopped the Glendale train.

It was on a Wednesday night, the moon was shining
   bright.
He stopped the Glendale train.
And the people all did say for many miles away,
It was robbed by Frank and Jesse James.

It was on a Saturday night, Jesse was at home,
Talking to his family brave,
Robert Ford came along like a thief in the night,
And laid Jesse James in his grave.

The people held their breath when they heard of
   Jesse's death,
And wondered how he ever came to die,
It was one of the gang called Little Robert Ford,
That shot Jesse James on the sly.

Jesse went to his rest with his hand on his breast,
The devil will be upon his knee,
He was born one day in the county of Shea
And he came from a solitary race.

This song was made by Billy Garshade,
As soon as the news did arrive,
He said there was no man with the law in his hand
Could take Jesse James when alive.

The author was never found.

[ALSO SEE William "Bloody Bill" Anderson, Al Jennings,
William Clarke Quantrill.]

JAMESON, JAMES
Murderer, Burglar • (? -1807)

With his partner, James M'Gowan, Jameson earned his dubious living as a burglar in the Harrisburg, Pa. area. The pair's undoing occurred August 28, 1806, when they attempted to rob Jacob Eshelman of Hummelstown, Pa. He resisted and the burglars clubbed him to death with tree limbs.

They were quickly taken into custody; Eshelman's savings—$500—was found on their persons. They were sentenced to death. M'Gowan was hanged December 29, 1806, but Jameson escaped from the Dauphin County Jail. He was recaptured days later, discovered hiding under his mother's bed in Reading, Pa.

He was hanged January 10, 1807, in Harrisburg.

JENNINGS, AL
Trainrobber • (1863-1948)

Jennings began late as a robber and his exploits were anything but awe-inspiring: comic would be more like it. The four Jennings brothers—Al, Frank, Ed, and John—were roustabout cowboys who lived at Kiowa Creek, Oklahoma, near Woodward. Al first met a shoddy-looking outlaw named "Little Dick" about 1885 and was goaded into several awkward attempts at robbery, more on a dare than through a desire to steal and kill.

Al and his brothers first pretended to be U.S. marshals and levied a toll against gullible ranchers driving cattle through the still-wild Oklahoma Territory. They soon tired of this and tried to rob two trains near Woodward.

Jennings attempted to flag the engineer to a stop but was ignored; he was almost crushed by the locomotive. The second attempt was even more ridiculous. Jennings and his brothers rode alongside a roaring train for several minutes firing their pistols in the air as a way of signaling the engineer to halt. The engineer merely waved a friendly hello and kept going.

The boys finally stumbled on a small passenger train taking on wood at a water stop, and robbed the express car of $60. Of the four men in this band, Frank and Al Jennings were captured a day later by lawman Bud Ledbetter who never fired a shot. He ordered the brothers to throw down their guns and tie themselves up. They did.

Ed and John Jennings rode to a nearby town and entered a saloon where famed lawman Temple Houston was sipping whiskey. The Jennings boys began an argument with Houston, who promptly shot them both. Ed was killed outright; John was wounded and lived to return to his small ranch.

Both Al and Frank Jennings were given life sentences for their absurd robbery. Al was freed in five years, Frank in seven. In the mid-1890s, Al Jennings rode out of the Oklahoma Territory and traveled to California, where he permanently settled. In his muddled mind, he somehow transformed himself from a bungling bandit to a much-feared outlaw.

Sheriff Jim Herron of Oklahoma later stated: "Old Al Jennings was around California for years, stuffing dudes with nonsense and telling them wild yarns about himself in the early days." One of the stories Jennings told of himself was that he could, in his prime, hit a can tossed in the air from one hundred paces without ever missing.

Ex Rough Rider and World War I commander, General Roy Hoffman clucked his tongue at this Jennings tale. "I knew Al Jennings personally," he once said, "and his

Al Jennings of Oklahoma, the West's most awkward bandit. (Oklahoma Historical Society)

marksmanship was notoriously poor. He was one of the kind of fellows who could have qualified as the traditional bad shot who couldn't hit the side of a barn."

Jennings' lurid tales of the Old West were strengthened when, in 1948, 101-year-old J. Frank Dalton appeared, claiming to be the real Jesse James. Jennings, then 85, hurried to his side, took one look at the ancient pretender, and shouted to AP reporters: "It's him! It's Jesse!"

Both men posed holding pistols. Jennings stated that "there isn't a bit of doubt on earth," that Dalton was the true Jesse James. He neglected to inform the press that he had never met Jesse James and that Dalton had miraculously grown a new left middle fingertip, one which the real Jesse James had accidentally blown off while cleaning a pistol when he rode with "Bloody Bill" Anderson.

Jennings died months later, raving about deadly shootouts that had occurred only in his fruitful imagination. As a tribute to his ability as a teller of tall tales, Hollywood believed every word and made a motion picture based on his life . . . or the life he thought he had led.

JOHNSON, JOHN
Murderer, Robber • (? -1824)

Publicity surrounding the trial of murderer John Johnson in New York City was tremendous. His victim, James Murray, had been his roommate. Johnson, seeking Murray's purse, murdered him in his sleep by splitting his skull with a hatchet.

He wrapped the body in a blanket and carried it toward the harbor, intending to dispose of the corpse there. A curious policeman called to Johnson and the killer dropped his grim load and ran.

Murray was unknown and authorities seeking his identification displayed his corpse at City Hall Park for days, hoping that someone would recognize the body. Someone did and this led to Johnson's arrest and speedy trial on March 16, 1824. He confessed and was sentenced to death.

Johnson's execution was a circus-like affair in the heart of New York City. Fifty thousand spectators came to watch him hang at Thirteenth Street and Second Avenue, April 2, 1824.

JOHNSON, RICHARD
Murderer • (? -1829)

Frustration was the root of Johnson's murderous discontent. Though his strange mistress, Mrs. Ursula Newman, had given birth to his child, she refused to marry him. The peculiar woman even refused to admit that the child was his. When he demanded she give the child his name, Mrs. Newman laughed at him.

In a rage, Johnson grabbed a pistol loaded with buckshot and fired it into his beloved on the evening of November 20, 1828, killing her instantly (nine slugs were removed

A CORRECT COPY OF THE

Trial & Conviction of
RICHARD JOHNSON,
FOR THE
MURDER
Of Ursula Newman,

On the 20th Nov. 1828, by shooting her with a
pistol loaded with buck shot or slugs,
NINE OF WHICH ENTERED HER BODY;
TOGETHER WITH THE
Charge of the Court,
AND THE
CONFESSION OF THE PRISONER
Of his entention to have added Suicide to the Horrid and Appalling Murder for which he is to suffer an ignomenious
death, and his letter to a friend in Philadel-
phia previous to his Conviction.

NEW-YORK:
PRINTED AND SOLD WHOLESALE AND RETAIL, BY
CHRISTIAN BROWN.
No. 211 WATER-STREET, N. YORK.

The strange murder tale of Richard Johnson was recounted in this 1828
booklet. (N.Y. Historical Society)

217

from Mrs. Newman's body). Moments later, Johnson thought of committing suicide but discarded this idea.

Another report had it that Johnson suffered from a strange malady—that he imagined Mrs. Newman's child was his own (as he did many others'). According to this version of the story, her jibes at his fantasy were what caused Johnson to kill her.

He was tried in New York City and confessed to the crime. Johnson was hanged May 7, 1829 on Blackwell's Island. Dying on the gallows with Johnson the same day was Catharine Cashiere, a Negro servant who had gotten drunk and stabbed another woman, Susan Anthony, to death. (The judge who sentenced Catharine to the gallows made several testy remarks about the increasing number of saloons in New York City.)

JONES, WILLIAM ("CANADA BILL") Gambler • (? -1877)

A longtime card sharping partner of the notorious gambler George H. Devol, Jones was a habitué of the Mississippi river boats. His expertise with cards earned him the reputation as the greatest three-card monte player in the country. He was known as Canada Bill and Devol later described him in his memoirs as "medium-sized, chicken-headed, tow-haired, with mild blue eyes, and a mouth nearly from ear to ear, who walked with a shuffling, half-apologetic sort of gait, and, who, when his countenance was in repose, resembled an idiot . . . he had a squawking, boyish voice, and awkward manners, and a way of asking fool questions and putting on a good-natured sort of grin that led everybody to believe that he was the rankest kind of sucker—the greenest sort of country jake."

Canada Bill was anything but that. Born in England to gypsy parents, Bill migrated to Canada where he learned his card playing from a leading crook, Dick Cady. He fleeced the gullible there for years in three-card monte, the proverbial bent card utilized to tip him off as to which card to play. He ran his luck dry in Canada by 1850 and moved south.

First Bill moved to the Mississippi area. After meeting Devol in New Orleans, the pair worked the elegant paddle wheelers for years through the 1850s. By the Civil War, the bet-a-million gamblers had disappeared. At this time, Bill learned that Devol was attempting to con him out of their jointly pooled funds and departed for Kansas City, where he teamed up with another gambler, Dutch Charlie. One card swindle with wealthy bankers there brought the duo $200,000. Before the players could realize they had been taken, Bill caught the train for Omaha.

The network of railways between Kansas City and Omaha was budding and the trains were loaded with greenhorns begging to be cheated. Bill obliged them and worked the iron horse trade for more than fifteen years, employing his nefarious skills with three-card monte.

The Union Pacific line was hardest hit by this one-man gambling army and soon ordered its conductors to eject anyone playing three-card monte on board its trains. Canada Bill became indignant. The railroad was out to destroy his livelihood. He wrote the president of the line, offering $10,000 plus an annual percentage of his take to obtain the exclusive "franchise" to three-card monte playing on the Union Pacific rails.

Further, the gambler promised that he would only fleece wealthy travelers from Chicago and Methodist preachers who were known to carry large sums and whom he personally disliked. The president of the line declined to sell Bill the franchise.

In 1874, Bill traveled to Chicago and with gamblers Jimmy Porter and "Colonel" Charles Starr, established four infamously crooked gambling dens in the Red Light district.

"Canada Bill," king of cardsharps. (University of Wyoming Library, Union Pacific Collection)

There, Canada Bill amassed $150,000 within six months but, being an inveterate gambler himself, lost almost every penny to crooked casino dealers.

Bill ambled on to Cleveland where he met with little success; his reputation preceded him and he could find little action. His last stop was the Charity Hospital in Reading, Pa., where he died in 1877. Gamblers by the dozens attended the quick-hand artist's funeral. One even offered to bet $1,000 to $500 that "Bill was not in the box."

His gambler's eulogy was delivered dramatically by a friend:

"O, when I die, just bury me
In a box-back coat and hat,
Put a twenty dollar gold piece on my watch chain
To let the Lord know I'm standing pat."

KEATING'S SALOON, BATTLE OF

As Western gunfights go, the battle of Keating's Saloon in El Paso, April 15, 1881, was an awkward melee spawned by drink and racism. The events leading to this reckless shootout began weeks earlier when the notorious Manning brothers were suspected of rustling Mexican cattle and driving them across the border near El Paso to sell them at high prices.

Ed Fitch, a Texas Ranger, and two Mexican vaqueros named Juarique and Sanchez from the raided Mexican ranch, investigated the Manning spread. The Mexicans, who had gone off on their own, were shot to death by hidden gunmen. Seventy-five heavily armed Mexican riders then crossed the border and entered El Paso, their leader demanding an inquest and investigation.

On April 15, 1881, Gus Krempkau, a Spanish-speaking El Paso constable, acted as interpreter during the inquest. At noon, Krempkau left the judge's chambers and walked to Keating's saloon where he retrieved his rifle (no firearms were allowed at the inquest). Pushing out through the swinging doors of the saloon, Krempkau spotted George Campbell, a small-time outlaw and a friend of the Manning

221

brothers who was prone to excessive drinking and nurtured a surly disposition.

Campbell was standing in the middle of the street, shouting at the top of his lungs that El Paso's marshal should have arrested the armed Mexicans who rode into town earlier that day. The marshal was none other than the redoubtable Dallas Stoudenmire, one of the most feared lawmen in the Southwest. Stoudenmire, at the time Campbell began his play, was eating beef stew in the Globe Restaurant, two hundred yards away.

Krempkau was a peace-loving man who tried to avoid trouble when possible. He ignored Campbell's taunts and walked to his horse, tethered in front of the saloon, where he slipped his rifle into its scabbard.

Campbell weaved in the middle of the road, obviously drunk, eyeing Krempkau's back. He shouted: "Any American who would befriend the Mexicans should be hanged!"

Krempkau craned his head about and gave the roughneck a long look. "George," he said slowly, "I hope you don't mean me."

"If the shoe fits you wear it, Gus."

Krempkau ignored the remark, readying his saddle.

Another town drunk and troublemaker, John Hale, staggering from Keating's moments before had heard the heated words and suddenly decided to throw in with his friend Campbell. He dashed up to Krempkau with a drawn gun which he jammed under the lawman's arm. "Turn loose, Campbell," Hale called to his friend. "I've got him covered." Inexplicably, Hale then fired one bullet into Krempkau who sagged to the ground, shot through the lungs.

Hale blinked in amazement at the stricken Krempkau and then, obviously realizing the rashness of his act, ran behind a post in front of Keating's Saloon to hide. Marshal Stoudenmire came on the run when he heard the pistol shot. Two guns were in his hands.

Stoudenmire evaluated the situation immediately when he saw Krempkau dying on the steps of the saloon and Hale hiding behind the post. He fired two shots at Hale as he ran. One wounded a bystander. The second shot was perfect, hitting Hale in the head as he peered around the post, killing him.

Campbell sobered quickly when he saw Stoudenmire. To a crowd collected in front of him which he attempted to flag away with a drawn pistol, Campbell nervously yelled, "Gentlemen, this is not my fight!"

The mortally wounded Krempkau thought differently. He managed to pull forth his pistol and with his last drams of strength squeezed off all six rounds, wounding Campbell in the toe and wrist. Campbell dropped his gun into his other hand and aimed at Krempkau who slumped against the steps leading to the saloon and who was already dead.

Stoudenmire turned and fired three shots into Campbell who dropped to the dust. The marshal walked over to Campbell and rolled him over on his back. With his last breath, the outlaw moaned: "You big son-of-a-bitch, you murdered me."

Another barfly, Patrick Shea, who was completely drunk, ambled from Keating's, crossed the street on wobbly legs, and knelt down next to his friend Campbell. He picked up the outlaw's weapon, an attractive pistol he had much coveted, and said with slurred words, "George, d'ya want your gun?"

Marshal Stoudenmire spat into the street in disgust, wiggled his pistols in Shea's direction and said: "Move on, you little rat." Shea moved on.

Though three men were killed in this zany dispute, it was never learned who murdered the two Mexican riders.

KENNEDY, JAMES ("SPIKE")
Murderer • (1855- ?)

In the days Wyatt Earp clamped law down upon the wild Kansas town of Dodge City, the reigning queen of the saloons was Dora Hand alias Fannie Keenan, a stunning showgirl who sang and danced her way to local fame. Dora, once described as "the most graciously beautiful woman to reach the camp in the heyday of its iniquity," was much sought after by Dodge's mayor, James H. "Dog" Kelley.

Vying for the singer's attentions was the son of one of the wealthiest cattlemen in the West, James W. Kennedy, called "Spike" by his friends. Kelley had his bouncers toss Kennedy into the street one night in 1878 after the young gunslinger paid too much attention to his star attraction.

Just before dawn on an October morning, Kennedy returned and fired a single shot into Kelley's bedroom window. The bullet hit Dora Hand, asleep on a couch, killing her. Kennedy, without stopping to see whom he had shot, whooped it out of town on his pinto.

Four of the most renowned lawmen in Dodge City (or anywhere else) set out after Kennedy—Earp, Charlie Bassett, Bat Masterson, and Bill Tilghman. The frantic chase led across more than a hundred miles of open range. The lawmen rode extra horses in relays in a day and night pursuit. Kennedy rode a single mount and he rode him to death.

Near Meade City, Kennedy's horse collapsed. The report of his pistol cracking a mercy bullet into his mount brought the lawmen to him. A wild fight ensued with Kennedy holding off the four man posse, potshooting from behind his dead horse. Masterson, a crack shot, finally pumped a bullet from his rifle into Kennedy's arm. The young man was taken without further struggle. As the four lawmen walked toward him, he shouted across the dark plain: "You sons-of-bitches! I'll get even with you for this!"

Minutes later, Wyatt Earp told Kennedy: "Your shot killed Dora, not Kelley."

Kennedy fell to weeping and sobbed, "I wish you had killed me."

He was returned to Dodge City where he was quickly tried and acquitted "for lack of evidence." Spike Kennedy left Dodge forever after the trial, returning first to his father's ranch and then becoming a drifter along the many cow trails, disappearing in the 1880s.

KERRIGAN, MICHAEL
Bankrobber • (? –1895)

Known in New York underworld as Johnny Dobbs, Kerrigan was one of the most remarkable bankrobbers of his day, a burglar who entered privately-owned banks, cracked the safes in seconds, and was gone. The number of banks he did rob was never determined but it is known that he fenced more than $2 million in securities (of which he realized a third) over the bar of his saloon on Mott Street.

Kerrigan was a loquacious sort who was once asked by police why so many crooks centered their activities near police headquarters. "The nearer the church the closer to God," Kerrigan quipped.

High living, a series of expensive mistresses, and a gigantic thirst finally brought Kerrigan down. He died in 1895 in the alcoholic ward in Bellevue Hospital. One of the mistresses sold an expensive broach he had given to her, to pay for his funeral.

KERRYONIANS GANG

Exclusive to natives of County Kerry, Ireland, the Kerryonians existed in New York about 1825, one of the earliest organized criminal gangs. The members headquartered on Center Street (now Worth) at Rosanna Peer grocery store. The Kerryonians spent most of their time mugging and beating up Englishmen.

KNAPP, JOSEPH
Murderer • (? –1830)

Seafaring captain Joseph Knapp lived with his wife in a sprawling New England home at Salem, Mass. along with several other relatives, and a Captain Joseph White, another retired sea captain in his late eighties. White had accumulated great wealth and Knapp conspired to steal it, arranging for the aged captain's murder.

Enlisting the aid of his brother John Francis Knapp and Richard and George Crowinshield, Joseph opened a window in the White home on the night of April 6, 1830. Richard Crowinshield crept inside and made his way to White's bedroom. The old man still had enough strength to resist and Crowinshield was compelled to knock him out with a club. He then drove a stiletto thirteen times into White's chest, killing him.

The Crowinshield brothers, who had been suspected of other murders in the Salem area, were immediately questioned by authorities. Then a letter, written by a convict attempting to extort the Knapp brothers for their part in the murder (the convict had learned of the deed through the Crowinshields) fell into police hands.

The Knapp and Crowinshield brothers were all arrested and tried. Joseph Knapp was promised immunity if he testified against the others. He agreed and named Richard Crowinshield as the murderer. Crowinshield hanged himself in his cell. Then John Francis Knapp was tried, prosecuted by no less a personage than Daniel Webster, who considered the murder "a most extraordinary case."

It took two trials to convict Knapp; then he was hanged. Since Joseph refused to testify against his brother, he lost his immunity and was also tried and hanged. George Crowinshield was acquitted after his mistress and her friend testified that he was in bed with them at the time of the murder. Crowinshield was set free and died a natural death in Salem decades later.

LAPAGE, JOSEPH
Murderer • (? -1875)

A French-Canadian lumberjack, Lapage worked at odd jobs in New England. In 1874, Lapage killed and mutilated Miss Marietta Ball, a school teacher, near St. Albans, Vt.

A year later, Lapage hit seventeen-year-old Josie Langmaid over the head with a club as she was on her way to school in Pembroke, N.H. After dragging her body into the woods, Lapage decapitated the girl with an axe and then proceeded to mutilate her. He then ravished the corpse.

Lapage was apprehended, tried, and convicted. He was hanged in 1875.

LATIMER, IRVING
Murderer • (1866-1946)

BACKGROUND: BORN AND RAISED IN JACKSON, MICH. OF WELL-TO-DO PARENTS. COLLEGE EDUCATED. OCCUPATION, PHARMACIST. DESCRIPTION: 5'10", BROWN EYES, BLACK HAIR, SLENDER BUILD. ALIASES: NONE. RECORD: MURDERED HIS MOTHER 1/24/1889 FOR HER ESTATE (SOME REPORTS HAVE IT THAT HE ALSO MURDERED HIS FATHER PREVIOUSLY TO COME INTO CERTAIN INHERITANCE MONIES); TRIED AND CONVICTED OF MURDER IN THE FIRST DEGREE; SENTENCED TO LIFE IMPRISONMENT IN MICHIGAN STATE PRISON IN JACKSON; PARDONED 5/11/35; DIED IN ELOISE STATE HOSPITAL, 1946.

The web of invented facts which Irving Latimer spun round himself at the time of his mother's murder was intended to protect him with a foolproof alibi. Instead, it entrapped him.

That Latimer was a clever, handsome, dashing young man in 1889 there can be no doubt. Women at Jackson's high society balls vied for his attention. He was also known to the fair belles of that city as a bit of a rake. Yet, at 23, he was a pillar of the community. He owned his own drugstore and taught Sunday School.

It seems that Latimer's tastes were rich, for he had been sinking heavily into debt. His mother had advanced him $3,000 to pay some of his creditors.

But this loan had nothing to do with maternal indulgence. Mrs. Latimer, ever the straight-laced Victorian, held her son's note, a handwritten I.O.U. which she fully intended to collect on January 31, 1889. She never lived that long.

On the night of January 24, 1889, someone broke into the Latimer home through a cellar door. From the basement, the intruder carefully walked upstairs to the second floor, entered Mrs. Latimer's bedroom and, as the woman woke hazily from her sleep, reduced her head to a bloody pulp with a heavy instrument and then shot her. The invader, without disturbing her considerable jewelry and other valuables, then retraced his steps and left the premises again by the cellar door. The family watchdog, Gyp, made no attempt to stop the killer or sound a warning.

The next morning, curious neighbors who noted that Mrs. Latimer did not let Gyp outside for his morning ritual as was her habit, inspected the house. They found the broken cellar door. They pounded and rang for Mrs. Latimer but got no answer. Police were summoned and the body of Mrs. Latimer was quickly discovered. Where, authorities wanted to know, was Irving?

They were told that Mrs. Latimer's fun-loving son was in Detroit. One thing puzzled Jackson Police Chief John Boyle. He was unable to find Latimer at Detroit's exclusive Cadillac Hotel, where he was known to stay. Instead, he found the young man registered at the second-rate Griswold Hotel. Latimer rushed home as soon as he was notified of his mother's death.

Latimer's untimely trip aroused Boyle's suspicions from the beginning. Irving had told the boy who helped him in the drugstore that he was going to the big city to attend a funeral. Upon his return, Latimer denied that there had been any funeral. He said he only used that excuse because he didn't want his employee to know his business. His business? Irving admitted it was a girl, a peccadillo named Trixy. He said he was embarrassed to talk about getting emotionally involved with a professional tart.

The Police Chief nodded understandingly. Then he went to check on Latimer's story, systematically running down witnesses who might have seen him. There were many between Jackson and Detroit, Michigan, all unwittingly hostile to Latimer's claim.

In Detroit, Boyle found a porter at the Griswold who recognized Latimer from photos as the man he saw sneaking out a side entrance of the hotel at 10 p.m. on the night of the murder. Two conductors of the Michigan Central railroad then verified that it was Latimer who frantically hopped aboard the 10:10 p.m. train for Jackson that night, getting off at Ypsilanti and then catching another train to take him on to Jackson where he arrived shortly before midnight, a half hour before Mrs. Latimer's murder.

Solid witnesses then cropped up faster than those summoned by Scratch to face Daniel Webster in his dynamic duel with the Devil. Their statements damned the young Latimer phrase by phrase.

Another conductor for the railroad stated that at 6:20 a.m. on the morning of January 25, 1889, only hours after Mrs. Latimer had been slaughtered, before her neighbors became suspicious of her silent house, he had picked up a young man who demanded a sleeper on the Detroit-bound train, paid for it on the train, and dove into it, immediately drawing the curtains. A porter supported the conductor's remarks. The man was identified from photos as Irving Latimer. The young man's strange conduct was further emphasized when he leaped from the slow-moving train in West Detroit fifteen minutes before the train came to a halt in the main station.

Boyle went back to the Griswold Hotel. A chamber maid stated that she had gone into Latimer's room on the morning of the 25th to make up the bed. It had not been slept in. As she left Room 34 and walked down the passage, she turned to see Latimer, nervously scanning the hallway as he let himself into his room. A barber whose shop was next to the Griswold Hotel testified that at 10 a.m. the same morning, Latimer had entered his premises and demanded a shave. He wore no cuffs on his shirt (in those days cuffs were detachable as were the collars of shirts; Latimer prided himself on his shirtcuffs because of the diamond cufflinks he habitually sported). There was blood on his coat. Latimer told the barber that he had had a nosebleed earlier that morning.

Boyle's excellent investigative prowess turned up one more damning piece of evidence. Aside from the terrible beating Mrs. Latimer had taken about her head, an autopsy revealed that she had been shot twice. Two .32-caliber bullets were recovered from her brain. Boyle found a .32-caliber revolver in a desk drawer in Latimer's drugstore.

The young man was arrested. His marvelous cufflinks were in his pocket, but he possessed no cuffs. His shoes and clothing were splattered with blood. It was the nosebleed, Latimer explained.

At his trial Irving Latimer continued to defend his elaborately-constructed alibi. He explained his night flight to Ypsilanti as an effort to find his love-mate Trixy, who had run away from him in Detroit. He had then gone on to Jackson to get some sleep on a cot in the rear of the drugstore which was sometimes his habit. Early on the morning of the 25th, he had remembered that his clothes and bags were still in Detroit and he took the early train back there to retrieve them. He had not gone near his mother's house, he insisted, during the night of her murder.

No one believed Irving Latimer, least of all the jury. In a record twenty minutes they returned a verdict of first degree parricide and he was sentenced to life imprisonment, Michigan having no death penalty.

Latimer became a model prisoner. He was made a trusty, and pharmacist's aide. As such he had access to deadly drugs. On the night of March 26, 1893 Latimer served his guards a midnight lunch of sardines and lemonade. The lemonade was lethal; he had dosed it with prussic acid and opium. It killed one guard and rendered the other unconscious.

Irving escaped but was picked up days later. He hadn't meant to kill the guard, he explained. It was an "accident." Too much prussic acid got into the lemonade, he said. It wasn't his fault.

There would be no parole for Latimer now. He would rot in prison. The calm, finely-mannered inmate did his time well. By 1907 he had become a trusty again and was placed in charge of landscaping the prison grounds. By the mid-1920s he had become the prison's most celebrated old con, giving out interviews to the press on the decline of class prisoners: "We used to have train bandits, bankrobbers, safe blowers—all fairly intelligent men. Now what do we have? A mob of ignorant, half-educated boys who think they know it all."

Years dragged on and changes came. The state prison was moved to new quarters but Irving Latimer declined to go. His cell was virtually a modest apartment with books, plants, desk. He liked it there. It was his home. The state considered him a harmless old man and allowed him to stay on as a watchman for the deserted prison. In 1935, he was set free after spending 46 years in prison. He loitered about Jackson's Depression-torn streets, and was picked up several times for vagrancy. There was no place for him on either side of prison walls anymore. He was finally taken in by a state-run old people's home where he died in 1946 still claiming his innocence as a victim of circumstances, a man chasing an imaginary tart named Trixy down through five decades.

LE BLANC, ANTOINE
Murderer • (? -1833)

Arriving from France April 26, 1833, LeBlanc took a job with the Sayre family in rural New Jersey as a common laborer. He resented his lowly position, especially the fact that he was compelled to sleep in the woodshed.

On May 2, 1833, LeBlanc decided to better his way of life and invaded the Sayre home with intent to rob them. He beat both Mr. and Mrs. Sayre to death with a shovel and placed their bodies under a heap of manure.

Hearing noises in the Sayre house he rushed to the attic where he found the Negro maid and killed her. Visitors to the Sayre place apprehended him and he was quickly tried; he was executed on the gallows September 6, 1833 at Morristown, N.J.

LeBlanc was a roguishly handsome fellow who, apparently, had a way with the ladies. As one historian's account has it, his execution took place on the Morristown green and "twelve thousand persons were present, of which the majority were females."

LECHLER, JOHN
Murderer • (? -1822)

Mary Lechler was about as unfaithful a wife as one could be, particularly when her neighbor, a Mr. Haag, arrived at her front doorstep. Unfortunately, her husband John, who caught Haag and his wife in bed, was not an understanding fellow. He threatened to kill them both.

In desperation, Haag offered Lechler a large sum of money, writing out a promissory note. When he later refused to pay, Lechler went berserk, rushing home where he strangled his wife and then hanged her from an attic beam. He then charged to Haag's home, pistols in hand.

When Haag refused to come out, Lechler fired through his front door, shooting and killing Mrs. Haag.

Lechler was hanged in Lancaster, Pa. October 25, 1822.

LEE, JOHN D.
Murderer • (? -1877)

When Mormon Bishop John D. Lee became an Indian agent in Utah in the early 1850s, he had more on his mind than keeping the peace. Arming his wards and enlisting the aid of white renegades dressed as Indians, Lee began leading attacks on wagon trains heading for California.

With a large body of such men, Lee, in September of 1857, jumped a wagon train of 140 immigrants. The foreigners valiantly fought off the attack for almost three days. Then Lee sent word that if they surrendered to him, giving up their gold and some livestock, they could continue their trip.

The immigrants threw down their arms and came out of their wagon circle, only to be slaughtered at Lee's command. Only seventeen children were spared.

It wasn't until 1875 that Lee was accused of the Mountain Meadows massacre and was tried. His second trial proved him guilty and he was condemned to death. Lee was shot by a firing squad near Salt Lake City, Utah, March 23, 1877.

LESLIE, GEORGE LEONIDAS
Bankrobber • (1842-1884)

BACKGROUND: BORN IN CINCINNATI, OHIO, THE SON OF A BREWER. GRADUATED UNIVERSITY OF CINCINNATI WITH A DEGREE IN ARCHITECTURE, HONORS. MOVED TO NEW YORK AT THE CLOSE OF THE CIVIL WAR. DESCRIPTION: TALL, FAIR-COMPLEXIONED, SLENDER. ALIASES: GEORGE HOWARD, WESTERN GEORGE. RECORD: CONSIDERED BY NEW YORK CITY POLICE TO BE THE MOST SUCCESSFUL BANK ROBBER IN THE EAST FOR TWENTY YEARS, ROBBING AN ESTIMATED $12,000,000 FROM VARIOUS BANKING INSTITUTIONS WHICH INCLUDED THE SOUTH KENSINGTON NATIONAL BANK OF PHILADELPHIA, THE THIRD NATIONAL BANK OF BALTIMORE, THE SARATOGA COUNTY BANK OF WATERFORD, N.Y., AND THE WELLSBORO BANK OF PHILADELPHIA; ROBBED WITH GILBERT YOST A JEWELRY STORE IN NORRISTOWN, PA., IN 1970, CAPTURED, RELEASED ON BAIL, JUMPED BOND; LESLIE'S SCORES WERE THE OCEAN NATIONAL BANK OF NYC ON 6/27/69 ($787,879) AND THE MANHATTAN SAVINGS INSTITUTION ON 10/27/78 ($2,747,000); MURDERED BY MEMBERS OF HIS OWN GANG IN 1884.

At his mother's death, college-trained Leslie moved to New York in 1865. He was easily accepted into exclusive clubs because of his family's social distinction, and soon acquired the reputation of a bon vivant. But George Leslie, while top-hatting it with New York's four hundred, lived a double life, one which put him squarely in the social register and another that heralded him as a criminal genius in the underworld, a man destined to be called "King of the Bankrobbers."

Leslie's technique in robbing banks was fairly simple. He merely acquired the architectural plans of a bank from some of his social contracts to "study" and then determined where a break-in could be best achieved. If plans were unavailable, Leslie would visit a bank he intended to rob, pretending to be a new depositor. From his observations he would then proceed to draw intricate plans of the bank's interior.

New York Police Superintendent George Walling was suspicious of the youthful dandy from the beginning but proof of his involvement in some of the most shocking bank robberies of the century was lacking. Leslie was apprehended once, in Norristown, Pa., in 1870, while burglarizing a jewelry store with a common thief named Gilbert Yost, but his political contacts in Philadelphia had the case against him quashed. (Yost was convicted and went to prison for two years.)

To further ensure success in his robberies, the ingenious Leslie established social contacts with bank presidents and then convinced them to hire some "down and out chap of my slight acquaintance" as a guard or porter. These "chaps," of course, were members of Leslie's mob who included such infamous thieves as James "Jimmy" Hope, Abe Coakley, Shang Draper, Johnny Dobbs (nee Michael Kerrigan), Jimmy Brady, Banjo Pete Emerson, Red Leary, and Worcester Sam Perris.

Leslie would assemble these men in a Manhattan room which had been fitted to duplicate the interior of the bank to be robbed. He rehearsed his men in their various assigned tasks, criticizing them on their timing and movements. In addition to such training, Leslie went to master tool makers and, according to his own specifications, ordered the finest burglar equipment ever seen in America. The tools used to burglarize the Manhattan Savings Institution alone cost Leslie $3,000.

After completing several successful robberies, Leslie engineered the robbery of the Ocean National Bank at Greenwich and Fulton Streets on June 27, 1869. The take was overwhelming, even beyond the robbers' expectations—$786,879. Fortified with a staggering amount of money, Leslie settled down to plan the biggest robbery of his life.

He took three years in planning his attack on the mammoth Manhattan Savings Institution, one of the largest banks in the world. The bank's vault possessed one of the most intricate combination locks ever made. Leslie learned from a friend in one of the clubs he had joined, the style of the combination and then purchased a copy from its manufacturers, Valentine & Butler.

Leslie then spent hours practicing with the combination lock until he discovered it could be thrown out of gear and the notches of the tumblers aligned by boring a hole under the indicator and then working the tumblers with a hair-like piece of steel.

An unimportant member of his gang, Pat Shevlin, was placed in the bank as a guard through Leslie's connections and the master thief was allowed inside one night by Shevlin six months later. He and Shevlin placed a black screen in front of the vault and then Leslie went to work. He fiddled with the combination for hours before boring his hole under the indicator. It was dawn and he had not completed his task. He puttied up the hole and left, hoping to return the next night.

The tumblers, however, had not been replaced and bank officials found it impossible to open the vault the next morning. A new lock plate was installed that day and when Leslie returned he discovered he could not move the tumblers. Leslie left the bank in disgust, determined to rob it within a week with only the means left to him—force.

On October 27, 1878, Leslie returned to the Manhattan Savings Institution with four men—Pete Emerson, Jimmy Hope, Abe Coakley, and a strong man named Bill Kelly who was supposed to handle any situation involving a beating. The policeman on duty, John Nugent, had been bribed to be away from the bank area during the time of the robbery, and, if necessary, to cover the gang's retreat.

The gang gained access to the bank through the apartment of night watchman Louis Werckle, tied up the Werckle family, and then entered the bank's main offices.

There, Leslie and the others worked for three hours behind their black screen to break into the vault.

Patrolman Van Orden, on his way home from work, peered into the bank to see the black screen in front of the vault. Then he saw a cleaning man dusting desks. The cleaning man looked up at him with a smile and waved. Van Orden waved back and continued homeward, unconcerned. The cleaning man was master thief Abe Coakley.

Working their way into various compartments within the vault, the gang extricated a whopping $2,747,000 in cash and securities which they stuffed into satchels. As they escaped out a back entrance, one of these satchels was given to patrolman Nugent to carry.

Ironically, the gang failed to notice more than $2 million in cash encased in sacks on the vault floor behind. The cash realized from the robbery amounted only to $11,000. More than $2 million in bonds were non-negotiable, but it was still an enormous haul and Leslie's fame in the underworld as a super bankrobber was firmly entrenched.

Following the Manhattan robbery, Leslie acted as an adviser to bankrobbers for close to six years. His fee for approving plans and suggesting methods was $20,000 a robbery. Police figured that Leslie was the consultant on fifty or more of the nation's most sensational bank burglaries between 1879 and 1883 coast to coast.

Despite his criminal windfalls, Leslie was soon near broke, having spent small fortunes on his mistresses, Babe Irving, younger sister to gangleader Johnny Irving and, subsequently, Shang Draper's girl. Draper, a vicious thug, sought revenge when his girl left him for Leslie and he plotted the bankrobber's death. Draper, Johnny Dobbs, Worcester Sam, and Ed Goodie barged into Leslie's Brooklyn rooming house one night in 1884 and shot him through the head.

The badly decomposed corpse of the King of the Bankrobbers was found on June 4, 1884 by a patrolman on horseback at the base of Tramp's Rock near the Bronx River. New York society reeled in shock. Police Superintendent Walling only shrugged and said: "I told you so."

[ALSO SEE Fredericka "Marm" Mandelbaum.]

LONGLEY, WILLIAM P.
Murderer, Gunfighter • (1850-1877)

BACKGROUND: BORN AND RAISED NEAR EVERGREEN, TEX. NO FORMAL EDUCATION. ORIGINAL OCCUPATION, COWBOY. DESCRIPTION: 5'11", BROWN EYES, BLACK HAIR, SLENDER. ALIASES: UNKNOWN. RECORD: MORE THAN THIRTY MEN, INCLUDING SEVERAL NEGRO POLICEMEN, POSSE MEMBERS AND GUNSLINGERS, WERE KILLED BY LONGLEY IN THE EARLY 1870S: LAST MURDER ATTRIBUTED TO HIM WAS THAT OF RANCHER WILSON ANDERSON IN APRIL, 1875; CAPTURED TWO YEARS LATER AND HANGED AT GIDDINGS, TEX.

No gunfighter believed more intensely in the myth of the Old South (with the possible exception of John Wesley Hardin) than did William P. Longley, a devout hater of Negroes, Yankees, and carpetbagging lawmen. Almost all of Longley's brutal slayings were explained away by the gunman as merely arguments in which he was protecting the honor and dignity of the defunct Confederate "Cause."

Longley, who occasionally worked as a cowboy to earn money for bullets and gambling, rode through New Mexico, Arizona, and Texas, like a grim reaper on horseback. An accurate count of the bodies he left littering small Western towns is unavailable, but most sources credit this fast gunman with killing more than thirty men (a record only John Wesley Hardin topped—by ten).

A rancher named Wilson Anderson had feuded with Longley and his family for several years. When one of the gunfighter's cousins was shot from ambush in April, 1875, Longley returned to his birthplace, Evergreen, Tex., and killed Anderson, whom he suspected of his kinsman's murder.

He was caught about two years later and was sentenced to die on the gallows. Awaiting death in the small jail at Giddings, Tex., Longley wrote an embittered letter to the Governor of the state. One of his complaints was that gunfighter John Wesley Hardin received only twenty-five years in prison for his many killings and he, Longley, had been condemned to hang. Why? The Governor declined to respond and Longley was hanged on schedule.

Texas gunfighter William P. Longley.
(Denver Public Library)

Standing on the gallows in his Sunday suit, the goateed killer brought himself erect and said clearly: "I deserve this fate. It is a debt I owe for a wild and reckless life. So long, everybody!"

LOOMIS, GEORGE WASHINGTON, JR.
Murderer, Robber • (1813–1865)

BACKGROUND: BORN NEAR SANGERFIELD CENTER, N.Y., TO GEORGE WASHINGTON LOOMIS, SR. AND RHODA MARIE MALLETT. FIVE BROTHERS AND THREE SISTERS (ALL OF THE BROTHERS, GROVER, WILLIAM, WHELLER, PLUMB, DENIO, AND

ONE SISTER, CORNELIA, TURNED OUTLAW WITH "WASH"). DESCRIPTION: TALL, DARK, HEAVYSET. ALIASES: UNKNOWN. RECORD: ROBBED AND MURDERED THROUGHOUT THE MOHAWK AND CHENANGO VALLEYS FROM THE 1840S TO 1865, LEADING HIS BROTHERS IN RAIDS AGAINST LOCAL FARMERS FOR LIVESTOCK WHICH WAS RESOLD TO CITIZENS AND THE U.S. ARMY; KILLED IN A RAID AGAINST THE LOOMIS STRONGHOLD IN NINE-MILE SWAMP IN 1865 BY VIGILANTES LED BY CONSTABLE JAMES FILKINS OF NEARBY BROOKFIELD.

For a half century, the Loomis gang dominated the upper New York State area, concentrating their outlaw exploits in the Mohawk and Chenango Valleys. Their leader, George Washington Loomis, Jr., called "Wash" by his friends and family, was the offspring of a notorious horse thief who had plundered farms in Vermont and Connecticut in the 1790s.

Loomis' mother, a French Canadian, schooled her six sons in criminal pursuits early in life, encouraging them to pilfer anything they wanted. Wash later stated that his mother sanctioned "stealing little things. As long as we were not caught, it was all right. If we got caught, we got licked."

By the early 1840s, the Loomis farmhouse, a rambling two-story structure, became the home of bandits, escaped convicts, and wanted murderers, all in the employ of Wash and his brothers who raided neighboring farms at will, driving off livestock to be resold. Often they killed the inhabitants.

The Loomis brothers used their mother's home to store stolen furs, equipment, and food. Their unwed sister, wild Cornelia, rode with the boys in many of their murderous raids and attacked several farmers who dared to call her brothers outlaws.

The Loomis farmhouse was raided in 1857 by a band of vigilantes and huge quantities of stolen goods were found secreted in hidden panels and closed-off rooms. The brothers were taken to Waterville, N.Y. but indictments against them disappeared. During their trial, court records were burned nightly by their armed bands who broke into the courthouse. Witnesses against the Loomis brothers vanished, only to be found days later hanging from trees. The Loomis boys were released.

Grover Loomis was arrested for counterfeiting bills drawn on the Onondaga Bank in Oneida County but was soon released when his brothers beat up the local district attorney.

At the time of the Civil War, the Loomis gang concentrated on horse stealing. It was big business. The U.S. Army was paying top prices for horses. The Loomis bunch stole every horse in sight along the Mohawk Valley and moved them to New York City through their own shipping system—on "thief boats" along the Erie Canal. Once in NYC, their stolen goods were handled by aging prostitute and super fence, Fredericka "Marm" Mandelbaum, who became a millionaire by reselling hot goods.

No legal methods worked against the Loomis brothers, though Plumb and Grover had been arrested numerous times. The frustrated constable of Brookfield, N.Y., James Filkins, finally took matters into his own hands and led a posse to the Loomis farmhouse in 1865. The lawmen crashed through the barricaded door and fell upon Wash Loomis, beating him about the head with guns and pipes. He was literally stomped to death.

Plumb Loomis was also beaten and then thrown onto a large fire in front of the farmhouse. When the posse departed to search for the other Loomis brothers, Mrs. Loomis raced from her home and dragged her son from the fire. He lived.

Another raid against the farmhouse took place in Summer, 1867. This time, Grover and Plumb Loomis were strung up by their hands over fires until they confessed to the crimes vigilantes insisted they had committed. When Grover died in 1870, Denio Loomis took control of the outlaw band. Denio and Plumb Loomis died in the early 1880s but their sister Cornelia continued to plan and order raids. The last of the Loomis gang members disappeared after Cornelia's death in 1897.

Constable Filkins, who almost single-handedly fought this terror gang for forty years, outlived them all, dying peacefully in 1911.

[ALSO SEE Fredericka "Marm" Mandelbaum.]

LOWE, JOSEPH ("ROWDY JOE")
Gambler, Gunfighter, Procurer • (? -1880)

Rowdy Joe" Lowe showed up in the wide-open cattle town of Wichita, Kan. about 1870 where he opened a saloon. Joe's wife Kathryn, known as "Rowdy Kate," operated a whorehouse on the second floor of the saloon and carried, like her husband, two guns at her sides at all times.

Lowe's gaming tables were rigged; whenever customers mumbled complaints of being cheated, Rowdy Joe leaped over his bar and pistol-whipped the offender into unconsciousness. Lowe's reputation became so bad that he packed up Kate, her girls, his fixtures, and moved his bar to Newton, Kan. in 1871. No sooner was he established there than he was involved in a battle with a gunslinger named A. M. Sweet.

The gunman was attracted to Rowdy Kate and, on several occasions, had pawed her. Kate Lowe reminded Sweet that such hanky-panky was reserved for the girls in her husband's establishment, but the amorous gunfighter insisted on having Kate. Lowe, watching from behind his bar with his ever-present top hat askew on his head, reached for his pistol and drilled Sweet dead on the spot. The Lowes departed Newton shortly thereafter, returning to Wichita.

In 1873, it was the same story all over again. Another saloonkeeper, E. T. "Red" Beard, battled Rowdy Joe over Kate in an hour-long gun duel inside the latter's bar. Beard was finally killed in the smoke-filled dive after an estimated fifty shots had been fired. Lowe was released from custody after it was determined that no one had seen him shoot Beard although the two combatants were the only ones present in the bar during the shootout, the customers having fled to a more serene atmosphere.

Lowe was finally killed in Denver in a gunfight, again over his wife's ample charms. Rowdy Kate disappeared

Rowdy Joe Lowe, saloon keeper by trade, killer by instinct. (Kansas State Historical Society, Topeka)

days later. Rumors had it that she traveled to San Francisco and, under a different name, married a wealthy railroader who was a distinguished member of Nob Hill society.

LUETGERT, ADOLPH LOUIS
Murderer • (1848–1911)

BACKGROUND: BORN IN GERMANY, IMMIGRATED TO U.S. IN EARLY 1870S. SETTLED IN CHICAGO WHERE HE PURSUED SEVERAL TRADES INCLUDING FARMING, TANNING, AND EVENTUALLY SAUSAGEMAKING. MARRIED LOUISA BICKNESE IN 1880S. MINOR PUBLIC EDUCATION. DESCRIPTION: 6'3", BROWN EYES, BROWN HAIR, EXTREMELY HEAVYSET. ALIASES: NONE. RECORD:

A dolph Louis Luetgert was an unhappy man, a hard-working, powerfully built German immigrant bent on sweaty success. For years he had been building up his sausage factory in Chicago. His first wife died leaving him with one child. He married again to Louisa Bicknese. Why Luetgert married Louisa is uncertain; that he planned her grisly murder in a most unique way was very certain indeed.

Luetgert's sexual appetite was enormous. He made no bones about it. Any woman he could manage to engineer under his massive 240 pound frame in a love bed in his factory was merely another prize.

There was his wife's maid, Mary Simering. Luetgert slept regularly with her. There was also his mistress Mrs. Christine Feldt, a wealthy German woman. Luetgert slept regularly with her. Then there was Mrs. Agatha Tosch, who owned a saloon with her husband on Chicago's North Side close to the sausagemaker's factory. Luetgert slept regularly with her also.

As Luetgert pursued his lustful objectives, his business began to slip away from him. Though his huge factory on Hermitage and Diversey turned out great quantities of sausages, Luetgert discovered that he could not meet his supplier's costs. Instead of shoring up his losses, Luetgert and his business advisor William Charles planned to expand.

They attempted to secure more capital to enlarge the factory and suddenly, Luetgert had visions of becoming the sausage king of America. But by May, 1897, the plans came to failure. As usual Luetgert sought solace in sex orgies with his many mistresses.

As Matthew W. Pinkerton of the renowned detective agency judged: "He was an immoral man and was often visited by women of extremely doubtful character." An understatement at the least.

Louisa Luetgert, a normally placid, nondescript person, suddenly became outraged at her husband's extravagant sex life. The cold-eyed, egotistical German sausagemaker responded to her indignation by immediately taking her by the throat and choking her. Before the poor woman collapsed, the butcher thought better of his rage and released her. He noticed alarmed neighbors watching him through the parlor windows of his home. A few days later Luetgert was seen chasing his wife down the street, shouting threats, a revolver quaking in his hand. Again, his angry burst came to nothing.

Then the butcher began to plan. On March 11, 1897, the sausagemaker went to Lor Owen & Company, a wholesale drug firm, and ordered 325 pounds of crude potash plus 50 pounds of arsenic. This was delivered to his factory the next day.

On April 24, Luetgert asked one of his employees, Frank Odorowsky, known as "Smokehouse Frank," to come into his office. There he told the worker to remove the barrel of potash in the shipping room to the factory basement where there were three huge vats used to boil down sausage material.

"This is strong stuff, this potash," Luetgert warned his employee. "Be careful not to burn yourself."

"Smokehouse Frank" and another employee, following Luetgert's orders, crushed the potash into small pieces with a hatchet and a hammer. Both burned their hands and faces badly.

Luetgert and "Smokehouse Frank" then placed the "strong stuff" in the middle vat in the basement. The sausagemaker then turned on the steam under the middle vat until the material dissolved into liquid.

On May 1, 1897, Luetgert called his night watchman, Frank Bialk, gave him a dollar and told him to go to a nearby drugstore and buy a bottle of celery compound. When the watchman returned with the medicine, he was amazed to find the door leading to the main factory barricaded. Luetgert appeared and took the medicine.

"All right, Frank, go back to the engine room," he said.

At ten that evening Luetgert again summoned the watchman and sent him back to the drugstore to buy a bottle of Hunyadi water.

While the watchman was running errands, Luetgert worked alone in the factory basement. He turned on the steam under the middle vat about a quarter before nine.

As she was later to testify, a young German girl named Emma Schiemicke, who was passing the factory on the night of May 1, at about 10:30 p.m. with her sister, saw Luetgert leading his wife up the alleyway behind the factory.

Luetgert stayed in the basement of his factory until two the following morning. Watchman Bialk found him fully dressed in his office the next day.

"Should I let the fires go out under the vat?" he asked his employer.

"Bank the fires at fifty pounds of steam pressure," the huge man told him. The watchman went down to the basement. There he saw a hose running water into the middle vat. On the floor in front of the vat was a sticky, glue-like substance. Bending down, Bialk noticed that the substance appeared to contain flakes of bone.

He thought nothing of it. Luetgert used all sorts of waste meats to make his sausage. Following the weekend, May 3, "Smokehouse Frank" also noticed the unusual slime on the floor of the basement. He ran to his employer, surprised.

"I don't know what that is, Mr. Luetgert. Somebody maybe came into the factory and—"

Luetgert spoke rapidly: "Don't say a word, Frank, don't say anything about it, and I'll see that you have a good job as long as you live."

The sausagemaker's employees went to work cleaning the brown slime from the floor. They scraped the gooey substance into a nearby drain that led to a sewer. The larger chunks of waste they placed in a barrel.

"What do I do with the stuff that won't go down the drain," Odorowsky said to Luetgert.

"Take the barrel out to the railroad tracks and scatter it around out there."

Odorowsky obeyed.

The following day, Diedrich Bicknese, Louisa's brother, came to Chicago and called on her at home. The maid, Mary Simering, told him that Mrs. Luetgert was not home. He came back later and his sister still had not appeared.

That evening, he found Luetgert at home and demanded to know where his sister was.

Luetgert calmly told the brother that his wife had disappeared, that she left the house on May 1 and had never returned.

"Why didn't you go to the police?"

"I don't want a scandal," Luetgert replied. "I paid five dollars to two detectives to find her."

Bicknese then seriously began to search for his sister. He went to Kankakee, Illinois, thinking she might be visiting friends there. He found nothing. He returned to Chicago and discovered that Louisa still hadn't returned home. Then he went to the police.

Police Captain Schuettler had to summon the sausage-maker twice to the station. He knew the butcher well and also knew about his violent arguments with his wife. When Luetgert arrived, the captain began to question him.

"You made a vigorous appeal to me to find a lost dog for you not long ago. Why did you not report the absence of your wife?"

Luetgert was calm. "I expected her to come back. I wished to avoid any disgrace. I'm a prominent businessman and can't afford to have this sort of scandal about my household."

The police allowed Luetgert to return to his factory. Then they began dragging the river and searching the alleyways of Chicago. On May 7, police visited the factory and interrogated watchman Bialk and "Smokehouse Frank."

Their story of the running water and the slime found in front of the middle vat in the factory's basement sparked Captain Schuettler's imagination. By May 15 he was back at the factory and began a thorough search of the basement, particularly the middle vat.

Schuettler's discovery was one of the most gruesome in the annals of murder. The middle vat was two-thirds full of brownish fluid. They drained the vat after using gunny sacks to act as filters. The catch was awful.

They found several pieces of bone and two gold rings. One was a small, badly tarnished friendship ring; the other was a heavy clean ring with the initials "L.L." engraved on it.

Both rings had been worn by Mrs. Luetgert.

Adolph Louis Luetgert boiled his wife's body down to sludge in his Chicago sausage factory; discovery of her teeth led to his arrest and conviction (N.Y. Historical Society)

Under analysis, the bones discovered in the vat were definitely human—a human third rib, part of a humerus or great bone of the arm, a bone from the palm of a human hand, a bone from the fourth toe of a human right foot, fragments of a human temporal bone, a bone from a human ear, and a sesamoid bone from a human foot.

After Luetgert was arrested and brought to trial, he maintained these bones were those of animals, that he purchased these scraps to boil down to make soft soap by which he could clean up his factory.

The defense's argument, of course, was ridiculous, argued the prosecution. Why would Luetgert buy $40 worth of potash and waste materials to scrub down his factory when $1 (at that time) worth of soft soap would have done the job?

All this circumstantial evidence was crowned by witnesses who damned the heavy German sausagemaker.

Luetgert's mistresses turned on him in womanly rage. First came Mrs. Agatha Tosch who stated that she asked Luetgert where his wife was shortly after she had disappeared while he was gulping huge amounts of beer in her saloon.

He became pale and excited, she said, and blurted: "I don't know. I am as innocent as the southern skies!"

The jury smiled grimly. It was obvious to everyone that if Luetgert didn't know where his wife was there was nothing over which to claim his innocence.

Mrs. Tosch further told the jury that Luetgert once stated that he hated his wife and that "I could take her and crush her." Another time, the witness said, Luetgert sent for a doctor to attend his sick wife. At that time, sitting in Mrs. Tosch's bar, he told her, "If I had waited a little longer, the dead, rotten beast would have croaked!"

Another witness, a woman, reported that the sausagemaker told her that "If it were not for Mary Simering I would not stay at home."

Then Luetgert's favorite mistress, Mrs. Christine Feldt took the stand. This was the woman for whom he felt, or once stated he felt, true love: "If you forsake me, Christine, I will take my own life; I do not care to live."

Christine Feldt, unfortunately for the sausagemaker, did not feel the same way about him.

She produced all the mawkish, love-gushing letters the heavyset man had written to her. He blushed in court, the only change in his calm demeanor throughout his two lengthy trials.

Mrs. Feldt also stated that Luetgert had given her $4,000 for "safe-keeping" shortly before Mrs. Luetgert's disappearance. The crushing evidence came when the sausagemaker's mistress also stated that Luetgert had given her a blood-stained knife without explanation the day after his wife vanished. Mrs. Feldt produced the knife.

Though the butcher never admitted his guilt, the evidence overwhelmingly supported the fact that Luetgert had murdered his wife and then boiled her body down to a gluey residue in his sausage machine.

He was sentenced to life in prison, where he died still claiming his innocence.

LUTHERLAND, THOMAS
Murderer • (? –1691)

A convicted felon, Lutherland was sent as a bound servant from England to work in New Jersey. Not long after his arrival, he was convicted of stealing. Months later, John Clark, a boat trader, was found dead and his supplies stolen. It was an obvious murder.

The goods from Clark's trading boat were found in Lutherland's home. The superstition rampant in the New World at that time was evidenced at Lutherland's trial. The corpse of John Clark was brought forth and the accused man was ordered to touch it. If Lutherland was guilty, the court reasoned, the body would bleed. It did not, but Lutherland was sentenced to die anyway, being executed February 23, 1691.

MC CONAGHY, ROBERT
Murderer • (? -1840)

Plagued with family problems, McConaghy lost his mind May 30, 1840, and slaughtered his wife's family after an argument. He strangled his mother-in-law, Mrs. William Brown, and beat and shot her four children whose ages ranged from 10 to 21 years old.

Quickly taken into custody, McConaghy stubbornly refused to confess his guilt during his trial. He was sentenced to death on the gallows. On the day of his execution, November 6, 1840 at Huntington, Pa., the rope broke as McConaghy dropped through the trap door. He was carried up to the scaffold again and, as another rope was placed about his neck, he loudly confessed his murders.

He again shot down into space, this time a self-admitted killer. The second rope held; McConaghy joined his hapless relatives.

Mass murderer Robert McConaghy was described in this 1840 pamphlet as being hanged twice for the slaying of his six relatives. (N.Y. Historical Society)

TRIAL, CONFESSION AND EXECUTION

OF

ROBERT McCONAGHY,

FOR THE

Murder

OF

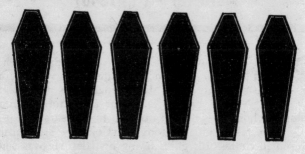

SIX

OF

HIS RELATIVES

IN BROAD DAY-LIGHT.

McConaghy was executed a few weeks since, and did not make his Confession until he was once suspended ; the rope broke and let him down, after which he made a full Confession.

Price 12½ cents.

MANDELBAUM, FREDERICKA
("MARM") Fence • (1818–1889)

BACKGROUND: BORN IN NEW YORK, 1818. MARRIED WOLFE
MANDELBAUM, GAVE BIRTH TO TWO DAUGHTERS AND ONE SON.
MINOR PUBLIC EDUCATION. DESCRIPTION: 5'1", BLACK EYES,
BLACK HAIR, FAT (APPROX. 250 LBS.). ALIASES: MARM MANDEL-
BAUM, MOTHER MANDELBAUM. RECORD: OPERATED THE MOST
SUCCESSFUL FENCING OPERATIONS IN THE EAST COAST, CEN-
TERED IN NYC, FROM 1862 TO 1884, HANDLING AN ESTIMATED
$12,000,000 IN STOLEN GOODS; FENCED THE NEGOTIABLE
BONDS TAKEN IN THE MANHATTAN SAVINGS INSTITUTION
THEFT ON 10/27/78; HANDLED ALL THE STOLEN GOODS—AN
ESTIMATED $500,000 WORTH—SENT TO HER BY THE NOTORIOUS
LOOMIS GANG OF UPSTATE NEW YORK THROUGH THE 1870S;
INDICTED FOR GRAND LARCENY AND RECEIVING STOLEN
GOODS IN 1884; FLED TO CANADA WHERE SHE DIED SOMETIME
IN 1889.

Marm Mandelbaum was as colorful a crook as they came, an authentic forerunner to Damon Runyon's "Apple Annie," except that she operated on a scale so vast police were never able to determine the exact amount of stolen goods she handled in her twenty-two years as America's super fence. They estimated around $12,000,000 but the sum was likely higher.

Marrying early in life to Wolfe Mandelbaum, a drifter, Marm produced three healthy children and then decided in her halcyon years to enter a life of crime. At forty-four, Marm purchased a three-story brownstone house at 79 Clinton Street and spread the word through underworld contacts she had established that she would handle any kind of stolen goods available, from diamonds to horses. The boodle flowed into her home from dawn to dusk.

Within the space of two years, Marm had become a millionaire and had safely fenced $4 million in stolen loot. Grateful thieves who wished to remain in her favor then began to steal the most exquisite furniture and furnishings from the landed gentry of the East to give as gifts to Marm.

She accepted these and furnished her house with them; it became the showplace of the underworld.

The most important criminals of the era flocked to Marm Mandelbaum's place, attending her famous balls and fetes. George Leonidas Leslie, who became America's first super-bankrobber and who fenced millions of dollars in securities through Marm, was usually in attendance; so were Banjo Peter Emerson, Mark Shinburn, Shang Draper, and the infamous burglars, Bill Mosher and Joseph Douglas. Mosher and Douglas, at the behest of king of the kidnappers, William Westervelt, had abducted little Charley Ross from his home in Germantown, Pa., July 1, 1874 and held him for ransom. They subsequently turned him over to Westervelt, from whose custody he disappeared.

Shinburn was one of Marm's favorite burglars; he brought her so much stolen goods that she put him under exclusive contract to her. He was a deft safecracker and burglar who detested the company of other crooks. They were beneath him, he told Marm, ordinary scum with haphazard talents. For years he fenced his stolen wares through Marm, sent money to relatives in Germany, and eventually retired in Monaco under the auspicious title of Baron Shindell.

With her fencing racket so lucrative, Marm invested time in promoting the cause of female criminals, teaching lady pickpockets, burglars, and confidence workers how to improve their trades. Her graduates included Black Lena Kleinschmidt, Ellen Clegg, Kid Glove Rosey, Old Mother Hubbard, Sophie Lyons, and Queen Liz.

Two of her graduates, Sophie Lyons and Black Lena, went on to the big time. Sophie, married to a bank burglar named Ned Lyons, ultimately became the most famous confidence woman in America, plying her trade exclusively in Pullman cars. Black Lena blackmailed her way to wealth, moved to Hackensack, N.J., and entered high society under an alias.

Marm went on to establish a female Fagin school on the third floor of her home. Here, a staff of experienced criminals taught youngsters how to pick pockets and become expert sneak thieves. She later introduced them to the professional methods of safecracking, blackmailing, and burglary.

The reign of Marm Mandelbaum came to an abrupt end when a reform party came to power in New York in 1884 and indictments against her for grand larceny and handling stolen goods were drawn up. Marm's famous legal firm of Howe & Hummell were powerless to prevent the indictments and she fled with her furnishings, family, and an estimated $10 million to an unknown spot in Canada.

There, she lived out her days in quiet luxury, traveling to New York in disguise, reports have it, to visit some of her fond underworld associates. Marm died a nostalgic woman.

[ALSO SEE George Leonidas Leslie, George Washington Loomis, Jr.]

MARTIN, MICHAEL ("CAPTAIN LIGHTFOOT")
Highwayman • (1775–1822)

BACKGROUND: BORN IN CONNEHY, IRELAND, 4/9/75, TO A WEALTHY LANDOWNER. MINOR EDUCATION. IMMIGRATED TO THE U.S., 6/17/18. ORIGINAL OCCUPATION, BREWERY OWNER. DESCRIPTION: TALL, MUSCULAR. ALIASES: CAPTAIN LIGHTFOOT. RECORD: BECAME A HIGHWAYMAN IN IRELAND, CIRCA 1792 IN COMPANY WITH ANOTHER, MORE EXPERIENCED BANDIT KNOWN ONLY AS "CAPTAIN THUNDERBOLT"; THE TWO MEN ROBBED COACHES, TRAVELERS AND PUBS THROUGHOUT IRELAND AND SCOTLAND FOR CLOSE TO TWENTY-SIX YEARS; MARTIN LEFT IRELAND ON 4/12/18 TO AVOID CAPTURE AND IMMIGRATED TO THE U.S.; ROBBED COACHES AND LONE TRAVEL-

The life of a highwayman in the late Eighteenth Century was a full time occupation that called for nerve, daring, and an unquenchable thirst for adventure. Boys of that era thought of becoming highwaymen just as youths in America would later imagine themselves firemen, baseball players, or cowboys. In this sense, Irish-born Michael Martin could be considered normal.

At age seventeen he ran away from his Connehy farm to Dublin where, in his own words he met and befriended "profligate men and women." Though he was soon compelled to return to his father's farm, Martin was wooed into a life of crime when a traveler stopped to water his horse, a man known throughout Ireland as the boldest bandit on the roads, "Captain Thunderbolt."

Martin rode off with the older man and for twenty-six years, became Thunderbolt's righthand man, riding stirrup to stirrup with him on countless raids and hold ups in Ireland and Scotland. Martin, who had taken on the sobriquet "Captain Lightfoot," fled to America in 1818 aboard the brig *Maria* when government troops were put on his trail.

Landing in Salem, Mass. on June 17, 1818, Martin decided to live an honest life, first buying a farm which went broke, and then a brewery which no one patronized. An ill-starred love affair finally caused him to return to crime.

Dressed as a Quaker and armed with two pistols and a swordcane, Martin began to ride the roads of Connecticut, where in early 1819 he robbed a traveling merchant of $70, hitting the man on the head for good measure.

For three years, Martin roamed at will, robbing coaches and travelers for small sums. His territory was vast, all of New England. No one was safe from his hold ups. Martin even robbed Indians as far north as Canada. Rewards for his capture offered $50 to any brave man who could bring in "the most notorious scoundrel."

Martin, or "Captain Lightfoot," as he still liked to be

The public hanging of highwayman Michael Martin from an old woodcut.

called, stopped one of the governor's coaches in 1821 and held up the passengers. When a woman handed him her watch he quickly returned it, stating, "I do not rob women, ma'am." It was the kind of beau geste in which Martin delighted, thinking himself, as would Jesse James and Pretty Boy Floyd centuries later, to be an American Robin Hood.

The governor of Massachusetts exploded upon hearing that his personal coach had been pilfered by the highwayman. He ordered an all-out manhunt which culminated in Martin's bloodless capture in a barn outside Springfield. Injured, he had fallen asleep after eluding several posses. A fall from his horse caused him to break his shoulder. He had then stolen a horse to continue his flight.

A posse of farmers delivered Martin to the Letchmere Point jail near Cambridge, Mass. in October, 1821. Here, he was condemned to die as a horse thief, a capital offense in those days. Days later, he broke out of his chains and smashed through three jail doors, but was soon recaptured in a cornfield.

Days before his execution on December 22, 1822, hundreds of curious spectators gathered near Letchmere jail to see him die. Writers of the period were on hand to describe the handsome highwayman as "romantic and unreal."

His death was real enough. He was placed upon a horse-drawn cart beneath a tree limb with a noose around his neck (which he unconcernedly helped to adjust). Taking a piece of cloth from his pocket, Martin looked at the executioner. "When shall I drop the handkerchief?" he asked politely.

"Whenever you're ready," came the reply.

Martin studied his audience, a crowd of hundreds who gasped as he held the handkerchief aloft in the crisp, cold air. With a shrug of indifference, Michael Martin let the wispy cloth slip from his fingers. The cart driver snapped a whip, the horse jerked forward, and Captain Lightfoot was gone.

MASON, EBENEZER
Murderer • (? -1802)

Insanity was deep in Mason and the neighbors of William Pitt Allen, for whom he worked, knew it. Mason always responded in a surly fashion at every order Allen gave him. The fact that Allen was his brother-in-law only increased Mason's resentment, which bubbled over into murder on May 18, 1802, when Allen told his in-law to hurry as he was scraping muck from a farm wagon.

Mason turned on Allen with an iron shovel in his hand and struck him dead. Ebenezer Mason was executed October 7, 1802, at Dedham, Mass.

MASON, SAM
Robber, Murderer • (? -1803)

A rough river man, Mason robbed and killed for several years along the Natchez Trace. After being captured in Natchez and sent from that city in tar and feathers, Mason organized a vicious band of cutthroats and plagued the residents with rapes, robberies, and murders from 1800 to 1802.

He was finally tracked down by a professional bounty hunter, Bill Setten, who brought the outlaw's head back from the wilderness in a jar as a way of proving his kill. Setten, however, received no rewards from the governors of Mississippi and Louisiana who had offered huge amounts for Mason's capture. The bounty hunter was accused of being none other than Wiley Harpe, one of the murderous Harpe brothers who had pillaged the countryside for years.

Though he mightily protested his innocence, Setten was hanged on February 8, 1804. The bounty hunter's true identity was never established, but many thereafter believed they had hanged the wrong man, especially when reports of Wiley Harpe's presence in the area continued long years after the execution.

MATHER (OR MATHERS), DAVID ("MYSTERIOUS DAVE")
Murderer, Robber • (1844- ?)

Mather was considered a "killer of killers" during the 1880s, a rough, uncompromising gunslinger who, upon telling a man he would kill him, "was sure to do it."

An unknown background and a tight lip earned Mather the name "Mysterious Dave." Some of his exploits were not as cryptic. It was known that he had been a horse thief and had been suspected of robbing trains in Texas and New Mexico. Mather possessed a violent temper and would not tolerate the slightest of threats. While serving as a constable in Las Vegas, N.M. on January 25, 1880, Mysterious Dave came upon a drunken railroad worker named Joseph Costello. Mather ordered him to move off the street and the drunk fumbled for his gun. Mysterious Dave shot him through the heart, an abrupt act which no doubt made the Las Vegas residents apprehensive of his law enforcement policies and led to his dismissal as a constable.

Mather was next seen in Dodge City, Kan. in the company of such hell-raisers as Charlie Basset, riding into the roaring cattle town about April, 1880. Stories told of him by street gossips had it that Mysterious Dave had broken three friends out of a New Mexico jail; had stuck up a whorehouse in Fort Worth, Tex., barely saving his life from an avenging madam who attacked him with a butcher knife and shotgun; and had been involved in a number of killings throughout the Southwest.

His reputation notwithstanding, Mather was appointed Assistant Marshal in Dodge in June, 1883. He was soon replaced through an open election which favored a new marshal, William "Bill" Tilghman, who would prove to be one of the finest lawmen in the Old West. Tilghman replaced Mather with Thomas Nixon, a famous buffalo hunter who had reputedly brought down 120 of the great beasts in one day, a record far in excess of that claimed by Buffalo Bill Cody.

Nixon and Mather both owned saloons in Dodge City. They went into a price war. Nixon gave his customers two beers for a quarter. Mather then offered the same at twenty cents. Nixon then reportedly bribed a distributor to cut off Mather's supply of beer. Mather strapped on his guns and went looking for Nixon.

Mysterious Dave Mather, a killer of killers, was the terror of Dodge City in the early 1880s. (Western History Collection, U. of Okla. Library)

The Assistant City Marshal was warned that Mysterious Dave was looking for him and on July 18, 1884, waited in hiding near Mather's saloon until he came outside. Nixon sent a bullet whizzing past Mysterious Dave and then fled down an alley.

Nixon, who at first thought he had killed Mather, was brought in for questioning but released when Mysterious Dave refused to make a formal charge against him. David Mather had other plans through which to enact his revenge. On the night of July 21, 1884, Mather found Nixon lounging outside a saloon on Front Street, came silently up behind him and said in a near whisper, "Hello, Tom." He then pumped four bullets into Nixon's back, killing him instantly.

Gambler and gunfighter Bat Masterson rushed from a nearby saloon and cradled the dead man's head in his arms. They had been friends. Before Masterson could bring about his own revenge, Mather was arrested by Tilghman and subsequently tried for the murder of Nixon. The trial took

261

place at Kinsley, Kan. Mather's lawyers claimed he could not receive a fair trial in Dodge. The jury played out the rules of the West. Though Mather had murdered Nixon in cold blood, the jury felt that the dead man had initiated the argument by firing the first shot.

Mather was acquitted and shortly thereafter vanished as mysteriously as he had appeared in the wild frontier towns.

MEACHAM, JEREMIAH
Murderer • (? -1715)

On the morning of March 22, 1715, Jeremiah Meacham climbed to the roof of his house outside of Newport, R.I. for no apparent reason. He sat there for several hours brooding while his family—his wife and her sister—begged him to come down.

Suddenly, Meacham, who had no history of violence, jumped from the roof and killed both women with an axe. He tossed their bodies into the house and set it on fire.

Meacham was hanged at Newport, April 12, 1715.

MERRICK, SUDS
Robber • (? -1884)

---

errick, along with Tommy Shay, James Coffee, and Terry Le Strange, was the organizer of the notorious Hooker Gang which robbed virtually at will in the Fourth Ward of New York City during the late 1860s and early 1870s. At one time Merrick had at least one hundred experienced thieves working for him, dominating an area from Fourteenth Street to the Battery.

The gang specialized in looting cargo boats docked in the East River. In 1874 Merrick led three of his top crooks—Tom Bonner, Sam McCracken, and Johnny Gallagher—on board a canal boat operated by Thomas H. Brick. The robbers tied up Brick and took hours carrying off everything on the boat that wasn't nailed down.

Police interrupted the quartet as they were about to depart, and all were captured, except Merrick, who fled. His three best men were sent to Auburn prison for long terms, and as a result, Merrick lost face with the other Hooker gang leaders and quit. He struck out alone, burglarizing and mugging for almost ten years until he was mysteriously killed in the Bowery in 1884.

MINA, LINO AMALIA ESPOS Y
Murderer, Thief • (1809-1832)

BACKGROUND: CLAIMED SPANISH HERITAGE AND TO BE THE SON OF THE SPANISH GOVERNOR OF CALIFORNIA, CONSIDERING HIMSELF A "DON." DESCRIPTION: 5'2", BROWN EYES, BLACK HAIR, SLIGHT BUILD. ALIASES: CAROLINO ESPOS. RECORD: KILLED WEALTHY PHILADELPHIAN DR. WILLIAM CHAPMAN BY ADMINISTERING MASSIVE DOSAGES OF ARSENIC TO HIM IN HIS FOOD IN 1831; TRIED AND CONVICTED 2/25/32 IN DOYLESTOWN, PA.; EXECUTED 6/21/32.

In the early fall of 1831 a slender, dark-eyed Spaniard who called himself Carolino Espos visited the home of Dr. William Chapman, headmaster of a prominent Philadelphia school. The young man explained that he was the son of the Spanish governor of California and that he was trying to rejoin his family in the West but lacked the funds to do so. He bluntly asked if he could board with the family until funds arrived to make his journey possible.

The socially conscious Chapmans agreed, or rather, Mrs. Lucretia Chapman, an attractive woman in her forties who was quite charmed by Mina, insisted that he stay in their home. Dr. Chapman, a weak-willed man, accepted this strange arrangement without argument. In the following weeks Mina was seen by the Chapman children and servants embracing and kissing Mrs. Chapman, who appeared quite receptive to the Spaniard's advances.

Dr. Chapman remained the complete gentleman and looked the other way, silencing the stories whispered to him by his household help.

Within five weeks of his arrival at the Chapman residence, Mina went to a druggist in Philadelphia and ordered a quarter pound of arsenic. The druggist wanted to know how Mina intended to use the poison.

"It is for the stuffing of birds," the Spaniard replied.

The next day, Dr. Chapman ate a heavy meal and retired early, feeling sick. His illness continued for four days before he died. Oddly enough, Mina insisted on personally shaving the corpse before it was buried.

Two weeks after Dr. Chapman died, Mina married Mrs. Chapman in New York. Then small treasures in the Chapman household began to disappear, and even the family's silver vanished. Mina, of course, had stolen the goods (along with Mrs. Chapman's jewelry and certain bank assets). Swindles in which Mina posed as Chapman to complete financial deals alerted the Philadelphia police.

Authorities suspicious of Mina ordered Dr. Chapman's body dug up and an autopsy performed. Massive amounts of arsenic were discovered in the corpse, and both Mina and Mrs. Chapman were arrested and tried.

A weeping Lucretia sobbed that she had been victimized

and hoodwinked into loving a thief and murderer. Mrs. Chapman was acquitted of murder by a chivalrous jury.

Mina was promptly convicted and labeled a notorious foreign cad who had violated an American home and marriage. He was hanged.

MOLASSES GANG

Jimmy Dunnigan, Blind Mahoney, and Bill Morgan were the founders of the zany Molasses Gang whose members operated throughout New York City in the early 1870s. The gangsters were basically store thieves and pickpockets, and their gang name came about through their simple, comic method of robbery.

Dunnigan, Morgan, and Mahoney would enter a store and hold out a soft hat, asking the proprietor to fill it with sorghum molasses. Yes, they knew it was crazy, they said, but it was a bet, you see, to determine if they were right in guessing how much molasses the hat would hold. The proprietor usually shrugged and filled the hat.

When full, one of the gang members would grab it and force it over the proprietor's head, the molasses blinding him until the others could rob the till and depart. Members were rounded up about 1877, and the gang ceased to exist.

MUDGETT, HERMAN WEBSTER
Murderer, Robber, Arsonist • (? -1896)

BACKGROUND: BORN AND RAISED IN GILMANTOWN, N.H., OF YANKEE LINEAGE. STUDIED MEDICINE AT ANN ARBOR MEDICAL

SCHOOL IN MICHIGAN. WORKED AS A DRUGGIST IN SOUTH CHICAGO IN THE EARLY 1890S. PROPRIETOR OF THE INFAMOUS "MURDER CASTLE" DURING THE CHICAGO FAIR OF 1893. DESCRIPTION: APPROXIMATELY 6', BROWN EYES, SANDY HAIR, HEAVY BUILD, MUSTACHE, IN HIS THIRTIES. ALIASES: H. H. HOLMES, H. M. HOWARD. RECORD: ARRESTED ON SUSPICION OF MURDER 11/17/94 IN BOSTON, MASS. (SUSPECTED, AND LATER PROVEN GUILTY, OF MURDERING MORE THAN TWO HUNDRED WOMEN IN CHICAGO) TRIED FOR THE MURDER OF BENJAMIN F. PITEZEL IN THE COURT OF OYER AND TERMINER AND GENERAL DELIVERY JAIL AND QUARTER SESSIONS OF THE PEACE, PHILADELPHIA, PA., 10/28–11/2/95; SENTENCED TO DEATH BY HANGING; EXECUTED ON THE GALLOWS OF MOYAMENSING PRISON 5/7/96.

He was the criminal of the nineteenth century, the archfiend of America and the all-time mass killer who slaughtered by the dozen. And he was the nicest man you'd ever want to meet.

Born Herman W. Mudgett, this subtle, charming murderer dropped his given name early and adopted the more rakish Harry Howard Holmes (one of many aliases). A sharp-minded but lazy student in New Hampshire, Holmes was always scheming ways to profit by the stupidity of others.

As a student of medicine at the University of Michigan, he finally struck pay dirt . . . or cemetery ground. Holmes hit upon the idea of taking out large insurance policies under different names.

Next, he would filch cadavers from the university's dissecting room and plant the bodies in various spots. Then he would collect the insurance on the unrecognizable bodies (he was by then a master of acid methods). His fortunes grew.

But this nineteenth century ghoul was caught one night dragging the body of a young woman from the medical lab. A campus policeman was astounded. "My God, what are you doing there?" he demanded.

Holmes cracked a crooked smile and answered, "Taking my girl for a walk, you idiot."

The body was returned to the university morgue, and

Holmes, dragged before a sputtering dean, aghast in his nightgown, was expelled immediately.

He shrugged, packed his bags, and headed for Chicago. Once there, he became, among many other names and disguises, Dr. Harry Howard Holmes. His time was spent ingeniously as a swindler—later he would graduate to being a professional polygamist, rapist, and sadist, and a mass murderer unequaled anywhere in the world.

At first, Holmes made his money by purchasing furniture on credit, then selling it overnight. It was easy, fast work, but it required constant changing of addresses. Dr. Harry was the movingest man in Chicago.

He soon tired of the furniture "race," and, not letting his medical background go to waste, landed a job in a drugstore on Chicago's South Side. By then he was a tall, handsome, and utterly charming gentleman with a long, well-waxed mustache and piercing snake eyes.

His looks, manners, and knowledge of medicine made business boom. It got so good that Holmes bought the drugstore. But operating a legitimate business was not enough for Holmes. He found honest success boring.

Holmes instituted a program of alcoholism cures, special self-bottled elixirs of colored cinnamon water. He also dashed off fictional get-rich-quick stories and published them in pamphlet form. The money rolled in.

There were moments when Harry would stare coldly at the empty lot across the roadway from the drugstore on 63rd Street. Once, caught eyeing the vacant property, he murmured, "I want that vacant lot . . . I've got plans."

He purchased the land the next day and then went to work designing one of the strangest buildings ever erected on the American continent. It had turrets, bay windows, and several entrances.

The three-story building was a monstrosity, crazily conceived, but it was all according to Holmes's plan. During the construction there was some talk about his strange behavior. No sooner would one work crew finish a section of the building than they would be fired and another crew of workmen hired.

Systematically, Holmes was creating a madhatter's castle that would go undetected. When completed, this crazy-quilt

Herman Webster Mudgett, alias H. H. Holmes, America's most prolific murderer, he claimed the lives of at least two hundred victims. (UPI)

structure had hidden rooms, concealed stairways, trap doors, false walls and ceilings. There were closets and rooms without doors, and doors that opened up to solid brick walls. There was an elevator that had no shaft, and an elevator shaft without an elevator. And there was a chute that led to the basement.

In the basement Holmes installed a mammoth dissecting table made of huge planks, a giant stove-crematory, and yawning pits that could be (and were) filled with quicklime and acid. Now Dr. Harry was ready.

Murder may have been on his mind, but money was the plan. Holmes went to several employment agencies and asked for secretary-typists. "He liked nice, green girls fresh from business college," one account states.

The parade of pretty young girls began through Dr. Harry's horror house. He explained away all this activity with a simple excuse: "The World's Fair [of 1893] is coming and that means tourists. That's why such a big building. Rents will go high with tourists coming into Chicago. By me, it's smart business."

But it was the devil's business . . . in a devil's house. As each pretty young thing was hired, Holmes began instant suggestive advances, which always ended with him leading the young girl up the stairs to his bedroom on the third floor.

There, after properly wooing her, and with the promise of marriage drooling from his lips, Holmes would convince each girl to sign over her insurance and savings and to make out a will in his favor.

As a reward, he allowed each would-be wife to spend an entire night in his bed. He would awaken early, go to his "laboratory" on the same floor, and return to the bedside with a container of chloroform. As the girl dreamed in ecstatic reverie, Dr. Harry gently deepened her sleep with a heavy dose of the anesthetic.

Holmes would then lift his victim carefully, almost lovingly and carry her to the elevator shaft, into which he rudely dumped her. Slipping a glass lid over the shaft, he sat down and waited until the girl became conscious. He watched silently with snake eyes gleaming as she awoke and realized the trap, clawing helplessly, frenzied and hysterical, at the doorless walls.

"It's time," he would say and retrieve a hose which he inserted into a small hole in the glass lid. He then pumped lethal gas into the horror shaft and settled back to watch the girl gasp out her final breath.

The next move required some strength, but Holmes was always up to it. He would loop a rope around the girl's neck and drag her up, then unceremoniously threw her down his special chute and listen to the body slide its way to the basement.

Down the wooden steps he would stomp through a concealed trap door in his personal bathroom. Once in the basement, its walls lined with containers of deadly gases and poisonous powders, Holmes would go to work on the dead girl, using many of the surgical tools that hung on the walls. He dissected the body methodically on his large bench. Those parts of the anatomy that attracted him most were pushed into one heap (he would later take them to his third-floor "lab" for grisly experiments), and the rest of the body was hacked and sawed to pieces. These unwanted remains would then be dropped into the huge stove for cremation.

As he stirred the fires slowly, he would notice hunks of body that refused to burn. These he placed into the vats on the concrete floor and poured quicklime and acid over them.

His daily chore complete, Dr. H. H. Holmes fiendishly gathered up the pieces of body saved and, humming a peculiar melody (overheard often by his janitor), began his climb upward to his quarters, hands outstretched and clutching his quivering "specimens."

Meanwhile, the World's Fair roared open and Chicago was jammed with tourists. Nobody noticed the girls—reported to approach the incredible number of 150—who went into Holmes' odd castle, never to be seen again.

Sometimes Holmes did away with all formality and merely butchered the girls alive and screaming. Who could hear? One of his rooms was completely soundproof, lined with asbestos.

In 1893 an alarmingly beautiful young woman, Minnie Williams, left her hometown in Texas to come to the World's Fair, seeking a career as an actress. She was to spoil everything for Dr. Holmes.

Minnie had been left a hefty piece of land by her rancher father, valued at $60,000, no mean sum in 1893. The first building she went to after reading an ad was the "crazy-looking house" on 63rd Street.

Dr. Harry welcomed her with open arms as a new boarder. When he learned of her assets, he advanced like the proverbial bull, taking her again and again in his elegantly appointed bedroom. He loved her, he adored her, he revered her, he cherished her. And Minnie believed him.

But when it came to turning over her land to Holmes, Minnie balked. First, she had to write her sister Nannie back in Texas and tell her about her wonderful husband-to-be.

Fine. Write sister Nannie.

Nannie showed up in Chicago weeks later, and Holmes,

wearing the best finery of the day, was a perfect gentleman. He squired the two Texas beauties to the World's Fair. They also went shopping in the fashionable stores in the Loop.

Days later, when the girls were shopping alone, they ran into one of Nannie's friends. She introduced her lovely sister, saying, "Minnie is soon to be Mrs. Holmes."

"Holmes?" the friend said. "That's curious. I know a woman who lives in Wilmette, the wife of a Dr. Harry Holmes. Are they related?"

The sisters blinked in amazement at each other. Could they be?

That night Minnie, remembering that her betrothed owned property in Wilmette and often went there on business (sometimes staying overnight), confronted Dr. Harry.

The janitor who worked in the building (he was never allowed into the basement or any of the special rooms) heard Minnie and Holmes arguing.

"You're married, aren't you, Harry?" he heard the young girl say. "That woman in Wilmette . . . she's your wife . . . isn't that so, Harry?"

"Ridiculous, absurd. Who told you such nonsense?"

"It's true, it's true, it's true, isn't it, Harry?"

The janitor heard no more.

Of course it was true. Dr. H. H. Holmes did have a wife in Wilmette, comfortably tucked away in a luxurious $50,000 house. What of it? He also had a wife in Indiana. There was a Mrs. Holmes in Philadelphia, too. Well, the woman in Philadelphia wasn't really a wife anymore. She was dead, hacked to bits years ago.

One thing was certain: Minnie would not be Mrs. Holmes Number Four. The night after the janitor overheard the argument, the two Texas sisters disappeared. The groom lamented. Handsome Harry had been jilted, he said to all.

One of those consoling Harry was a petty thief named Ben Pitezel. The smalltimer was not unaware of the good doctor's line of work. In fact, after this gruesome story was finally pieced together by a remarkable detective, it was learned that Pitezel had often helped his benefactor in his bizarre Murder Castle work.

Holmes complained to Pitezel that his horror house was

not taking in enough loot. "Lord knows, I've worked hard, Ben. But the damnable place has cost me $50,000 to operate. I'm going broke in this business!"

Yes, life was rough for Holmes, but he pulled himself together and cooked up another wild scheme. Pitezel would travel to Philadelphia, Holmes explained, and set himself up as a wealthy patent agent, taking out a $10,000 insurance policy. Once established, Holmes would show up, steal a corpse from the local morgue, disfigure it beyond recognition, and leave it to be discovered in Pitezel's home. They would then claim the insurance and be back on their feet.

"A sound plan, Harry." Pitezel even went further and offered the loan of his wife and three children, eight-year-old Howard, Alice, fourteen, and Nellie, thirteen, for a cover. The bereaved widow, Pitezel's own wife, would claim the phony body.

Pitezel packed and rushed off to Philadelphia to begin his career as a patent agent. Holmes, however, decided to pick up some quick money first. He torched Murder Castle so badly that it had to be boarded up. Then he attempted to collect the insurance on the building.

Overcurious police inspectors messed up this plan. They insisted on examining his structure before the insurance company paid off.

Holmes, standing in a police station, never lost his composure. He was indignant. "Now, see here. I'm a tax-paying, law-abiding citizen and I'm entitled to my claim."

"Of course, Dr. Holmes, but we must inspect the premises. It's a formality. You'll have to unlock your building."

"That's an insult. Are you accusing me of something?"

"Of course not. It's only a formality, doctor."

What must have been in the mind of Herman Mudgett at that moment? What visions of those awful rooms, that hideous basement, and the ghastly fragments hidden there must have flashed through his mind? Dr. Harry thought better of it and told the police he would have to reconsider; he was busy and would return later.

He never did. Instead Holmes headed for Texas and tried, unsuccessfully, to obtain Minnie Williams' $60,000 property, but the Texas lawyers representing the estate were too shrewd for him. They demanded proof that Minnie was his wife and had died by natural causes.

Holmes hung around Fort Worth for weeks trying to figure an angle, until his money ran out. Then, this highly intelligent criminal made his first mistake. Acting like an ordinary thief, he stole a horse, his only means of getting out of Texas, and fled.

St. Louis was as far as he got. Once there, a common swindle backfired and Holmes was arrested for the first time in his life. He gave the name of H. M. Howard. He shared a St. Louis cell with the notorious train robber (they were still running wild in those days), Marion Hedgepeth.

Mr. "Howard" asked the bandit if he knew of a reliable, crooked lawyer, explaining his impending insurance scheme with Pitezel, who was waiting in Philadelphia. He offered $500 to Hedgepeth for the right lawyer and told him he would pay after he received the insurance money. The bandit gave him the name of Jeptha D. Howe. Soon, Holmes was out on bail and skipped off to Chicago to prepare for his next murderous adventure.

On Tuesday, September 4, 1894, a Mr. Perry, who had set up a patent office and whose only known client was a Mr. Holmes in Chicago, was found very dead, his face charred beyond recognition. A pipe, a box of matches, and a benzine bottle were found nearby. Poor Mr. Perry. How unfortunate. He blew most of his face away on his back porch while lighting his pipe too close to the benzine bottle. Poor soul.

A medical examiner grew suspicious. He inspected the body and reported that Mr. Perry had died of poisoning. A coroner's jury, however, ruled death by accident.

Almost immediately, attorney Jeptha D. Howe stepped forward representing Mrs. Benjamin D. Pitezel. The woman said that the dead man was really her husband—Ben Pitezel. They were claiming the insurance. But the company had second thoughts. So the insurance people wrote Perry's only client, now back in Chicago, the ubiquitous Mr. Holmes.

Would he come and identify the body? Certainly, if he were to be paid a fee. It was agreed, and, incredibly, Holmes went to Philadelphia to identify the body of his ex-partner in crime. He brought Ben's fourteen-year-old daughter, who made the identification through rivers of tears, and the insurance was paid. The couple disappeared.

It was then that convict Hedgepeth blew the whistle on Mr. "Howard," telling the warden of the St. Louis jail how he gave Holmes the name of the crooked lawyer to set up the phony insurance deal.

"So I give him the name of my lawyer. And that's the last I seen of him. He got out on bail the next day and skipped out. I heard by the grapevine that he collected the insurance money but he ain't been near me to pay the five hundred dollars!"

H. H. Holmes' "Murder Castle" in which he slaughtered a reported two hundred or more gullible females during the time of Chicago's World's Fair. (N.Y. Historical Society)

That's when Philadelphia policeman Frank P. Geyer, a super-detective by anyone's standards, was hired by the insurance people to track down the nefarious Mr. "Howard."

Geyer inspected boarded-up Murder Castle, but did not enter. He checked the Illinois license records and they led back to the University of Michigan. There he was given Holmes' birthplace—Gilmantown, New Hampshire.

Nobody in Gilmantown had ever heard of Holmes. Geyer described the handsome, tall man with the glib tongue. "That fits Herman Mudgett to a T," one officer said, and Geyer was directed to the Mudgett home.

Mrs. Mudgett explained that her son was away, busy. "He's an inventor, you know."

"Yes, I know," the wily detective said. "He's invented some marvelous things. Do you know where I can find him?" She told Geyer that Herman was in Boston on business, and the detective caught up with him there on November 17, 1894. He was with Mrs. Pitezel and both were arrested.

Mudgett refused to be returned to Philadelphia, and under questioning, Mrs. Pitezel admitted that she didn't have the insurance money. She had signed it over to Herman.

Then a warrant for Mudgett's arrest arrived from Fort Worth for horse stealing. "Take your choice," Geyer told Mudgett. "It's back to Philadelphia or to Texas for horse stealing."

Mudgett sweated. Horse stealing was a hanging offense in Texas. "I'll go back to Philadelphia." Once in Philadelphia, Mudgett told incessant lies. He said that Pitezel was alive in South America and that he had stolen the corpse known as Mr. Perry from a medical school. The records were checked, and the medical-school-cadaver story was thrown out.

Next, Mudgett said, "All right. The man was Pitezel. He was supposed to steal a cadaver, lost his nerve and got despondent. So he drank chloroform. When I discovered that, I decided to make it appear an accident so his poor widow could collect the insurance."

"What about the Pitezel children? We can't find them."

"I've told you everything, so help me God."

God, on the other hand, was far from helping Mudgett. Again, Geyer went to work, tracking through all the cities Mudgett had dragged the helpless, hopeless Pitezel children—Chicago, Detroit, Cincinnati.

In a rented house in Indianapolis, leased by Mudgett (as Holmes), Geyer sifted through the ashes in a large stove. He found bones and the skull of a small boy—Howard Pitezel. In Toronto he discovered another Mudgett-rented house and in its basement a trunk containing the two Pitezel girls. They had been locked inside, and gas, piped into the trunk, had killed them.

"It was a foul murder!" raged Herman Mudgett when Geyer confronted him. "Who was the fiend?"

Geyer only stared at the good-looking face behind the bars, a face that hid the real sight of a monster. He still had no proof linking Mudgett to murder. Then he remembered the big house in Chicago.

With the help of Chicago police, Geyer broke into Murder Castle, and in the stench-reeking basement, grown men dug, fainted, then dug again until they had unearthed the remains of *over two hundred corpses.*

"Untrue! A lie! Villainous slander!" Mudgett yelled, but they had him on the Ben Pitezel murder, for he did, it was proved, kill his partner in crime. It was all over . . . or was it?

Herman Mudgett invited the press in and confessed in detail to murder after murder in Murder Castle. He described his gory slaughterhouse, and as the papers sopped up his words and spread his name across a shocked nation, he reveled in his terrible fame. "My sole object," he said in a gross misstatement, "is to vindicate my name from the horrible aspersions cast upon it."

The date of his hanging cut short his "memoirs"—he had only gotten to victim number twenty-seven—and on May 7, 1896, Herman Mudgett, alias Dr. Harry Holmes, staggered up the thirteen steps to the gallows.

As the noose was slipped around his neck, there came a high, almost inhuman voice wailing, "As God is my witness, I was responsible for the death of only two women. I didn't kill Minnie Williams! Minnie killed her—"

At that moment, the trap sprang open and the large, heavy rope sliced into Mudgett's last words, silencing him forever. But what did he mean with that last, unfinished statement? Did Minnie kill her sister? Was she in league with her killer-lover?

We shall never know . . . which is exactly what this archfiend of the century may have wanted after all. Was it the truth or a lie on his lips at the last. The final baffling mystery left unsolved—that would fit Herman Mudgett to a T.

[ALSO SEE Marion Hedgepeth.]

MURIETA, JOAQUIN
Bandit • (? -1853)

Practically nothing is known about this most glamorous of California bandits except that fiction writers have heralded his exploits for a hundred years with only threadbare facts to sustain their lurid and ample imaginations.

At the time of Murieta's raids, California was a wild place where upstanding citizens lost their identities in the pandemonium of the gold rushes. It was all but impossible to keep factual records of elusive bandits like Murieta.

There is little doubt, however, that he did exist, robbing gold miners of their hoarded treasure and stopping stages to pilfer passengers. The bandit's one-man crime wave in the early 1850s caused the governor of the state to offer a $1,000 reward for his capture, dead or alive.

One Harry Love, a captain of the Texas Rangers, promised California authorities that he would bring in the bandit. After several expeditions, Love did bring in something—the head of a Mexican preserved in a jar, which the ranger insisted was that of Murieta. The head was displayed in

An artist's rendering of the legendary Joaquin Murieta, California's most notorious bandit. (Denver Public Library)

Stockton, California, on June 24, 1853, for the gawking curious.

Rumors persisted for a dozen years following Love's trophy hunt that Murieta was still riding and looting in the California hills. The rumors then faded into gentle folklore.

MURREL, JOHN A.
Bandit • (1794- ?)

He was known to readers of the *Police Gazette* as "the great Western Land Pirate," but John Murrel was, in reality, a murderous bandit with a head full of fanciful schemes and a massive ego. Murrel was one of the first horse bandits to organize a gang of cutthroats who robbed and terrorized those living along the Natchez Trace.

In 1834 Murrel met a youth named Virgil Stewart in his travels, and the two men journeyed several miles through the wilderness together. During the trip, Murrel, who passed himself off as a harmless merchant, told Stewart of an "elder brother" who had become a bloodthirsty bandit.

At their camp stops, Murrel painted grisly pictures of killings and robberies committed by his "elder brother," who also stole slaves and resold them. Those slaves who gave him trouble, Murrel said, were killed. One slave, Murrel pointed out, gave his brother so much trouble about being resold that "he took the nigger out on the bank of the river which ran by the farm and shot him through the head and then got rid of him . . . He cuts open the belly and scrapes out the guts, and then he fills him full of sand and throws him into the river to feed the eels . . ."

Hours later, while Stewart was still shivering from such cold-blooded stories, Murrel leaned a shadowy face into the light of a campfire, smiled, and said: "I might as well be out with it. I'm the elder brother I've been telling you about."

Murrel then admitted to Stewart that he had committed countless robberies along the Trace and had killed a number of men who resisted him. He terrified the young man when he outlined his plans for taking over the city of New Orleans by leading a slave revolt. Many of the slaves he had stolen, Murrel said, he had kept and armed for this purpose. When he had accumulated enough slaves to form an army, he would take over the states of Mississippi and Louisiana. He vowed he would kill every aristocrat he found, a class of people he bitterly blamed for beginning his criminal career, and at whose hands he had been beaten and whipped and branded a horse thief. "My blacks will cut all their throats . . . we will swim in rivers of blood!"

Murrel, who thought to recruit Stewart for his insane cause, took the young traveler to his camp, where dozens of armed blacks were drilling as soldiers and preparing for Murrel's coming attacks on nearby settlements. Stewart slipped away during the night and informed authorities of the madman's plot. Murrel was taken without a fight, tried, and sent to the Nashville prison for ten years. His abortive slave revolt began without a leader and soon collapsed following a number of murders along the Natchez Trace.

Murrel was released from prison about 1842 and disappeared.

NEWTON'S GENERAL MASSACRE

This fight began in early August, 1871, on the eve of a referendum concerned with issuing $20,000 in county bonds to help build a long stretch of track for the Wichita and Southwestern Railroad, particularly that section which reached through Newton, Kansas.

Two lawmen were assigned to keep the peace on election day, August 11, 1871. One was a brawler known as Mike McCluskie (alias Art Delaney). The other was gunfighter and gambler William Wilson (alias Billy Bailey). Each man hated the other. McCluskie, some said, was jealous of Wilson's reputation as a gunslinger, belittling the fact that Wilson had gunned down three men in previous duels.

That night in the Red Front Saloon, the two men began to argue over who would buy the drinks and were shortly in the street shooting at each other. Wilson died of his wounds within hours, and McCluskie was warned to flee since the slain man had many friends in Newton. McCluskie departed, but returned on August 19, 1871, and immediately retired to Tuttle's Saloon to drink himself abusive.

Hugh Anderson, son of a wealthy cattleman and longtime friend of William Wilson, led a band of Texans into the bar at 2 a.m. the following morning, shouting vengeance. McCluskie was then hit by a blizzard of bullets and fell dead. His young friend, T. Riley, picked up McCluskie's guns and blazed away at the Texans, killing three of them.

Riley, it was said, was spared death because he was consumptive.

The twenty-minute slaughter took the lives of five men and was referred to as "Newton's General Massacre" by a local paper whose editor sadly concluded, "It was worse than Tim Finnegan's wake."

NINETEENTH-STREET GANG

A juvenile mob led by an unholy terror named Little Mike, the Nineteenth-Street Gang operated as pickpockets and sneak thieves in the area about East Thirty-fourth Street and Second Avenue in New York City. At the time of the gang's existence in 1875, this teeming tenement section was known as Misery Row and Poverty Lane.

Little Mike preyed on storekeepers, cripples, and other children, stealing what he could from them. He was particularly fond of leading other Catholics in his gang in raids against Protestant missions and schools. The apprentice thug would throw rocks through the windows of these institutions and, while classes were going on, thrust his gnomelike head through the jagged opening and shout: "Go to hell, you old Protestants!"

Mike and his minions disappeared by the early 1880s, much to the relief of everybody in the neighborhood.

NORTH, JOHN
Gambler • (? -1835)

O ne of the most corrupt gamblers of the ante-bellum South, North ran a notorious saloon-brothel-gambling-house in Vicksburg, Mississippi. North's place was in the center of the criminal-infested Landing area, from which he proposed the taking and looting of Vicksburg. Hundreds of gamblers and thieves rallied to his plan, but the army of criminals was foiled by an alert vigilante group who invaded the Landing on July 6, 1835.

Dozens of gamblers were hanged, but North escaped. He was found the following day and hanged on the highest hill overlooking Vicksburg with practically the entire town looking on. He was not cut down for twenty-four hours. North's crooked roulette wheel was "tied up to his dangling body" as a warning against dishonest gamblers.

OCUISH, HANNAH
Murderer • (1774-1786)

A Pequot Indian girl, Hannah was abandoned at an early age and turned to delinquency in nearby New London, Connecticut. In late 1786 she was arrested for murdering Eunice Bolles, a six-year-old child who, according to reports, angered Hannah by accusing her of stealing her strawberries.

The stern New England court quickly condemned her to death following her murder confession (which she made only after she was confronted with the body of the dead Bolles girl). The half-witted girl hardly responded to the court's sentence. On the scaffold the day she was hanged, December 20, 1786, a contemporary account indifferently stated that "she said very little and appeared greatly afraid, and seemed to want somebody to help her."

O.K. CORRAL, GUNFIGHT AT THE

By the time Wyatt Earp and his brothers assumed the duty of upholding the law in Tombstone, Arizona, in 1881—the site of the wild shoot-out at the O.K. Corral—the lawman was the most legendary peacemaker in the West. He had appeared in a dozen wild cow towns since 1873, taming them with his fists, his guns, and his considerable verbal persuasion. For most, Earp had no peers; not even the feared Wild Bill Hickok approached the magnitude of his exploits. To some, he was a mean, bushwhacking murderer who gloried in his gunslinger reputation.

Earp was first heard of in Ellsworth, Kansas, in the summer of 1873, when he backed down a motley crew of Texas gunmen (so the story goes) led by quick-tempered Ben Thompson. Earp assumed the duties of sheriff for one day to clean up the town. The following year Earp was made marshal in Wichita and soon dismantled such gunworthies as the Clements brothers, Abel Head, "Shanghai" Pierce, the rowdy cattle baron, and brutish George Peshaur.

Then came Dodge City, which could justly claim the first Boot Hill in the West. Earp became Dodge's chief deputy at $2.50 per month and earned every penny of it, along with his three aides, Bat and Jim Masterson and Joe Mason. Earp moved to the goldfields around Deadwood, South Dakota, in 1876, but the area was panned out. He returned to Dodge and pinned his star on once again.

Outlaw barons placed a $1,000 reward for anyone who would put Earp in Boot Hill in 1876. Gunman George R. Hoyt tried to collect one night by furiously riding up to the Comique Theater where Earp was lounging after watching comedian Eddie Foy. Hoyt banged six bullets into the railing where Earp sat. The lawman coolly withdrew his pistol and, taking careful aim, shot Hoyt from his skittish horse. The would-be assassin died a month later of lead poisoning.

Wyatt Earp, the legendary lawman, brought the fight to the outlaw McLowery and Clanton brothers at the O.K. Corral in Tombstone, Ariz., 10/26/81. (Kansas State Historical Society, Topeka)

Earp left Dodge in 1879 and, at the request of Sheriff John E. Behan, rode to distant and chaotic Tombstone, Arizona, founded a dozen years before by prospector Edward Schiefflin, who struck a vein that ultimately yielded more than $30,000,000 of silver. With Wyatt rode his brothers James and Virgil and the dentist-turned-gunfighter John H. "Doc" Holliday. Morgan Earp followed a month later.

Why Behan had bothered to ask Earp to be his deputy at all was never learned. Though Earp had ostensibly been brought in to keep the peace and quell the almost daily riots incurred by the deadliest outlaws of the era, Behan spent his efforts in pooh-poohing the mayhem. Much to Earp's disgust, Behan coddled and patronized the worst gunmen in the territory, attempting to befriend such killers as Curly Bill Brocius, Johnny Ringo (Ringgold), Frank and Tom McLowery, and the three Clanton brothers led by their murderous father, N. H. Clanton.

Behan refused to patrol the streets at night; that chore was left to the Earps and town marshal Fred White. One evening in October, 1881, White and Virgil Earp attempted to arrest Curly Bill Brocius, Pony Deal, Ike and Billie Clanton, the McLowerys, and Frank Patterson when the gunmen began to shoot up the town.

Brocius pretended to surrender his pistol to White, but used a gun-spin to bring the butt of his gun back to his own hand and shot White dead. Virgil Earp knocked Brocius senseless and dragged him to jail.

Later that year, Earp was made deputy U.S. marshal and his chief concern became the protection of the Oriental Saloon, a wide-open gambling spa. The casino's owners paid Earp $1,000 a month to make sure nobody wrecked the place, a daily goal of other saloon owners.

Within months, Earp's friends Bat Masterson and Luke Short came from Kansas to obtain jobs as dealers in the Oriental and, if necessary, back Earp's play against the outlaw faction.

Outside of a few drunken fights, Earp had little to do in Tombstone until the spring of 1881. The Wells Fargo Stage was then held up and its driver, Bud Philpot, shot to death. Shotgun rider Bob Paul told Earp that the raiders had been Luther King, James Crane, Harry Head, and Bill Leonard, all friends of the Clantons.

Alone, Earp rode after Luther King and captured him. When he brought the bandit back to Tombstone, Sheriff Behan ordered Earp to turn King over to him. "He's my prisoner, Wyatt," Behan insisted. Earp reluctantly turned King over to Behan's custody, and the prisoner escaped two days later.

Then the Clantons stated that Doc Holliday had really led the raid against the stagecoach. Dance-hall trollop Big Nose Kate Fisher (later Doc's lover), who had stayed up all night drinking with the Clantons, made a deposition to the effect that Holliday bragged to her about committing the holdup. Holliday, who was not much given to defending himself with anything other than a six-gun, pointed out that the $80,000 the stage had been carrying at the time of the holdup had not been taken by the outlaws.

"If I had pulled that job," Holliday said wryly to a board of inquiry, "I'd have gotten the eighty thousand." He sauntered out of the jailhouse and into the Oriental. No one dared challenge Holliday, considered one of the meanest, fastest guns in the West.

Holliday, who had a record of grim gunfights in Denver and Dodge City, was consumptive and excessively nervous. It took very little prompting to draw him into a gun duel. According to his sometime friend Bat Masterson, Holliday "had a mean disposition and an ungovernable temper, and under the influence of liquor was a most dangerous man. . . . Physically [Holliday] was a weakling who could not have whipped a healthy fifteen-year-old boy in a go-as-you-please fist fight, and no one knew this better than himself, and the knowledge of this fact was perhaps why he was so ready to resort to a weapon of some kind whenever he got himself into difficulty. He was hotheaded and impetuous and very much given to both drinking and quarreling, and, among men who did not fear him, was very much disliked."

Trouble with the McLowery-Clanton gang plagued the Earps throughout the summer and early fall of 1881. Ike Clanton began to tell the tale that Wyatt Earp had attempted to bribe him to turn in Head, Leonard, Crane, and King, and he refused. When Earp confronted Clanton, a notorious loudmouth, the outlaw denied his words. Hours later, Clanton stated: "He offered me the reward for them fellows, all he wanted was credit for capturin' 'em." In June, 1881, Head and Leonard were killed by the Haslett brothers in Eureka, New Mexico. Crane died fighting Mexican regulars in August of that year while attempting to rustle cattle near Huachita.

The feud between the Earps and Clantons boiled over on the night of October 25, 1881, when Doc Holliday (by this time deputized as a deputy U.S. marshal) had a run-in with Ike Clanton. The two were eating steaks in a lunchroom. Morgan Earp sat at the end of the counter with his hand inside his coat, as if resting it on a gun butt. Holliday looked up from his platter. "Still say I robbed that coach, Ike?"

Clanton gave Holliday a sideways glance and snorted an unintelligible reply.

"You're a son-of-a-bitch of a cowboy," Holliday said.

Clanton pushed his plate back, stood up slowly, and walked outside. There he saw Virgil and Wyatt Earp. Morgan Earp and Holliday followed him outside and, according to some reports, taunted him. Clanton turned

Wyatt Earp's intrepidly loyal back-up man was John H. "Doc" Holliday, consumptive, a fast draw, a deadly killer. (Western History Collection, U. of Okla. Library)

to Morgan Earp and said, "Don't shoot me in the back, will you, Morg?" He then walked away into the darkness.

Later that evening Clanton joined Tom McLowery and Sheriff Behan in a saloon and played cards until dawn. About 9 a.m. the following morning Clanton approached Virgil Earp in the middle of the street and said: "If you were one of them threatening me last night, you can have your fight." He then walked away.

About noon Virgil and Morgan Earp spotted Clanton and stopped him. Their argument ended when Virgil Earp withdrew his six-gun and slammed it against Clanton's head. The two lawmen then dragged Clanton to the courthouse, where he was fined $25 by Judge Wallace for carrying concealed weapons. Tom McLowery barged into the courtroom shouting oaths. Wyatt Earp stepped up, took out his pistol, and cracked McLowery on the side of the head. He then dragged the outlaw into the street and threw him into the gutter.

An hour later, a town drunk came up to the Earps, all

assembled at the courthouse. Doc Holliday stood nearby holding a shotgun. The barfly said: "There are some men want to see you fellas down at the O.K. Corral."

"Who are these men?" Wyatt asked.

"The McLowery brothers, the Clantons, and Billy Claiborne."

Wyatt turned to Morgan Earp and said, "Let's go."

Then began the most famous gun battle in the history of the West. The three tall, mustachioed Earp brothers, dressed all in black, and Doc Holliday, cradling a shotgun in his arms, moved solemnly down the street abreast of one another, heading for Fremont Street and the O.K. Corral. It was the final showdown, and the lawmen had prepared for it for days.

Sheriff Behan, who was getting a shave, raced from a barbershop, the lather still on his cheeks, when he heard of the impending fight. He tried to argue the Earps out of the showdown, but he was brushed aside.

When the lawmen turned the corner to Fremont Street and entered the O.K. Corral, they saw five men waiting for them—Billie and Ike Clanton, Tom and Frank McLowery, and Billy Claiborne.

"You sons-of-bitches, you have been looking for a fight and now you can have it!" roared Wyatt Earp (according to Sheriff Behan's later testimony).

Virgil Earp, who was the town marshal, said: "You men are under arrest. Throw up your hands."

Billie Clanton and Frank McLowery dropped their hands to the pistols at their sides.

"Hold it, I don't mean that," Virgil Earp said. "I've come to disarm you."

Behan, who witnessed the entire confrontation, claimed that Billie Clanton shouted: "Don't shoot me, I don't want to fight." He also later stated that Tom McLowery brushed back his frock coat and said: "I am not armed."

For a moment the two groups glared at each other. Then Wyatt Earp and Billie Clanton went for their pistols. Earp's gun came out of a specially made coat pocket with a leather lining heavily waxed for a fast draw. Clanton and Frank McLowery drew their pistols from holsters. Clanton fired at Wyatt and missed. Wyatt fired at Frank McLowery and hit him in the stomach.

Ike Clanton, the braggart and instigator of the fight, panicked and ran up to Wyatt, grabbing him by the sleeve. "Don't shoot me!" he screamed. "Don't kill me! I'm not fighting!"

"The fighting has now commenced," Earp stoically told him. "Go to fighting or get away." Clanton ran across the street and down an alley.

Though mortally wounded, Frank McLowery managed to stagger across the open lot behind the O.K. Corral, into the street, and onto a sidewalk where he fired off a shot that barely missed Wyatt Earp.

"Throw up your hands!" Virgil Earp continued to shout, but the outlaws kept firing. Billy Claiborne threw up one hand when bullets came dangerously close to him. He sent a shot toward Virgil Earp and then raced down the street and hid inside C. S. Fly's photographic studio. Tom McLowery, who allegedly said he was unarmed, advanced against Morgan Earp and Doc Holliday, firing a very real pistol as he went. Two shots threaded Doc's coat sleeve just as Holliday raised his ugly shotgun and fired both barrels into McLowery, who died in his boots.

Before the second McLowery died, he squeezed off a round that tore into Morgan Earp's shoulder. Billie Clanton, nineteen years old and alone in the Corral, shifted his pistol from his shattered right hand, which had been hit by either Virgil or Morgan Earp, to his left and fired off several shots at the Earps, hitting Virgil in the leg. As he fired he ran in the same direction that Claiborne had fled, collapsing in front of Fly's gallery. By then he had been hit by at least four more bullets from the Earps' roaring pistols. One of Clanton's last shots creased Holliday's back.

Wyatt Earp, the only lawman uninjured, jogged after Clanton and stood over him as the boy tried to lift his pistol to shoot. Clanton kept repeating, "God, God, won't somebody give me some more cartridges for a last shot . . ." Then he died.

From thirty to fifty shots had been fired in the two-to-three-minute gun battle. Three of the outlaws—Frank and Tom McLowery and Billie Clanton—were dead.

Lawmen Wyatt Earp and Doc Holliday were arrested after warrants were sworn out by Sheriff Behan and Ike Clanton. Virgil (discharged as deputy U.S. marshal) and

Morgan Earp, killed after the O.K. Corral battle by Ike Clanton's friends. (Arizona Society of Pioneers)

Morgan were not arrested and were bedridden with serious wounds. After a short hearing before Justice of the Peace Wells Spicer, Earp and Holliday were exonerated.

The outlaw clan struck back from ambush within months, when an unknown gunman shot Virgil Earp in the side on the night of November 28, 1881, as he was entering the Oriental Saloon. He was crippled for life. Ike Clanton added new guns to his cause, and on the night of March 17, 1882, Hank Swilling, Pete Spence, Frank Stilwell, and Florentino "Indian Charlie" Cruz hid behind a stack of kegs and shot Morgan Earp in the back, killing him, as he played pool in Hatch's Saloon.

Wyatt and Doc Holliday accompanied the wounded Virgil Earp and the body of Morgan Earp on board a train bound for California. James Earp, who had been severely crippled in the Civil War and did not serve as a lawman, went with them. The Earps were going to their family home in Colston, California. Doc Holliday and Wyatt Earp got off the train at Tucson, where they were joined by another Earp brother, Warren, and three noteworthy lawmen—

Virgil Earp was crippled for life after the gun battle. (Arizona Society of Pioneers)

Texas Jack Vermillion, Turkey Creek Jack Johnson, and Sherman McMasters.

Wyatt had been warned that Stilwell and the others planned to ambush the Earp family on the train after it pulled out of Tucson. As the train took on passengers Wyatt and his friends scoured the area around the tracks. Earp, according to his own version, spotted four figures crouching on a flatcar and began shooting at them. One, Pete Spence, ran across the roadbed, and Earp killed him with a single shot.

Earp came face to face with Stilwell, his brother's murderer, in the dark. The famous marshal later stated: "Stilwell caught the barrel of my Wells Fargo gun with both hands . . . I forced the gun down until the muzzle of the right barrel was just underneath Stilwell's heart. He found his voice. 'Morg!' he said and then a second time, 'Morg!' I've often wondered what made him say that . . . I let him have it. The muzzle of one barrel was just underneath the heart. He got the second before he hit the ground."

One by one, Earp tracked down his brother's killers.

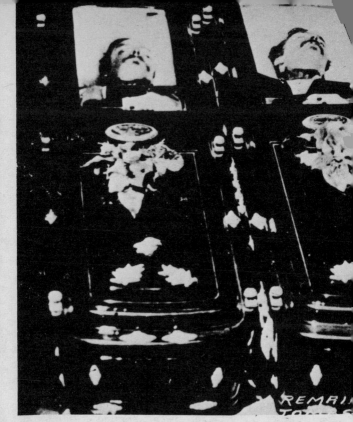

REMAI

He found Indian Charlie Cruz outside of Tombstone and killed him after forcing the outlaw to draw on a count of three. He caught up with Curly Bill Brocius at Iron Springs and shot him to pieces. On the western side of the Whetstone Mountains, Wyatt ran down Johnny Ringo and killed him in a close duel, according to one historian.

Then Earp hung up his guns and retired to the peaceful town of Colston, California, to live out a storybook life and mull through awful memories. His close friend and back-up man in a dozen gunfights, John H. "Doc" Holliday, died four years after the gunfight at the O.K. Corral. He was thirty-five, and the cause of death was tuberculosis.

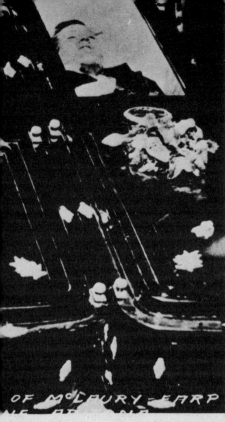

Three dead outlaws resulted from the gunfight in Tombstone. Shown in their caskets are (left to right), Tom McLowery, Frank McLowery, Billie Clanton. (Arizona Historical Society Library)

Next to his bed was his shotgun, his nickel-plated six-gun, and a bowie knife he had worn about his neck for ten years.

After a final shot of whiskey, Holliday worked himself up on one elbow and looked at his bare feet. "Dammit," he yelled. "Put 'em back on." The nurses of the Glenwood Springs, Colorado, sanitorium searched frantically but were too late. Holliday died with his boots off.

[ALSO SEE Curly Bill Brocius, Ben Thompson.]

OLD BREWERY

Erected in 1792 and originally known as Coulter's Brewery, the Old Brewery was situated in the center of what is now White, Leonard, Lafayette, and Mulberry streets in New York—the old Five Points section. The brewery was a five-story brick building originally painted yellow. Through the years, its dilapidated appearance, according to one writer, "came to resemble nothing so much as a giant toad, with dirty, leprous warts, squatting happily in the filth and squalor of the Points."

In 1837 the cavernous building was transformed into a tenement house with more than 100 rooms. The long hallway between rooms was called Murderer's Row. Irish immigrants inhabited the top floors, Negroes were in the twenty basement rooms. Dozens of children born in the Old Brewery did not see sunlight or inhale fresh air until their teens.

Murder was a pastime at the Old Brewery, a nightmare world in itself, dangerous to enter and lethal to leave. Anyone foolish enough to enter the building was marked for death. Anyone leaving would be stoned or strangled by citizens fearing the building's barbarous inhabitants.

It was truly a nether world of nauseating poverty and compassionless people who were more animal than human. In a fifteen-foot room, ten years prior to the Civil War, twenty-six persons dwelled. When a small girl rashly displayed a penny she had been given, she was murdered for it and her body tossed into a corner, where it stayed unburied for five days. Her mother, weak from starvation, finally managed to scrape out a miserably shallow grave with a spoon and fork and place her child in it.

Negroes, many of whom had reached New York via the slave escape route, came to dwell in the Old Brewery, where they took white wives. Sexually, the place was a free-for-all, flourishing with incest, miscegenation, rape, homosexuality. Almost every denizen of the Old Brewery pursued a criminal trade—pickpocketing, burglary, professional murder.

The Notorious Old Brewery squatted at the hub of the Five Points; literally thousands were murdered in its murky chambers before it was destroyed in 1852.

Drunken revels never ceased; loud voices, the banging of doors, the smashing of bricks, continued on a twenty-four-hour basis. The building fairly shuddered with the most frightening and ghastly sounds imaginable—wails, whines, shrieks, insane laughter, screams, catcalls, hoots. The mad cacophony could be heard from blocks away.

One historian estimated that there was a murder per night in the Old Brewery for an unbroken period of fifteen years—5,475 lives snuffed out without one police investigation. Police did venture into the building occasionally, but never in numbers less than fifty and then only at great peril to their lives.

It was said that many scions of once-great American families who had fallen into disrepute went to live and die in the Old Brewery. Harman Blennerhasset, the man who had so archly sided with Aaron Burr to create an American dictatorship, lost his son to the Old Brewery.

In 1852 the powerful Ladies Home Missionary Society, with the backing of financier and philanthropist Daniel Drew, bought the Old Brewery for $16,000, erecting a mission on the site a year later. Pandemonium erupted when the city police came to eject the Old Brewery's inhabitants on December 2, 1852. Like rats, the murderers—some wanted by the authorities for twenty years—fled into police nets. Women and children cried with joy to be released from the foul social and economic prison. When the grisly work of destroying the building began, workmen removed a hundred sacks of human bones from between the walls and under the floors.

OLIVE, ISON PRENTICE ("PRINT")
Murderer, Gunfighter • (1840-1886)

BACKGROUND: BORN IN MISSISSIPPI IN 1840. MINOR PUBLIC EDUCATION. SERVED IN HOOD'S TEXAS DIVISION DURING THE CIVIL WAR. ORIGINAL OCCUPATION, CATTLE OWNER AND RANCHER. DESCRIPTION: TALL, SWARTHY, HEAVYSET. ALIASES: NONE. RECORD: INVOLVED IN SEVERAL KILLINGS IN TEXAS FOLLOWING THE CIVIL WAR; MURDERED LUTHER MITCHELL AND AMI KETCHUM, HOMESTEADERS, AT CLEAR CREEK, NEB., IN NOVEMBER, 1878, CLAIMED THE TWO WERE ENCROACHING ON HIS VAST CATTLE RANCH; PLACED ON TRIAL WITH FREDERICK FISHER, FOUND GUILTY OF MURDER AND SENTENCED TO LIFE IMPRISONMENT IN THE NEBRASKA STATE PENITENTIARY; FREED, 1880, ON A TECHNICALITY AND SCHEDULED TO BE RETRIED (A NEW TRIAL NEVER OCCURRED); KILLED IN 1886 IN TRAIL CITY, COLO., BY JOSEPH SPARROW.

Following in the tradition of Abel Head "Shanghai" Pierce, Olive became one of the super cattle barons of the West before homesteaders and farming communities sprang up in the middle of his vast herds and ranges. He ruled his enormous lands by the gun and the lynch rope. His cowboys were hired not only as expert cowpunchers but for their prowess with a pistol.

Violence had been a way of life with Olive, called "Print"

by his friends, since his childhood in Mississippi. While still a youth, Print moved with his parents to Texas. When the Civil War broke out, he was one of the first to enlist in the Confederate Army, serving with distinction in Hood's Texas Division and participating in such bloody actions as Gettysburg.

Following the war, Olive moved back to Texas and raised a gigantic herd of cattle which he drove northward. Some of his beef was sold and the rest kept as stock with which to raise even greater herds in the then untamed ranges of Nebraska. Olive cut out a huge territory along the Platte River there, lands that stretched for hundreds of miles. He hired an army of killer cowboys to run his cattle and protect his barony.

Two intrepid homesteaders, Ami Ketchum and Luther Mitchell, moved into Nebraska's Custer County, controlled by Olive, and with their large families established neighboring farms. Olive, along with his brother Robert, who had fled Texas to avoid arrest by the Texas Rangers on a murder charge, rode into Mitchell's farm at the head of a sizeable body of men in November, 1878.

The farmers had been prepared for just such a raid after receiving repeated warnings from Print to "get out or get killed." A gun battle erupted in which Robert Olive was killed and the cattlemen driven off.

Through his bribed officials (Olive owned everything in sight along the Platte), Print had Mitchell and Ketchum arrested and then turned over to him. Olive proceeded to mete out his own brand of frontier justice. In a deserted spot near Clear Creek, Olive ordered the two farmers bound with ropes. He then shot Mitchell in the back, saying "That's the way you gave it to my brother."

Both farmers were strung up by their necks from a nearby tree. The lynching did not satisfy the cattle baron, so he ordered a large fire built beneath the swaying, dead bodies. When members of a vigilante committee arrived, they found the corpses charred almost beyond recognition.

Public anger at such raw power and brutality rose against Olive, and, under pressure, the governor ordered his arrest and trial for murder. Olive and one of his top lieutenants, Fred Fisher, were found guilty and sentenced to life imprisonment at the Nebraska State Penitentiary. The outcome of the trial so enraged the hundreds of cowboys who worked for Olive that it was feared they would storm the courthouse where the cattle baron was being held.

No less a personage than President Rutherford B. Hayes was called upon by Nebraska's governor to order troops into the territory to prevent Olive's release by his private army. Several mounted companies of soldiers were sent in to deliver Olive and Fisher to jail.

Print Olive boasted he would never stay in prison, and he was right. He spent a large fortune on legal maneuvers, and two years after being put behind bars, he was released. The state supreme court ruled that his trial, and that of Fisher, were improperly conducted since they were not held in Custer County, scene of the Mitchell-Ketchum slayings.

While Olive was in prison, his empire waned. His herds had diminished following incessant raids by rustlers (many of whom were his former employees). An influx of settlers challenged his supremacy, and hatred for him in the Platte River communities was rampant. He took what was left of his herds and crossed into Kansas in 1882.

Kansas, too, was overrun with farmers, members of a farming federation known as The Grange, which all but destroyed Olive's influence in Dodge City, where he attempted to establish himself. Selling his beef, Print moved on to Colorado and purchased a saloon in Trail City.

The once mighty cattle baron came to an unexpected end in 1886 when a cowboy, one Joe Sparrow, who was disgruntled over the fact that Olive owed him $10, entered his saloon and shot him, without warning, in the head. Olive died while standing up, a startled look on his face.

PARSONS, REUBEN
Gambler • (? -1875)

Parsons, who moved from New England to New York in the 1850s, was known as the "Great American Faro Banker." He was responsible, more than any other, for the rise of infamous sharpers such as John Frink and Henry Coulton, who he backed in dozens of gambling houses. He and Frink inaugurated the policy game in America.

One historian described Parsons thusly: "Plain in his dress, and unassuming in his manners, he associates but little with his class, and is seldom publicly seen in any of his gaming houses, of which, although the actual proprietor, he stands in no fear or danger of legal prosecutions, as it cannot be shown that he is the winner of a dollar."

Parsons retired to a life of wealthy leisure in 1861, but caught the gambling fever a dozen years later when he speculated hundreds of thousands of dollars on Wall Street. He was wiped out in 1875, the year of his death.

PHILLIPS, JAMES JETER
Murderer • (1844-1868)

A well-educated and moderately wealthy young man, Phillips grew tired of his wife, a woman ten years his senior. On the pretense of inspecting his estate in Henrico County, Virginia, Phillips convinced his wife to accompany him in a buckboard. He stopped on a deserted road and shot her with a derringer, throwing her body into a ditch.

Approximately three months later, Mrs. Phillips' body was discovered and her landowner husband charged with murder. He confessed and was quickly executed.

PIPER, THOMAS W.
Murderer • (? -1876)

As sexton of the old Warren Avenue Baptist Church in Boston, Thomas Piper had complete access to church buildings and grounds. For years it was rumored that Piper was "not quite right" and had attacked several young girls in the neighborhood, but nothing could be proved against him.

Late in 1875 Piper enticed a young girl, Mabel H. Young, into the tower of the church. There, he turned on the five-year-old child and beat her to death with a cricket bat.

Police discovered the body and soon picked up Piper as a suspect. He was convicted by overwhelming evidence and sentenced to death on the gallows. He was hanged in 1876 after authorities learned that he had murdered at least one other young girl and had, indeed, attacked and raped several children.

PLUG UGLIES GANG

Organized about 1825 in New York City in the Five Points section, the Plug Uglies took their name from the giant plug hats they filled with rags and straw to protect them in gang battles. It was an all-Irish gang at the beginning, and and its members were required to be at least six feet tall.

Each member walked the streets in the symbolic plug hat and carried a brick in one hand and a mammoth club in the other. He usually wore a pistol in his belt and considered his giant hobnailed boots an additional weapon with which to stomp robbery victims and enemies to death.

The Plug Uglies were afoot during the period in which The Chichesters, Roach Guards, Shirt Tails, and Dead Rabbits gangs operated, their leaders being some of the most notorious gangsters in New York. This gang participated in the death-dealing New York City draft riots in 1863 which claimed the lives of hundreds.

The Plug Uglies disappeared about 1900, its members amalgamated into the Five Points gang, the last important street gang in New York before the Prohibition gangsters took over.

PLUMMER, HENRY
Murderer, Robber • (? -1864)

Plummer headed one of the most vicious gangs of outlaws and murderers in the early Washington Territory. The area in which he and his men operated, the town of Bannock being their headquarters, later became the Idaho Territory and then part of Montana.

Nevada City, California, was the scene of Plummer's first criminal escapades in the late 1850s. The killing of a man married to the woman he was wooing was laid at Plummer's door, and he was found guilty of the murder. Plummer, a man of imposing appearance and considerable charm, had, however, important political contacts, and through these he wangled a pardon from the governor of California.

No sooner was he freed than Plummer joined a gang of bandits and robbed a stage. One man was killed in the robbery, and Plummer was again arrested for murder. There would be no pardon this time, which the outlaw knew, and he soon arranged an escape. After breaking out of the Nevada City jail with the help of friends, Plummer rode into the goldfields of Washington Territory.

He established headquarters in Lewiston, now in Idaho, and gathered about him the deadliest cutthroats and outlaws in the territory. Plummer acted out the role of a concerned citizen whenever a robbery was committed and donated sums of money to hire lawmen to patrol the community. Under this leader-of-the-community cover, Plummer directed his bandits in one theft after another. In 1861 one member of his gang was captured and a lynch mob formed in the middle of Lewiston's main street. The outlaw Charlie Forbes, was a quick-draw artist who wore his pistol scabbard in the middle of his gun belt and served as Plummer's right-hand man.

Upon seeing Forbes being led down the street to be hanged, Plummer raced to the front of the mob and held up his hands. He delivered an impassioned speech about fair play and "justice" for Forbes. "This man deserves an impartial trial," Plummer insisted.

A shopkeeper in the crowd shook his fist. "Not to hang this man is cowardice!" he yelled at Plummer.

Henry Plummer only stared at the man and then went on with his plea, which convinced the vigilantes to return Forbes to Lewiston's gimcrack jail, from which he easily escaped days later. The pesky shopkeeper was shot to death the following week by members of Plummer's gang at the outlaw leader's orders.

When the Lewiston area was sufficiently plundered, Henry Plummer and his most-trusted aides rode to Bannock, a boom town squatting among the thriving goldfields. Again Plummer played the role of upstanding citizen while organizing the outlaws in the territory into a small army, numbering at times close to two hundred men. Between directing his carefully planned robberies and murders, Plummer found enough time to work for his own election as sheriff of Bannock, which he won on May 24, 1863. He was not only the town's leading lawbreaker but the law itself.

Wholesale robberies, looting, and stickups followed Plummer's election. His men, absurdly dubbed "The Innocents," attacked stagecoaches almost daily, particularly those marked with an X in chalk, the symbol placed by Plummer's paid informants and spies who worked for the stage lines and knew in advance of the gold shipments each stage would be transporting. Plummer grew rich, and the residents of Bannock grew enraged. Their new sheriff, leaders of Bannock's vigilante committee concluded, was not only ineffective but had to be involved directly with the robberies.

Vigilantes then captured some of the outlaws in Plummer's employ, and they identified him as their leader. Plummer, Forbes, and two others were promptly arrested and lynched on January 10, 1864. Before the hanging, outlaw leader Plummer protested loudly, claiming innocence—"You wouldn't hang your own sheriff, would you?"

Plummer's question was answered with alacrity when one young man in the crowd dashed to the rope dangling from Bannock's odd-looking gallows (three heavy timbers resembling an inverted U) and trailing to a noose around the outlaw's neck, and gave it a violent yank. Others quickly joined the young man, and the vigilantes hauled Henry Plummer up into the air and death.

The irony of the execution was that Plummer had ordered the construction of the gallows before his election as sheriff to prove to the populace that he meant to deal severely with lawbreakers. Two dozen members of Plummer's gang were subsequently hanged from this makeshift gallows, a grim accolade to Plummer's false intent.

POOLE, WILLIAM
("BILL THE BUTCHER")
Murderer, Gangster • (? -1855)

As one of the leaders of the Bowery Boys—a gang of notorious thugs who operated illegal rackets and administered political drubbings in the Lower East Side of New York for seven decades, from 1830 to 1900 —Poole was a brawler and strong-arm slugger who took particular delight in bashing in the heads of any member of the Tammany political group.

Poole, along with such feared bruisers as Tom Hyer, once American heavyweight boxing champion, worked for and was paid handsomely by the Know-Nothing Party. By 1855 Poole headed a gang on New York's West Side, having close to two hundred professional criminals along Christopher Street under his command.

A former butcher, Poole was a six-foot-tall, 200-pound killer who had dispatched many foes with carving knives. On the night of February 24, 1855, Poole entered Stanwix Hall, a new and splendidly gilded bar in the hub of Manhattan's night life at Prince Street and Broadway, across from the old Metropolitan Hotel.

Moments after entering, Poole, in the company of Charley Shay and Charley Lozier, two of his minions, began to argue with three Tammany toughs—Lew Baker, Jim Turner, and Paudeen McLaughlin (whose nose had been bitten off in a to-the-death fight with Five Points gangsters).

McLaughlin threw a drink into Bill the Butcher's face and called him a "black-muzzled bastard." Turner threw off his coat and pulled a pistol, but his draw was so poor he shot himself in the elbow, whereupon he screamed horribly and fainted. Someone threw a drink into Turner's face. He revived and fired off a shot at Poole, who was advancing toward him, hitting the giant in the leg.

Lew Baker then drew a pistol and said: "I guess I'll take you anyhow," and fired twice. One shot hit Poole in the abdomen, the other went through his heart. The powerfully built man, though mortally wounded, got up from the floor, grabbed Baker, and hurled him against the bar, breaking his arm. Poole, in a daze, grabbed a carving knife from the free-lunch service area and shouted at the terrified Baker: "I'll cut out your heart!" He then collapsed as his assassins fled.

Fourteen days later, with his gang members at his bedside, Poole died. His endurance with a bullet in his heart was a source of wonder to the medical profession. At the last moment he jackknifed from his bed and shouted: "Goodbye, boys. I die a true American!"

Poole's death marked the first of the lavish gangster funerals in the United States. Because of his strong affiliation with the Know-Nothings, five thousand of his cronies and political associates marched behind his flower-bedecked hearse, and ten brass bands heralded his approach to Greenwood Cemetery in Brooklyn.

His killer, Baker, attempted to flee by boat to the Canary Islands, but a sloop was sent after him and he was arrested and returned for trial. After several involved legal and political battles, he was acquitted.

Poole, however, emerged triumphant in death. His last words inspired several melodramas in which he was pictured in the last act as a heroic martyr draped in The Stars and Stripes and shouting patriotically, "Goodbye, boys. I die a true American!"

"Bill the Butcher" Poole (on floor of Stanwix Hall saloon) receives a bullet in the heart from his murderer Lew Baker.

PRESCOTT, ABRAHAM
Murderer • (1816–1836)

On June 23, 1833, when Mrs. Sally Cochran refused to make love to Prescott, the enraged youth, then eighteen, picked up a stake and beat the woman to death with it. His long trial was a sensation. His defense argued that Abraham was a somnambulist (the first attempt at utilizing such a defense) and had killed Mrs. Cochran in his sleep! The suspicious jury and court refused to countenance such a plea (insanity was still widely considered to be variance of devil possession) and ordered Prescott hanged.

A large throng gathered at Pembroke, New Hampshire, not far from the scene of the killing, to witness Prescott's hanging. When the mob learned that the youth had received a temporary stay of execution, riots occurred, causing several injuries.

Prescott was moved to Hopkinton and was there hanged, on January 6, 1836, without pomp and ceremony.

PROBST, ANTOINE
Murderer • (? -1866)

Probst worked as a hired hand for Christopher Deering, a wealthy farmer whose estate was outside Philadelphia. Following several bouts of drunkenness, Probst was fired. He brooded over losing his job and then begged it back from the kindhearted Deering.

One spring night in 1866 Probst grabbed an axe and slaughtered the entire Deering family in their beds, including a female house guest and a hired boy, eight persons in all.

He was quickly apprehended and confessed the murders immediately. He was hanged, and as was the custom of the day, parts of his body were turned over to medical colleges for examination and study. Oddly enough, Probst's eyes were removed and carefully examined to prove that the retina of his eye retained the last image seen before death. The "experiment" was a failure.

PURRINTON, JAMES
Murderer • (? -1806)

Purrinton was a retired army captain who suddenly went berserk on the night of July 8, 1806, and slaughtered his entire family—his wife and seven children. He had been meditating and reading his Bible, which was allegedly found open to a passage by Ezekiel: "Slay utterly old and young, both maids and children."

The mass murderer then slit his own throat, thus saving Maine authorities the expense of a trial.

QUANTRILL, WILLIAM CLARKE
Murderer, Outlaw • (1837–1865)

**BACKGROUND: BORN IN CANAL DOVER, OHIO, 1837. MOVED TO
UTAH IN 1857 AND THEN TO KANSAS IN 1859. ORIGINAL OC-
CUPATION, TEACHER, DESCRIPTION: 5'9", BROWN EYES, BLACK
HAIR, SLENDER. ALIASES: CHARLES (OR CHARLEY) QUANTRILL,
CHARLES HART. RECORD: WANTED BY AUTHORITIES IN KANSAS
IN 1859 FOR HORSE STEALING AND MURDERING SEVERAL
PROSLAVERY FARMERS, ALSO NAMED AS A SLAVE STEALER;
JOINED CHEROKEE INDIANS AS A RENEGADE AND HELPED TO
ATTACK AND KILL REGULAR U.S. ARMY TROOPS AT WILSON'S
CREEK IN 1861; ORGANIZED GUERRILLA BAND TO FIGHT UNION
FORCES OSTENSIBLY UNDER CONFEDERATE BANNER IN DE-
CEMBER, 1861; BURNED AND LOOTED THE TOWN OF OLATHE,
KAN., 9/6/62; RAIDED LAWRENCE, KAN., 8/21/63 WITH 450 MEN
WHEREIN HE ORDERED THE MURDER OF MORE THAN 150 DE-
FENSELESS MEN AND BOYS, BURNED AND LOOTED THE TOWN;
LOOTED A WAGON TRAIN NEAR BAXTER SPRINGS, TEX., IN
OCTOBER, 1863; KILLED IN EARLY MAY, 1865, IN KENTUCKY IN
A FIGHT WITH UNION TROOPS.**

Quantrill left his quiet home in Ohio when he was
about twenty and journeyed west. His education
was better than most youths his age, and he sometimes taught Bible school. Life in rural Ohio, however, was

not for him. He longed for adventure and traveled as far as Utah in 1857, where he stole horses to earn a living. He moved back to Kansas two years later and, posing as an antislavery Jayhawker, raided several farms, claiming he wanted to free slaves. The slaves taken into his custody from such raids (along with considerable livestock) were resold to other slaveholders.

When the law appeared to be closing in on Quantrill, he retreated to the refuge of a schoolhouse, where he assumed the duties of a teacher. In December, 1860, Quantrill persuaded five young Quakers to raid the farm of Morgan Walker, located in Jackson County, Missouri, telling the ardent abolitionists that their goal was to free the slaves Morgan owned. His true aim was to resell the slaves at a good price elsewhere.

Hours before the raid, and for reasons never made clear, Quantrill informed slave owners of the impending raid. He then led the Quakers into an ambush which resulted in three of their number being killed. When the slaveholders surrounded Quantrill, he calmly leaned forward on his saddle and, as torches flickered, prosaically told his wary captors that he was from Maryland and was proslavery. He said that he had journeyed to California with an older brother who had been killed by Quakers; he himself had been left for dead. "I have spent my days trailing my brother's murderers," he lied, "and the three dead men you see before you were part of that band."

He was not only believed but became an immediate folk hero to the slave traders. His reputation was such that at the time the Civil War broke out, Quantrill had no trouble in enlisting several men to his pro-Confederate guerrilla banner. These included such arch-murderers as William "Bloody Bill" Anderson, George Todd, and Fletcher Taylor. Coleman Younger and Frank James also joined him. Jesse James, who was too young to enlist at the war's beginning, joined Quantrill's group in 1864.

Quantrill's aim was anything but serving the Confederacy. He busied himself during the war with murder, arson, and robbery, all performed under the guise of fighting for the South. With Todd, William Haller, and William H. Gregg as his lieutenants, Quantrill led his first bloody raid against Olathe, Kansas, which he burned to the ground

Civil War raider William Clarke Quantrill slaughtered 450 helpless men and boys at Lawrence, Kan., 8/21/63. (State Historical Society of Missouri)

after carting away gold, cash, and jewelry. A dozen un-armed men were shot to death at his command.

Elected captain by his men, Quantrill never officially existed as an officer in the Confederate Army, though he did journey to Richmond once to seek an appointment with President Jefferson Davis. Later, in 1864, when regular

313

Confederate officers in Texas challenged his authority, he produced a commission signed by President Davis.

With a band of 450 men, Quantrill set out for Lawrence, Kansas, in August, 1863. Lawrence was a peaceful farming community and the home of James Lane, the notorious Jayhawker and senator. Quantrill had encouraged his men to kill without mercy in this raid to teach Lane a lesson (ever the teacher) and promised his followers that the old Jayhawker would be returned to Missouri and publicly executed by being burned at the stake.

As Quantrill's men moved through Kansas, they ordered residents at gunpoint to lead them through unknown territory and around Union Army camps. These guides were summarily killed once they had performed such duties. The raiders reached Lawrence on August 21, 1863.

Swooping into town, Quantrill and his men found no garrison to oppose them. They searched frantically for Lane, but he had heard their rebel yell and had escaped by running in his nightshirt into a cornfield, where he hid during the massacre.

Men such as Bill Anderson and John McCorkle were particularly bloodthirsty, seeking revenge for the deaths of their sisters. The sisters of both men, along with dozens of other wives, mothers, and daughters of Confederate sympathizers, had been rounded up by Union General Thomas C. Ewing and confined in a three-story building in Kansas City weeks earlier. The top floor, where the women were imprisoned, collapsed, and many of the women were crushed to death, among them Matilda Anderson and Christie McCorkle Kerr.

These and other grievances, real or imagined, spurred Quantrill and his men to mass slaughter. More than 150 men and boys were rounded up in Lawrence. Their hands were tied behind their backs, and then their wives and daughters were made to watch as they were shot to death. The killing went on for two hours and became the worst massacre of the Civil War. William Clarke Quantrill rode among the bodies of the slain, ordering men to shoot those who appeared to be still alive. He then ordered the burning and looting of the town. Several hours later, his band of men, half-drunk in Lawrence's saloons (these were not put to the torch), received word that Union troops were approaching. Quantrill and his guerrillas rode hurriedly from the smoldering ruins, leaving only one man behind. He was hopelessly drunk and was promptly lynched by the enraged citizenry once the raiders were out of sight.

Lawrence proved to be Quantrill's high point. From Kansas he rode to Texas, where he attacked several defenseless wagon trains and murdered dozens of travelers, robbing them of their goods. He became anathema to the Confederacy and was shunned by regular Southern officers. With a slowly diminishing band of men, he first made his way back to Missouri for a few skirmishes with Union troops and then moved to Kentucky with a band of about twenty men. Quantrill's plan was to surrender to Union troops there. Knowing the war was coming to an end, he intended to pass himself and his men off as regular Confederate troops, receive a legal pardon, and avoid the certainty of hanging if he capitulated in Missouri or Kansas.

The plan failed. Union troops under the command of Captain Edward Terrill intercepted Quantrill and his men and destroyed them in early May, 1865. William Clarke Quantrill was found dead on the field with a bullet in his back, shot while running away.

[ALSO SEE "Bloody Bill" Anderson, Jesse James.]

RAYNOR, WILLIAM P.
Gunfighter • (? -1885)

E l Paso, in its wildest days, was the scene of more
than one mass shoot-out. In the spring of 1885 two
gunfighters met their death there over imagined insults and through unprofessional carelessness. Famed lawman Wyatt Earp was a witness to the whole affair without
ever drawing a pistol.

Bill Raynor, called "the best-dressed bad man in Texas,"
was spoiling for a fight on the night of April 14, 1885,
as he sat playing faro in the notorious Gem Saloon, site
of dozens of gunfights and killings.

Faro dealer Bob Cahill made an odd movement with
his hands to which Raynor called attention, stating that
Cahill was "a bit too fancy." Cahill said nothing, obviously
frightened of the older man, who had been involved in
several shootings and was known as a fast-draw artist.
Raynor pushed away from the table and joined his friend
Charlie "Buck" Linn. Both men had been law-enforcement
officers at one time or another—Raynor had been an El
Paso constable and Linn was presently a city jailer who

was thought to be "crazy" when drunk. The two proceeded to get drunk.

Wyatt Earp, who was visiting a friend in the town, was standing at the bar, quietly drinking. Raynor moved toward him and mildly insulted the lawman. Earp looked at Raynor and said: "I'm not armed." The marshal brushed back his long coat to reveal no pistol at his side. Earp pointed out that he wanted no part of a man who was obviously "glory-hunting."

Raynor then turned his attention to "Cowboy" Bob Rennick, who was playing faro with Cahill. Raynor made several caustic remarks about Rennick's white cowboy hat. Rennick said nothing except to point out that he, too, was unarmed. With a snort of disgust, Raynor moved into the billiard room of the Gem Saloon. Rennick took several drinks and then growled, "I've been imposed upon enough and won't stand for it." He took a pistol from Cahill. Raynor, sitting in a position in the billiard room where he had a full view of Rennick's actions, came running into the saloon with his guns drawn. He fired five or six shots at Rennick, who calmly knelt down and shot twice. Both bullets hit Raynor, one in the shoulder and another in the stomach.

The gunfighter, moaning as he moved, staggered outside past the stoic Earp and managed to stumble aboard a passing horse-drawn streetcar. Collapsing on a seat, he shouted to the driver to tell his mother that he "died game." He was taken to a doctor.

Raynor's friend Linn, who had been drinking in another saloon, then raced into the Gem thinking Cahill had shot his drinking companion. The youthful faro dealer had been warned that Linn was on the prod for him. Before Linn burst through the Gem's swinging doors, Earp gave Cahill a quick lesson in gunfighting.

"He'll come shooting," Earp told him. "Have your gun cocked but don't pull until you're certain what you're shooting at. Aim for his belly, low. The gun'll throw up a bit, but if you hold it tight and wait until he's close enough, you can't miss. Keep cool and take your time."

Cahill had the drop on Linn when the latter burst into the saloon. The faro dealer asked Linn to drop his weapon, which he refused to do. Then both men began firing, until Linn fell to the floor with a bullet in his heart.

Gunfighter Bill Raynor, though mortally wounded, lingered near death for hours. Talk in the Gem Saloon had it that when he recovered, Raynor would kill Cahill and Rennick. Both men rode into Mexico to hide. A courageous drunk at the bar suddenly shouted, "Bill ought to have been killed years ago. I'm damned glad he got it." No one at the bar said a word. The drunk quickly sobered at the sound of his own words, placed his drink on the bar, and moved toward the door. He turned and thoughtfully remarked: "If Bill gets well, what I said don't go."

Raynor died an hour later, much to the relief of El Paso's citizens.

REAVIS, JAMES ADDISON
Swindler, Forger • (? -1908)

BACKGROUND: BORN IN RURAL GEORGIA, DATE UNKNOWN. MINOR PUBLIC EDUCATION. MARRIED "SOFIA LORETA MICAELA," CIRCA 1882; DIVORCED IN THE LATE 1900S. ORIGINAL OCCUPATION, STREETCAR CONDUCTOR. DESCRIPTION: TALL, SLENDER, BEARDED. ALIASES: BARON DE ARIZONAC, CABALLERO DE LOS COLORADOS. RECORD: FORGED PROPERTY TITLES IN ST. LOUIS IN THE LATE 1860S TO EARN COMMISSIONS; FROM 1868 TO 1870 FORGED DOCUMENTS, CHARTERS, AND LAND GRANTS ALLEGING THAT HUNDREDS OF MILES OF TERRITORY IN THE STATE OF ARIZONA WERE DEEDED TO ONE MIGUEL DE PERALTA, A HISTORICAL PERSONAGE OF HIS OWN INVENTION; POISONED DR. GEORGE WILLING IN PRESCOTT AND SUBSEQUENTLY LAID CLAIM TO THE "PERALTA LANDS"—10,800,000 ACRES IN ARIZONA WHICH HE STATED HE HAD PURCHASED FOR $30,000 FROM WILLING, WHO HAD PURCHASED THE RIGHTS OF THESE LANDS FROM A PERALTA DESCENDANT FOR $1,000; BEGAN TO COLLECT HUGE SUMS FROM RAILROADS AND MINING FIRMS INSIDE THE AREA OF HIS "BARONY"—SOME REPORTS FIXED AMOUNTS AS HIGH AS $300,000 ANNUALLY FOR A DEC-

Of all the swindles ever perpetrated in the United States, none was so painstakingly pieced together over such a long period of time as the one concocted by master forger James Addison Reavis. Where most swindlers are content to bilk money from their victims, Reavis laid claim, through delicately forged documents, to a tract of land half the size of the state of Wisconsin and for a decade exacted staggering tribute while frenzied experts and exasperated courts attempted to prove him a fraud. His swindle was in the grand design, and its success was achieved by sheer gall, superb acting, and obdurate patience.

Little is known about Reavis' background. He first appeared on the muster rolls of the Confederate Army during the Civil War, a lowly private with good manners and a penchant for escaping duty. It was at this time that Reavis discovered his ability to forge signatures. He carefully copied the signature of his commanding officer on a pass, and it was accepted by sentries guarding the post. Employing this peculiar talent regularly enabled Reavis to miss most of the war.

About a year after the war ended, Reavis was in St. Louis working as a streetcar conductor. Times were hard, but through his considerable skill as a salesman, Reavis managed to quit the horse-drawn trolley and open a small real-estate business. The few customers who did patronize broker Reavis were not particular how he settled their affairs.

One man stated that there was some question about his ownership of a considerable piece of property. He offered Reavis a hefty commission if he could manage to obtain a quitclaim on the land. The clever forger produced a document of ownership so authentic-looking that it was accepted in court and filed. Reavis got his commission and a new vocation in life. He went on to doctor records and create deeds so quickly that he aroused the suspicion of authorities. To avoid arrest, Reavis closed his handsome bank account and moved West.

A high liver, he was broke by the time he reached Santa Fe. There he applied for a clerical job in the records division of a special commission to handle Spanish and Mexican claims on lands annexed by the United States following the Mexican War. This country had agreed by treaty to honor all legitimate claims and turn back the proper lands to true owners. It was in Santa Fe that Reavis developed the most intricate swindle in American crime.

Essentially, Reavis began to forge ancient Mexican and Spanish documents, creating out of nothing a Spanish nobleman named Miguel de Peralta. In his unique clerical position he was privy to the types of documents and scrolls produced by monks and Spanish padres who had laboriously penned out lands grants, marriage certificates, and family histories of Spanish royalty hundreds of years in the past.

Reavis studied the delicate paper and parchment employed in such documentation. He experimented with inks and even whittled quills modeled after those used by royal Spanish historians.

Reavis' fictional Spanish don was related to King Ferdinand. The master forger's vivid imagination portrayed Peralta as a grandee of Spain, a knight heaped with regal honors and possessing an ancestry resplendent with princely titles, enormous wealth, and a very distant strain of the blood royal.

Obsessed with his intricate swindle, Reavis spent years manufacturing documents to prove the existence of the Peraltas; he also created whole families who had descended from the Peraltas. He then prepared the most significant documents involved in his stupendous swindle, those giving the descendants of Peralta a vast tract of land in Arizona, more than ten million acres, which had once been within the province of Spain.

About 1870 the myriad travels of James Addison Reavis become virtually impossible to trace, though it is known that he journeyed to Guadalajara, Mexico City, Lisbon, Madrid, and Seville. How he financed such expensive travel for a period of seven or eight years is unknown, but he did arrive in the ancient capitals of Europe, and there, quietly and stealthily, he lodged his forged documents concerning the Peralta family in archives, libraries, and monasteries where such state papers were zealously preserved and guarded.

Sometime in the late 1870s, Reavis appeared in Prescott, Arizona. There he met and most likely murdered a Dr. George Willing by giving him poison. Willing was another unwitting accomplice to Reavis' grand scheme. Reavis would later claim that Willing, for a mere $1,000, had purchased rights to a vast section of land from Miguel Peralta (whose history was also linked to the original Peraltas by fake documents), a direct descendant of the Spanish nobleman. Reavis then bought the rights to the grant from Willing and his heirs for approximately $30,000. He had the forged documents, of course, to prove it.

In 1881 Reavis filed his claim with the Surveyor General of the United States. His petition was backed up with certified copies of his falsified documents. He then appeared in Phoenix, which was within his claimed realm—as were the cities of Tempe, Silver King, Pinal, Florence, Globe, and Casa Grande—posting notices and demanding taxes and tribute of those living on his land. He also sent word to the powerful Southern Pacific Railroad and the equally commanding Silver King Mine that his rights had been trespassed and that his gold and silver had been mined illegally.

The best legal minds in the country went to work on Reavis' carefully manufactured documents and, after minute inspection, woefully conceded that the "Red Baron Arizona," as Reavis came to be called, was the real owner of the finest lands in the state.

Reavis' ten years of acicular forgery and secret travels finally paid off. The Southern Pacific gave him $50,000 as a down payment for the right of way along its rail lines; the Silver King Mine paid him $25,000 to continue mining Reavis-owned ore. Thousands of Arizona settlers, ranchers, and businessmen were thrown into a frenzy. Reavis levied claims against their lands and properties, and they were forced to pay.

James Addison Reavis became wealthy overnight, his

barony in Arizona yielding hundreds of thousands of dollars each month. Worried that the government would send experts throughout the world to analyze the specious documents he had planted, Reavis found a Mexican waif, sent her to a finishing school, dressed her in jewels and finery, and passed her off as a direct Peralta descendant. He then married his ward and moved into a luxurious hotel in New York, collecting his fabulous rentals all the while.

The marriage produced two sons, twins, who were always attired in princely fashion and escorted by a host of servants wherever they went. And the Reavis family went far and wide, traveling, as would royalty, to Europe where the king of Spain greeted them like long-lost relatives.

For ten volatile years, the Reavis claim withstood all manner of challenges by experts. In 1891, however, Spanish historian and linguist Mallet Prevost followed the trail Reavis had made ten years before and meticulously examined the documents he had planted in monasteries and state libraries. Using special chemicals and a microscope, Prevost found that the first few pages of each document granting lands to the Peraltas were genuine but that succeeding pages were made of parchment much more modern than the documents claimed to be. There was a noticeable difference in ink, too. The genuine script employed by the monks of Spain was written in iron ink, and the doctoring of certain phrases, wherever the name Peralta was mentioned, was penned in dogwood ink.

Reavis was hauled into the Land Grant Court in Santa Fe and exposed as a fraud. He was indicted and tried in 1895 and sentenced to six years in the state penitentiary. Released in 1901, he was a pauper. He had spent his fortune lavishly for a decade, boldly thinking his swindle would never be revealed. His wife had divorced him and gone to live in Denver with her sons, where she disappeared.

Penniless and addle-brained, Reavis spent his remaining years haunting the streets of Santa Fe. A stoop-shouldered man in a threadbare suit, he spent most of his hours reading about his own exploits during his heyday. He was found dead in his shack in 1908.

RED SASH GANG

During the range war between cattlemen and home-steaders, from 1887 to 1892, the Red Sash Gang (so named because of the red sashes they wore) became the most notorious band of rustlers and killers in Wyoming's Powder River territory. The gang was headed at times by gunslinger Frank M. Canton and Major Frank Wolcott. Members preyed on settlers and accounted for a number of murders, the most infamous being the shooting of Nathan Champion and his foreman Nick Rae at the Champion Ranch on April 8, 1892.

Champion and Rae, after barricading themselves in their ranch house, were shot to death by a large party under the command of Wolcott. The house was put to the torch and the two men fled. A gunslinger known as The Texas

Gunfighter Frank M. Canton, Red Sash Gang member, was driven half mad with the terrors of the Johnson County, Wyo. range war of 1887-92. (Western History Collection, U. of Okla. Library)

Kid killed Rae, and Champion was shot down in cold blood by other killers in the raiding party.

The war became so bloody that it reduced the hardened Frank Canton to a nervous wreck. He had nightmares of killings and gunfights and found it impossible to sleep, often leaping from his hotel bed and screaming so loud that he awakened boarders with: "Can't you hear them, boys? . . . Get to your horses! . . . Get to your guns!"

The U.S. Army arbitrated the dispute under martial law in 1892, until the Johnson County war ended and the Red Sash gang disappeared.

RENO BROTHERS

BACKGROUND: BORN AND RAISED IN INDIANA. MINOR PUBLIC EDUCATION. FOUGHT IN THE UNION ARMY DURING THE CIVIL WAR. THE BROTHERS WERE CLINTON, FRANK, JOHN, SIMON, AND WILLIAM. ORIGINAL OCCUPATIONS, FARMERS. DESCRIPTION: ALL TALL AND SWARTHY. ALIASES: TRICK RENO (FRANK RENO), WILK RENO (WILLIAM RENO). RECORD: ORGANIZED CRIMINAL BANDS IN SOUTHERN INDIANA INTO ONE UNIT FOLLOWING THE CIVIL WAR, PREYING UPON FARMERS AND SMALL TOWNS, MURDERING SEVERAL PEOPLE; ROBBED WITH SEVERAL BANDITS THE OHIO AND MISSISSIPPI RAILROAD AT SEYMOUR, IND., 10/6/1866, THE FIRST TRAIN ROBBERY IN THE HISTORY OF THE U.S. ($10,000); ROBBED THE FOLLOWING YEAR THE DAVIESS COUNTY TREASURY IN MISSOURI ($22,000); JOHN RENO CAPTURED SHORTLY THEREAFTER BY PINKERTON DETECTIVES AND SENTENCED TO TWO YEARS IN JAIL; ROBBED THE HARRISON COUNTY BANK IN MAGNOLIA, IOWA, IN 1868 ($14,000); ROBBED THE JEFFERSON, MISSOURI, AND INDIANAPOLIS RAILROAD 5/22/68, WOUNDING AN ENGINEER WHO DIED OF INJURIES RECEIVED IN THIS HOLDUP ON 12/7/68 ($96,000 IN CASH, GOLD, AND GOVERNMENT BONDS); WILLIAM, FRANK, AND SIMON RENO AND CHARLES ANDERSON, A MEMBER OF THE GANG, LYNCHED BY VIGILANTES AT THE NEW ALBANY COUNTY JAIL IN SEYMOUR, IND., 12/11/68.

The Renos, as far as Western outlaws go, didn't last long. They robbed and murdered throughout southern Indiana with sorties into Iowa and Missouri for little better than two years, yet their single strike against the Ohio and Mississippi Railroad on October 6, 1866, marked them for distinction in criminal history. It was the first train robbery in America, an act popularly and mistakenly attributed to Jesse James.

On that night, the brothers and several others in their recently organized band waited for the fast express outside Seymour, Indiana. When the train slowed for a curve, Frank and John Reno flagged it down. A startled messenger was made to open the Adams Express car, and the robbers hauled away $10,000 in gold and cash. William Reno labored for close to an hour to open the safe, but it was too sturdy for him and he gave up only after cursing, kicking, and emptying his pistol at it.

In the spring of 1867 the brothers rode into Daviess, Missouri, and robbed the county bank of $22,000. Jesse and Frank James would relieve the same bank of considerably less money years later. The Renos then rode home to Indiana with the Pinkertons hot on their trail. The detective agency had been hired to protect Adams Express car shipments.

The brothers weren't hard to find. They operated openly around Seymour and brazenly made the train station their meeting place. There, while the outlaws were gathering one day to plan another strike, Allan Pinkerton and six men swooped down on them and captured John Reno. It was more of a kidnapping; Pinkerton did not wish to take on the entire clan at the time and tricked Reno into getting aboard a departing train before the gang became alerted. The outlaws blinked in surprise and stood empty-handed as the train pulled out of the station with one of their chieftains under arrest.

Incensed, Frank Reno loaded his men onto another train and ordered the engineer to run down the flyer. A frantic chase ensued, but the outlaw train was diverted onto another track at Quincy, Illinois, and Pinkerton successfully delivered Reno to authorities. He was sent to jail for two years.

The loss of one brother did not deter the gang, who

struck again in 1868, robbing the Harrison Bank in Magnolia, Iowa, of $14,000. Pinkerton again pursued them and, with a large posse, surrounded them in their Council Bluffs, Iowa, camp. The bandits were packed into a small jail but escaped *en masse* on April 1, 1868. One rather capricious member of the gang had painted on the side of the jail before departing the galling words: "APRIL FOOL."

At least two dozen men reportedly participated in the Reno-led raid against the Jefferson, Missouri, and Indianapolis Railroad flyer that was stopped on the night of May 22, 1868, outside Marshfield, Indiana, where a guard was wounded fatally when the outlaws forced the express car door. The amount stolen from the express car was a staggering $96,000 in gold, cash, and government bonds, one of the largest amounts ever taken in a train holdup, far surpassing anything ever stolen by the James gang.

Frank Reno, the acknowledged leader of the gang, was an elementary robber. He reasoned that the previous successes enjoyed by the band in robbing trains around Seymour would continue indefinitely. Pinkerton detectives, who had studied the gang's predictable moves for some time, were of the same mind. They spread the report that $100,000 in gold would be shipped through Seymour. When the outlaws stopped the train and threw open the express car doors, a well-armed posse opened up on them, wounding several men. The bandits fled with the detectives in close pursuit.

Simon and William Reno were taken quickly. Pinkerton operatives tracked Frank Reno and four of his men—Michael Rogers, Miles Ogle, Charles Spencer, and Albert Perkins—to Canada, where they were arrested and returned to Indiana for trial.

Housed in the New Albany County Jail, the Reno brothers and one of their lieutenants, Charlie Anderson, never saw the inside of a courtroom. Vigilantes, angered over the two years of terror and killing the brothers had conducted throughout the area, broke into the jail on the night of December 11, 1868. Sheriff Fullenlove was wounded as he attempted to protect his prisoners.

At gunpoint, two deputies turned over the keys to the cells, and one by one, the Renos were dragged out and hanged from a second-story tier. Frank Reno prayed and

Frank Reno and his brothers committed the first train robbery in American history. He was later hanged by vigilantes. (Pinkerton, Inc.)

begged. He was hanged from the tier and died immediately of a broken neck as his body was hurled over the railing. William Reno reminded the vigilantes that his father's ghost would haunt them. He, too, was hanged and died in seconds.

When Simon Reno's turn came, he put up a bone-crushing fight, swinging as a bludgeon an iron sink he had torn from the wall of his cell in desperation. He knocked several vigilantes senseless, and then, his arms weary, he dropped his makeshift club. He was hanged while cursing his executioners. Charlie Anderson, without a whimper of protest, joined the three swaying corpses moments later.

Seconds after the vigilantes departed, Simon Reno, hanging by his neck, suddenly revived. While prisoners screamed for the wardens to help, he fought frantically with the rope that was slowly choking him to death. For a half hour Simon attempted to grab the rope and pull himself upward overhand, but the feat required superhuman strength and, giant though he was, he had expended his energy in his fight with the vigilantes. The absence of the wounded Fullenlove and his deputies was never explained. They arrived in the cell block about an hour later, and by then Simon Reno, in full view of the prisoners, had slowly strangled to death.

The mass execution ended the gang's power around Seymour. The vigilante committee issued a warning to other outlaws who might be inspired to follow in the footsteps of the Reno brothers. The committee's proclamation read: "Having first lopped off the branches, and finally uprooted the tree of evil which was in our midst, in defiance of us and our laws, we beg to be allowed to rest here, and be not forced again to take the law into our own hands. We are very loth [sic] to shed blood again, and will not do so unless compelled in defense of our lives."

RICHARDSON, LEVI
Gunfighter • (1851-1879)

The gunfight between Levi Richardson and Cockeyed Frank Loving in Dodge City's Long Branch Saloon was one of passion-struck motives and reached comic proportions before its conclusion. The Wisconsin-born Richardson, who worked in Dodge as a freight handler, had a solid reputation as a feisty gunfighter, having dispatched several men who had mistaken his awkward gestures and clodlike manner for sluggishness and ineptitude with a six-gun. He was fast on the trigger.

Loving was a cool-headed, handsome young gambler of twenty-five who had no gunfights to his credit. The two men had known each other for years, and Richardson had played poker in games where Loving served as the dealer. Then they fell in love with the same girl.

In early March, 1879, Richardson passed Loving on the street. The two men argued about their dance-hall Delilah and Levi hit Loving across the face. Unarmed, Loving stalked off without a word. Richardson told a crony,

P. O. Beatty, that the next time he "would shoot the guts out of the cock-eyed son-of-a-bitch anyway."

Blood boiled over between the gunmen on the night of April 5, 1879. Richardson sauntered into the Long Branch at 9 p.m. with his .44 Remington pistol strapped to his side. Although Wyatt Earp, Bat Masterson, and other redoubtable lawmen who kept the peace in Dodge City had banned the wearing of all side arms north of the dividing line, the rule was ignored. Loving, after his first encounter with Richardson, had also gone armed at all times.

Ten feet separated the two as they stood at the bar sipping whiskey and watching each other in the mirror. Richardson mumbled some inaudible words from the corner of his mouth. Loving pushed away from the bar and faced his antagonist. "You damned son-of-a-bitch," Cockeyed Frank said. "If you have anything to say to me, say it to my face."

"I don't believe you will fight," Richardson replied and dropped his hand to his pistol.

"Try me and see," Loving gritted.

They moved away from the bar together, closing in until they were on opposite sides of a stove. Each man jerked out his pistol. For several seconds they dodged back and forth around the stove, neither firing and each man waiting for the other to be off-guard. Richardson then fired a shot which whizzed past Loving's head. The men were so close, according to one report, that "their pistols almost touched each other."

The experienced gunfighter, Richardson, then resorted to fanning his pistol—the sign of an amateur gunman —either in desperation or fear of Loving. After Richardson's fifth shot, Loving jumped on Richardson and emptied his pistol into him, hitting him in the chest. Richardson died almost immediately, and Loving was arrested.

After a brief hearing, the gambler was acquitted on the grounds of self-defense.

ROBINSON, PETER
Murderer • (1809-1841)

An impoverished farmer, Robinson could discover no way to redeem the mortgage on his home from businesslike Abraham Suydam, president of the Farmers' and Mechanics' Bank of New Brunswick, New Jersey. Being a simple-minded fellow, Robinson concluded that sheer brute force would solve his problem.

The farmer asked Suydam to his house and told him to bring the mortgage, implying that he intended to pay it off. As soon as the bank president arrived, Robinson clubbed him with a mallet and took the mortgage. He then dragged Suydam to his basement where he kept him tied up for three days. On the night of the third day, December 3, 1840, Robinson walked calmly to his cellar, dug a grave while Suydam watched, terrified, and threw the bank president into it. He stepped forward and bashed in his victim's skull with a shovel and then buried the body.

Friends discovered Robinson in possession of the mortgage days later and reported this curious fact to authorities, who knew full well that the farmer had no funds with which to retrieve this document. Robinson was arrested and quickly confessed to the murder (he was compelled to dig up the corpse himself).

Following a speedy trial, Robinson was hanged in New Brunswick on April 16, 1841. Bands played, families picnicked, and colorful bunting adorned the gallows.

ROMAINE, HENRY G.
Graverobber • (? - ?)

When wealthy New York department store owner Alexander T. Stewart died in 1876, leaving an estate of $30 million, great pains were made to protect his remains buried in the venerable churchyard of St. Mark's-in-the-Bouwerie. The Stewart family had been warned that the famous bank robber George Leonidas Leslie might attempt with his gang to dig up the remains of the merchant prince and hold them for ransom.

First, a guard was posted in the churchyard. For months the armed sentry marched back and forth on eerie night duty, but nothing happened. The guard was finally dismissed in early November, 1876. On the morning of November 17, 1876, the church's assistant sexton, Frank Parker, discovered that the marble slab covering the Stewart tomb had been turned over and that the remains of Alexander T. Stewart had been stolen.

In a day where the violation of graves was considered a mortal offense against God and man, the incident caused widespread publicity and public indignation. Stewart's heirs offered $25,000 as a reward for anyone who could recover the remains and capture the ghouls.

The following January, lawyers for the Stewarts received a letter signed by Henry G. Romaine, an obvious alias, stating that he and others in his grave-robbing gang possessed the Stewart bones and demanding a ransom of $200,000 for their return. After much haggling by mail and through intermediaries whispering at secret rendezvous along dark roads, Romaine and his gang accepted $20,000 as payment for the human artifacts.

Romaine and two others met a Stewart relative and turned over to him a sack of bones. As way of proof that the contents were truly the remains of Stewart, the masked Romaine displayed strips of velvet taken from Stewart's

An artist's conception of graverobber "Henry G. Romaine," ransoming the bones of millionaire Alexander T. Stewart in 1877.

coffin plus the silver handles from his specially built casket. The Stewart family took no chances with ghouls in the future, reburying the remains in the basement of the Garden City Cathedral on Long Island. An intricate alarm system of springs and bells was constructed and set up around the Stewart casket, lest anyone dare approach the expensive bones of Alexander T. Stewart in the future.

Romaine, whoever he was, went on to enjoy the fruits of his grim plunder, never being apprehended. Some historians identify him as Traveling Mike Grady, others as the bank robber Leslie.

RULOFF, EDWARD H.
Murderer, Burglar • (? -1871)

Ruloff was a man who prided himself on his cunning and glib ability to persuade others to his way of thinking. His background was extremely shadowy, but it is known that he lived for a while in Ithaca, New York, and that, sometime in 1846, he killed his wife and child, dropping their bodies into Lake Cayuga (they were never found).

Arrested for these murders, Ruloff smugly languished in jail knowing that the state had to produce a body to convict him of murder in the first degree. He was convicted of kidnapping his wife, but that was all. After serving ten years in prison, Ruloff was again tried for killing his child and convicted of murder. The court sentenced him to hang. He escaped before the execution could be carried out.

In his absence, a court of appeals reversed the death sentence, but by then, Ruloff, who had mastered several languages while in prison, began impersonating a professor, giving lectures at various colleges for large fees. The academic life bored Ruloff, so he enlisted the aid of two burglars and, for a decade, robbed stores and offices throughout New York. One August night in 1870 Ruloff was discovered in a Binghamton store by two clerks who slept there.

The surprised Ruloff turned his pistol on one of the clerks, Fred Mirick, and shot him dead; the trio of burglars ran from the premises and dove into the nearby Chenango River in an attempt to escape. Ruloff, an excellent swimmer, got away, but his accomplices drowned.

Days later, a man in rags begging for food was found wandering near the river. He was identified as Ruloff by the absence of the big toe on his left foot, the result of a previous accident. By the time of his apprehension, eight murders were attributed to Ruloff, who was promptly convicted of murdering the clerk Mirick and hanged. Physicians from Cornell University's medical college received permission to dissect the killer's brain, which was then compared with that of Daniel Webster's, an effort the great barrister would, no doubt, have found less than creative.

The murderer's skull remained on display at Cornell for many years; Ruloff had strangely returned to the place of his highest aspirations—college.

SAUL, NICHOLAS
Gangleader, Robber • (1833-1853)

Of the fifty gangs running wild through New York's troubled Fourth Ward in the 1850s, the Daybreak Boys were the most fearsome. It was compulsory for each member of the gang to commit at least one murder before being accepted as part of the mob. Leader Nicholas Saul, twenty, and his sidekick, William Howlett, only nineteen, had qualified many times over.

The Daybreak Boys gang got its name from the period of time when its members were most active, at dawn. They usually preyed upon the barges and sloops that were docked along the Hudson and East Rivers. Stealing cargo and cash from a captain's chest was but a prelude to killing the crew and scuttling the ship. Saul was ever conscious of future witnesses against him.

Skull cracking became a sport for this gang and soon the most desperate gangsters in New York joined its ranks—Slobbery Jim, Cow-legged Sam McCarthy, Sow Madden, Patsy the Barber. In the two years that Saul led the gang, its members committed at least forty murders and stole $200,000 in cash and goods.

Saul's fortunes ebbed on the night of August 25, 1852 when he, Howlett, and Bill Johnson invaded the brig *William Watson* anchored in the East River between Olive Street and James slip. While Johnson waited in a dinghy alongside the brig, Saul and Howlett climbed aboard, found the captain's chest, and were dragging it to the railing when a watchman, Charles Baxter, rushed them. Both Saul and Howlett drew their pistols and fired, killing Baxter with a bullet in the heart and one in the head.

A detective spotted the trio pulling to shore with their loot and called for aid. A squad of heavily armed policemen, twenty in all, rushed into Pete Williams' Slaughter House Inn where Saul, Howlett, and Williams had taken their spoils. It took almost three hours to arrest the gangleaders. When the cops entered the inn, two dozen Daybreak Boys engaged the police in a slugmatch, attempting to save their captain from capture.

Convicted of Baxter's murder, Saul and Howlett were hanged in the Tombs Courtyard on January 28, 1853. Before they were executed, two hundred of their fellow gangsters, as well as political big-wigs including Butcher Bill Poole and Tom Hyer, formed a line and passed the two men, already with ropes about their necks, enthusiastically shaking their hands and telling them what swell fellows they had been.

SCHILD, JOHN
Murderer • (? -1813)

A farmer in Reading, Berks County, Pa., Schild seemed obviously insane when, on August 12, 1812, he accused his wife of putting poison in his tea and, moments later, dashed to the barnyard where he wildly pursued chickens with an axe. Failing to catch any of the hurrying hens, the madman ran to his house and, wielding the axe, bashed in his father's skull and cut off his mother's head.

Schild then took to the house furniture with a vengeance, whopping it to pieces. He concluded his murderous tantrum by setting fire to his home. Naturally, his defense at his trial was that of insanity but this was thrown out and he was ordered to hang. Schild was executed January 20, 1813.

SHAEFFER, DANIEL
Murderer • (? -1832)

The only thing on handyman Shaeffer's mind was the voluptuous body of Mrs. Elizabeth Bowers, a well-to-do resident of Lancaster, Pa., whom he accosted in November, 1831. Entering the pretty young widow's home, Shaeffer extracted her promise not to resist him or scream out, but twice she asked him "not to kill" her.

Mrs. Bowers' statement obviously took hold in Shaeffer's mind and he suffocated her with a pillow after he had taken his pleasure. Neighbors finding the woman days later assumed she had merely died in her sleep and quietly buried her; Shaeffer escaped without suspicion. He could not, however, elude his conscience, and after listening to a moving sermon delivered from the gallows in Frederick, Md., where another murderer was to meet his fate, Shaeffer went to the local sheriff and confessed the killing of Mrs. Bowers.

The sheriff thought him drunk and threw him out of his office. Shaeffer persisted and his statement was finally and seriously written down. He was promptly tried, convicted, and hanged April 13, 1832.

SHERMAN, LYDIA
Murderer • (? -1879)

Mass poisoners Lucrezia Borgia and the Marchioness of Brinvilliers would have found it difficult indeed to match the sheer ruthlessness of America's Lydia Sherman, who admitted to killing at least eight persons. The true count was probably closer to an even dozen.

Lydia's first husband, Edward Struck, was dismissed from the New York City Police Department with a charge of cowardice. Struck took to drink and became violent when soused. Lydia's eighteen-year marriage with this man ended when she administered to him a fatal dose of arsenic in his soup. The poison seemed to solve her marital problems with such ease that Lydia decided to eliminate her responsibility to the four children she had borne. They were given lethal amounts of poison in their meals and died.

Authorities did not grow suspicious of the deaths since Lydia never made any insurance claims; her murdering was merely an expeditious way of canceling troublesome people—her family. The next to die was a man named Hurlburt, whom Lydia married after he promised her his estate following his death. His demise came fourteen months later.

A widower, Horatio Nelson Sherman from Derby, Conn., was her next victim. After marrying Sherman, a drunkard, Lydia grew to despise his two small children. She poisoned them to death. Then she poisoned Sherman.

With the death of Lydia's husband Sherman, doctors became suspicious and examined the body. The corpse contained heavy amounts of arsenic. Mrs. Sherman was arrested and broke down almost immediately, admitting the murders of two husbands (she stated that Hurlburt may have died because some arsenic "accidentally" got into his salad) and six children. In explaining why she murdered her first husband Struck, Lydia stated: "I gave him the arsenic because I was discouraged. I know now that that is not much of an excuse, but I felt so much trouble that I did not think about that." As far as Sherman, his two children and her own four offspring, Lydia simply reported that she felt that by giving them poison they "would be better off."

Convicted of second degree murder, Lydia Sherman, mass murderer, was given a life sentence and died in prison.

SHIRT TAILS GANG

An early New York gang, circa 1825, the Shirt Tails got their names from several sloppy members who habitually wore their shirts outside their pants. Basically sneak thieves and muggers, the Shirt Tails centered their activities around the Five Points section. In their battles with other gangs, the Shirt Tails generally sided with the more heavily-staffed Plug Uglies, Chichesters, and Dead Rabbits gangs. The Shirt Tails disappeared in the 1890s, making way for the last of New York's street-terror gangs, The Five Pointers.

SKAGGS, ELIJAH
Gambler, Con Man • (1810–1870)

Kentucky born, Skaggs mastered the art of card sharping before his twenty-first birthday. He could conceal cards on his person, make a pass, deal from the bottom of the deck and arrange card positions in the deck with such proficiency that even the most experienced gamblers of his time fell prey to his black art.

Nashville was Skaggs's first area of gambling activity. Here, he won enough money to attire himself in what became the almost traditional garb of professional gamblers. He was described by criminal historian John Morris thusly: "He appeared in Nashville, dressed in frock coat and pants of black broadcloth, a black silk vest, and patent leather boots, a white shirt with standing collar and around his neck was wound a white choker, while, resting on his cranium, was a black stovepipe hat, which completed his attire."

Elijah's game was faro and he schooled himself in every conceivable trick known to dealers. He studied dealers suspected of being dishonest and, if he could not detect them, would then take them aside and offer large amounts of money for their secrets; if they refused, he threatened to expose them. Skaggs began operating along the Mississippi, appearing in New Orleans and St. Louis. As his fortunes grew, enterprising Elijah added employed teams to work the riverboats, fleecing the gullible. He made an estimated $100,000 a month from his crooked faro games.

In 1847, Skaggs was a thriving millionaire but word about his crooked faro operations had spread—"the true character of his games leaked out, and a cry was raised against them throughout the country, till the name of Skaggs patent dealers, as they were termed, was a synonym for all sorts of frauds and dishonesty at the gaming table."

At thirty-seven, Elijah retired to a lavish plantation in Louisiana, but he lost his millions by banking too heavily in Confederate Bonds. When the South collapsed following the Civil War, Skaggs' fortunes went with it. He wandered through Texas for five years, dying a hopeless drunk in 1870.

SLADE, JOSEPH A. ("JACK")
Murderer, Gunfighter • (1824-1864)

BACKGROUND: BORN IN CARLYLE, ILL., IN 1824. NO PUBLIC EDUCATION. MARRIED, NO CHILDREN. SERVED IN THE U.S. ARMY DURING THE MEXICAN WAR, SEEING ACTION ON NUMEROUS OCCASIONS. ORIGINAL OCCUPATION, STAGECOACH LINE SUPERINTENDENT. DESCRIPTION: SHORT, HEAVYSET. ALIASES: NONE. RECORD: MURDERED JULES BENE (OR RENI) AT COLD SPRINGS, COLO., IN 1859; ARRESTED FOR SHOOTING UP THE U.S. ARMY POST AT FORT HALLECK, COLO., 1861, RELEASED; INDICTED BY A GRAND JURY ON A CHARGE OF ASSAULT WITH INTENT TO MURDER A FORT HALLECK RESIDENT, 1861; FLED TO VIRGINIA CITY, MONT., WHERE HE WAS HANGED BY VIGILANTES 3/10/64 FOLLOWING A WEEK-LONG SPREE OF "HURRAHING" THE TOWN WITH HIS PISTOL WHILE DRUNK. BURIED IN THE MORMON CEMETERY AT SALT LAKE CITY, UTAH, 7/20/64.

There was much of the Jekyll and Hyde in Joseph Slade, better known as Jack. When sober, he was the kindliest, most thoughtful of men. In his cups, Jack Slade was one of the most savage gunmen and killers the West had ever seen.

Born in the sleepy town of Carlyle, Ill., Slade moved away from home while still a youth and wandered the cowboy trails of the Southwest until joining the army during the Mexican War. He was hired by the Central Overland California and Pike's Peak Express Company in 1858 as a line superintendent.

Slade's position made him responsible for a long stretch of roadway the stage traveled, through Colorado. Company officials suspected that another superintendent, a French Canadian named Jules Bene, was stealing horses from the line and using the company offices at Julesburg, Colo. to shelter wanted criminals. The firm's general superintendent, Ben Ficklin, ordered Slade to investigate Bene's operation.

Julesburg was a hellish eyesore, a bloody blot on the map where a killing a day was usual even though the town

Gunfighter Jack Slade was one of the most feared men of the early West; he was hanged in Virginia City, Mont. by vigilantes, 3/10/1864. (Western History Collection, U. of Okla. Library)

never numbered more than 2,000 souls. Slade arrived full of business. He looked up an ex-overland employee, one Bene had fired, and found him to be extremely conscientious. Slade rehired the man and Bene, upon learning this, traced Slade down with shotgun in hand. Bene fired twice at close range into Jack Slade who thumped face first into the street. Three more blasts from Bene's shotgun tore into the fallen man.

"Bury him," was Bene's terse remark as he stood over Slade's body. The barbarous shooting, however, so incensed a crowd at the scene that several men turned on Bene, tied a rope about his neck, and prepared to hang him for murder. Ben Ficklin arrived and stopped the lynching. Amazingly, Jack Slade, shot five times, staggered to his feet still alive. Ficklin offered Bene his life if he promised to leave the state. Bene accepted and departed.

Inside of a year, Slade had fully recovered from his wounds and was back at work for the Overland Company. Then he received word that Bene had returned to the territory. Slade sent several cronies to locate him and Bene was shortly found at Slade's ranch near Cold Springs. It appeared that Bene was lying in ambush and waiting for Slade to appear so that he could kill him. The would-be bushwhacker was lashed to a post in front of Slade's home.

When Slade arrived, he stood before Bene and proceeded to take long pulls from a whiskey bottle. Between drinks, Slade used Bene for a target, shooting him in the legs and arms. "To hell with it," he finally said, and walked up to his victim, placed the barrel of his pistol in Bene's mouth and blew out the back of his head. Legend then has it that Jack Slade pulled out a knife and sliced off Bene's ears. Most reports state that Slade used one of these ears as a watch fob. The other he sold as a souvenir to have drinking money.

The bestial mutilation of Bene earned Jack Slade a neck-turning reputation, one that sent chills up the spines and, fortunately for Slade, down the hands of gunslingers who might otherwise have tried their luck with him. Whenever he entered a saloon, which was often, Slade would find a wide space at the bar. He reveled in the attention heaped upon him by greenhorns eager to look at his grisly watch fob.

Even the noted author Mark Twain found this tough, unfeeling killer fascinating. Twain, however, was fascinated by most gunmen and robbers; he once wrote that "some time ago I was making a purchase in a small town store in Missouri. A man walked in and, seeing me, came over with outstretched hand and said, 'You're Mark Twain, ain't you?'

"I nodded.

" 'Guess you and I are 'bout the greatest in our line,' he remarked. To this I couldn't nod, but I began to wonder as to what throne of greatness he held.

" 'What is your name?' I inquired.

" 'Jesse James,' he replied, gathering up his packages."

Of Jack Slade, Twain waxed fondly, following their meeting in 1861. Twain wrote that he discovered Slade to be "so friendly and so gentle-spoken that I warmed to him in spite of his awful history."

Slade's history degenerated further by the time his wife

Virginia had convinced him to move from Colorado to the rip-snorting town of Virginia City, Montana. There was little argument in moving on; Slade was on the run from an arrest warrant charging him with assault with intent to kill a Julesburg citizen.

At first, Slade tried his hand at running a small ranch outside of Virginia City, but his alcoholism increased and he soon became the cause of small riots, mass fights, and general bedlam.

A vigilante group, hardened by their harsh dealings with swarms of bandits who had raided their town, wanted no more trouble from Jack Slade. The tough gunman was ordered to leave Virginia City for good. He promised he would do exactly that, but made the mistake of stopping by a local saloon for a drink, which was followed by a bitter tonguelashing hurled against the bartender. Hands on his guns, Slade defied anyone to draw against him.

Several vigilantes rushed him, tied him up, and dragged him down the street. A rope was placed about his neck and then thrown over a sturdy beam holding a saloon sign. The tough killer realized his predicament and burst into great sobs. As the tears rolled down his bearded cheeks, Slade gasped, "My God! My God! Must I die like this? Oh, my poor wife!" A boy raced off to bring Virginia Slade to plead for the outlaw's life.

It was too late. The vigilantes were determined to make an example of this most feared of men. "Do your duty, boys!" someone in the crowd shouted and Slade was hanged. His body was taken to a local hotel and laid out. Slade's wife appeared and threw herself across the corpse. Weeping hysterically, Virginia Slade spat out insults to Slade's friends standing nearby. Why had they not, she demanded to know, shot her husband like a man rather than allow him to be hanged like an animal?

Days later, Mrs. Slade packed her husband's body in a tin coffin filled with raw alcohol to preserve the remains and set off for Slade's birthplace in Illinois where she intended the burial to be. The alcohol did not do its work; the body began to decompose and gave off a knockout odor by the time it reached Salt Lake City, Utah. Mrs. Slade buried the remains of her man in the Mormon

Cemetery there on July 20, 1864, a peaceful spot for those who had fled religious oppression but a most unlikely resting place for the imbruted Jack Slade.

SMITH, JEFFERSON RANDOLPH ("SOAPY") Gambler • (1860-1898)

Times were hard for Jefferson Randolph Smith as a boy in Georgia. The South had lost the Civil War and was in the desperate Reconstruction period when young Smith decided to run away from home; he moved to San Antonio where he became a cowpuncher. In his wide-sweeping travels from Texas to the northern cities of Kansas and Missouri, Smith met the famous gunmen, gamblers, and cattle barons of the West.

In San Antonio, Smith was relieved of six month's pay by an old shell game expert, Clubfoot Hall. The man's prestidigitation so impressed Smith that he began to hang about with card sharps and con men, learning piecemeal their nefarious trades. He mastered the pea-in-the-shell routine and three card monte. He then teamed up with a bunco artist named Taylor. Their con game was simple but it worked on the naive settlers and cowboys in Colorado.

Taylor would set up a soap stand in a small town and shout out to the residents that several of the bars of soap he was selling contained a twenty dollar bill inside the wrapper. Smith would rush up to Taylor, buy a bar of soap and excitedly unwrap it, shouting to the startled citizens that he had struck it, waving a twenty dollar certificate aloft.

Smith, by the time he arrived in booming Leadville, had naturally acquired the nickname "Soapy" from his routine. He ran his own soap stand game so profitably that he was able to hire several shills to help him con the curious crowds.

Leadville was a wild and different world from even the roaring cattle towns of Kansas and Texas. Smith once held a race between two prostitutes who ran naked down the town's main street; the winner received a quart of bonded whiskey. The town's leading residents protested not. When Soapy had a man arrested as insane because he spent all day in prayer, the citizens roared appreciation.

In 1892, Soapy opened a saloon, the Orleans Club, in nearby Creede, Colorado, following the rush of miners to that pesthole where silver veins two feet wide had been discovered. The Orleans Club stayed open 24 hours a day and Soapy freed the suckers from every cent in their pockets. Every game in his establishment was rigged and crooked. This brought about a few gunfights from vituperative customers, but Soapy displayed his own truculence by shooting several.

When the silver veins ran out in Creede, Soapy moved on to the gold rush scene in Alaska, establishing another saloon. Jeff's Place, in teaming Skagway. This grubby, mud-filled town was the crossroads of the great Alaska Gold Rush. Gold-fevered miners passed through the little hell-hole on their way northward to the gold fields and straggled back through it with saddle bags laden with nuggets and gold ore. Soapy got them going both ways.

One of Smith's money-producing devices was a ramshackled cabin with a huge sign atop its roof which read: "Telegraph Office." He charged each person $5 to send a telegram to the U.S. The money rolled in from prospectors desperate to inform their families that they had arrived safe in the golden kingdom, had struck it rich, or had been broken by their own hardscrabble dream and needed grubstaking.

No one noticed that there wasn't a single wire stretching from Soapy's telegraph office and that the messages tapped out incoherently by one of his sharpers disappeared into air at the final tap of the key.

Those who became suspicious of Soapy's rigged card games, pea-in-the-shell trick, and tilted roulette wheel, hid their gold in their mattresses. It did them no good. Soapy's roaming toughs merely held them up. Those who protested too much were shot and killed. Soapy virtually owned Skagway. Though not officially or clerically endowed with the authority, Soapy took upon himself to marry and divorce the lonely miners from his shill-bound dance hall girls. He administered justice as a self-appointed marshal and handled court cases, also as a self-appointed judge, from behind the bar of his saloon.

As Skagway grew, its permanent residents yearned for relief from Soapy's baronial dictatorship. Religious leaders arose and condemned him. One Methodist minister went so far as to solicit money from Soapy to help rid Skagway of its corrupting influences. The wily gambler smiled and then stood up on his bar, handing down to the preacher $1,000 in cash and announcing loudly that he personally backed such a noble effort.

The minister, guarded by Soapy's men, made the rounds that day in Skagway, telling saloon owners and prospectors that Soapy Smith was behind his drive to clean up the town. By evening, the preacher sweated heavily as he toted three large grain sacks brimming with more than $36,000, the fruits of his collection. At this point, Smith's guards merely relieved the preacher of the money for "safe keeping."

Soapy roared long and loud that night. "Thirty-six for one is pretty good odds," he told his junior partner, Wilson Mizner.

The reign of Soapy Smith roared to an end in July, 1898. Three days after he led the town's Independence Day parade astride a resplendent white horse, a vigilante committee called the Committee of 101, tired of trying to persuade the gambler to reform, stormed his saloon, and shot him to pieces.

Soapy Smith was laid to rest with honors. Three shells and a pea were ceremoniously tossed into his open grave.

SMITH, RICHARD
Murderer • (? -1816)

Smith, a lieutenant in the regular U.S. Army who was stationed near Philadelphia, met the beautiful and vivacious Mrs. Ann Carson in 1812. Her husband, Captain John Carson, had been away for two years on missions against the Indians and was presumed dead. Following a brief courtship, Smith married Mrs. Carson. Four years later, on January 20, 1816, Carson staggered out of the wilderness and made for his home.

Banging loudly on the door of his house, he announced himself to a befuddled Smith, who refused him entry. A scuffle took place and Smith drew a revolver, sending a ball into Captain Carson's brain.

While Smith stood trial for the murder, Ann Carson Smith attempted to boldly kidnap the governor of Pennsylvania, Simon Snyder, and hold him until her husband was released. The plot failed and Smith was promptly convicted, his prosecution all but directed by Judge Rush. The hapless lieutenant was sentenced to death and was hanged on a Philadelphia scaffold, February 4, 1816.

His wife, Ann, became embittered against all forms of justice and turned to crime, establishing a counterfeiting ring. As a daughter of a naval officer and the wife of two army officers, Ann knew well how to command her brigands. Her cohorts—William Butler, Sarah Maland, Sarah Willis, and a Dr. Loring—operated successfully for close to six years, passing phony notes throughout Pennsylvania.

The gang was finally captured in June, 1823, for passing counterfeit notes on Girard's Bank in Philadelphia and on July 12, 1823, all received stiff prison sentences. Ann died writing her memoirs in the Philadelphia prison in 1838.

SOCCO THE BRACER
Gangster • (1844-1873)

Born Joseph Gayles, Socco the Bracer was the chief lieutenant of the New York Patsy Conroy Gang. Under the command of Socco the Bracer were such ruthless thugs as Scotchy Lavelle, Kid Shanahan, Pugsy Hurley, Benny Kane, Wreck Donovan, Piggy Noles, and Johnny Dobbs (Mike Kerrigan).

River pirates mostly, the gang operated in the early 1870s from the Corlears' Hook district and preyed on cargo ships docked in the East River. Socco the Bracer was reported to have killed at least twenty men and always went heavily armed into the streets.

On the night of May 29, 1873, Socco the Bracer and two of his cohorts, Billy Woods and Bum Mahoney, robbed the brig *Margaret*. They made such commotion in stealing the captain's sea chest that the ship's crew was alerted and shot at them as they rowed for shore. Two policemen patroling the river in a rowboat gave chase through the fog-bound waters.

As the thieves neared shore, Socco the Bracer lit a lantern to find his way and one of the policemen, Officer Musgrave, traded shots with him. Socco the Bracer was hit below the heart. His two companions rowed furiously for the middle of the river where they unceremoniously tossed their leader overboard, thinking him dead. The water revived the wounded Socco and he held on to the boat.

The pursuing policemen could hear the gangleader somewhere in the mists begging his men to pull him into the boat. Woods said, "Aw, give 'em one in the knuckles." Mahoney, however, pulled Socco into the rowboat where he promptly died. "Ah, hell, *now* he's dead," Mahoney said and they threw Socco the Bracer once again into the churling waters. His body floated ashore four days later.

SONTAG BROTHERS

George and John Sontag, owners of a quartz mine in California, traveled throughout Wisconsin and Minnesota in 1892, holding up trains. Returning to California, the brothers, along with Chris Evans, held up another train near Collis Station in Fresno, California in August, 1892.

Local police and Pinkertons tracked down the three men days later and a deputy was killed and several wounded when the outlaws attempted to shoot their way out of the trap. George Sontag was captured and sent to Folsom Prison for life.

After robbing several stages and terrorizing the residents of the San Joaquin Valley, John Sontag and Evans were surrounded at their hideout and a terrific gun battle ensued. Evans was captured but John Sontag was killed, pierced

California trainrobber John Sontag (front, center) lies dead at the feet of the posse which tracked him down and shot him full of holes. (Western History Collection, U. of Okla. Library)

by two dozen possemen's bullets. When George Sontag heard of his brother's death he staged a one-man riot in Folsom Prison and was shot while trying to escape over a wall. Evans was sent to jail for life.

SPOONER, BATHSHEBA
Murderer • (1746-1778)

Bathsheba was the daughter of General Timothy Ruggles, who had served in several campaigns under Lord Amherst. His vast estates in Massachusetts were taken over by the colonials at the advent of the Revolution after Ruggles declared himself for the king. Ruggles went into exile in Nova Scotia but Bathsheba, who had married a squire named Joshua Spooner in 1766, remained behind.

Ezra Ross, a young revolutionary soldier returning from a battle, stopped by Bathsheba's Brookfield, Mass. home asking to be fed. The attractive Mrs. Spooner not only fed him but bedded him and a romance between the two blossomed. The thought of murdering her wealthy husband then occurred to Bathsheba and she tried to convince Ross to perform the deed. The young man was squeamish and Bathsheba enlisted the aid of two passing British soldiers, James Buchanan and William Brooks, to help perform the killing.

The trio waited for Joshua Spooner outside of his home on the night of March 1, 1778 and cracked his skull as he stepped into his porchway. The three men then dragged Spooner's body to a nearby well and threw it in. They were not clever men. All three were found days later wearing Spooner's clothing and carrying his watch and silver buckles.

In the first capital case of American jurisdiction in Massachusetts, the three men and Bathsheba were convicted and sentenced to death. Mrs. Spooner begged for her life on the grounds that she was pregnant with child. A group of midwives called in by the court examined her and stated she was not about to have a baby.

Bathsheba, her lover Ross, Brooks, and Buchanan were hanged at Worcester, Mass., July 2, 1778. Mrs. Spooner's body was then inspected and doctors discovered the midwives had erred. The fetus Bathsheba carried was already close to five months old.

SPORTSMEN'S HALL

From about 1845, Kit Burns owned and operated this notorious dive in the Fourth Ward of New York City. A three-story frame building at 273 Water Street, Sportsmen's Hall featured a stinking pit on its first floor, where fights to the death were held between terriers and enormous gray rats.

The infamous killer, George Leese, a leader of the Slaughter House Gang, frequented Sportsmen's every night. Leese was known as "Snatchem" because of his adroitness in lifting wallets from customers in the dive. He was described as a "beastly, obscene ruffian, with bulging, bulbous, watery-blue eyes, bloated face and coarse swaggering gait." Leese would pick up pin money by attending boxers who had been cut and slashed in matches. He would suck the blood from their wounds, once considered medicinal, for the right stipend.

Another denizen of Sportsmen's was Jack the Rat. The

A daily scene in Kit Burns' Sportsmen's Hall where thieves and killers hovered about the popular Death Pit to witness two terriers destroy each other.

peculiar entertainment this obnoxious character offered customers consisted of gnawing the head from a mouse for a dime. For twenty-five cents he would chew off the head of a live rat.

The place had an odd bouncer, a giant woman known as Gallus Mag. She was English and well over six feet. Gallus Mag carried several daggers and pistols in a belt strapped around her skirt and stalked through the saloon eager to cripple or kill any troublesome customer. This odd creature specialized in biting off the ears of those who caused disturbances. The ears were kept pickled in a jar behind the bar as a warning to boastful drunks.

There wasn't a police officer in the district who would speak to Gallus Mag, let alone stop her from beating someone half to death on the street. They shuddered at the sight of her as she walked down the alleyways, heavy-booted and snapping exposed galluses (suspenders). Sportsmen's Hall served as a gathering place for the most devastating gangs in New York during the Nineteenth Century—the Daybreak Boys, Border Gang, Patsy Conroys, Shirt Tails, Hookers, Buckoos, Swamp Angels, and Slaughter Housers all met there.

Seven murders were committed inside the hall within

two months during 1845. Such hulking murderers as Slobbery Jim, Patsy the Barber, and One-Armed Charlie clodmarched their way through the dimly lit passageways and gambling rooms of the hall seeking likely victims to rob and kill.

Sportsmen's Hall was torn down in 1870 as part of a redevelopment program in the district and the gangsters moved off to the Five Points section to continue their criminal careers.

STARR, BELLE
Horse Thief, Fence • (1848-1889)

BACKGROUND: BORN 2/5/48 AS MYRA BELLE SHIRLEY IN A LOG CABIN NEAR CARTHAGE, MO. TO ELIZABETH AND JOHN SHIRLEY. ONE BROTHER KILLED IN THE BORDER WARS (1860) WHILE RIDING WITH REDLEGS UNDER THE COMMAND OF JIM LANE AT SARCOXIE, MO. MOVED WITH THE FAMILY AT AGE 16 TO SCYENE, TEX., NEAR DALLAS. GRADUATED CARTHAGE FEMALE ACADEMY (EIGHTH GRADE). MARRIED OUTLAW SAM STARR IN 1876. TWO CHILDREN, PEARL (BY OUTLAW COLE YOUNGER) AND EDWARD (BY BANKROBBER JIM REED). DESCRIPTION: 5'1", BLACK EYES, BLACK HAIR, SLENDER. ALIASES: UNKNOWN. RECORD: HARBORED FUGITIVE COLE YOUNGER IN 1866; WITH JIM REED TORTURED AND ROBBED A SETTLER IN CALIFORNIA NEAR THE NORTH CANADIAN RIVER, STEALING APPROXIMATELY $30,000 IN GOLD; HEADED A BAND OF HORSE AND CATTLE THIEVES IN OKLAHOMA FROM 1875 TO 1880; TRIED WITH HER HUSBAND SAM STARR BEFORE JUDGE ISAAC PARKER IN FORT SMITH, ARK. AS HORSE THIEVES IN 1883, CONVICTED AND SENTENCED TO SIX MONTHS IN JAIL; ARRESTED IN 1886 FOR HORSE STEALING, DISMISSED FOR LACK OF EVIDENCE; SHOT AND KILLED BY AN UNKNOWN BUSHWHACKER NEAR BRIARTOWN, OKLA., 2/3/89.

Of all the legends of the Old West, that of Belle Starr, bandit queen, was the most totally fabricated. Belle was ridiculously romanticized by the dime novelists of the day. To them she was a daring and noble woman endowed with beauteous charms who fulfilled the role of a female Robin Hood. It was all far from the truth. Belle Starr was a cheap, free-living horse thief with the morals of an alley cat.

Born Myra Belle Shirley, the future "bandit queen" lived a docile life in Carthage, Mo. until she was twelve, attending the Carthage Female Academy and finishing eighth grade. Her father was reportedly a judge at one time or other and stemmed from Southern aristocracy.

To avoid the violence of the border wars between Redlegs and Slaveholders, John Shirley moved his small family to Scyene, Tex., about ten miles from Dallas. Six years later, Belle met and fell in love with bankrobber Cole Younger, right-hand man to Jesse James.

Horse thief Belle Starr playing the role. (Oklahoma Historical Society)

Cole was on the run, having just robbed the Liberty bank in Missouri. Belle took him to a small cabin squatting on the Oklahoma Strip, a place she renamed Younger's Bend, where they hid. Months after Cole rode away to rejoin the James gang, Belle gave birth to a daughter, Pearl. It was generally acknowledged that the child was Younger's offspring.

Next Belle took up with bankrobber Jim Reed. In 1869, Belle, Reed, and two others rode to California and, hearing that a wealthy prospector living near the North Canadian River had a huge cache of gold hidden in his shack, attacked him one night and tortured him into telling them where his riches were secreted. The band rode off with about $30,000 in gold.

Supplied with new wealth, Belle returned to Texas and sported about Scyene in long velvet gowns, plumed hats and a leather girdle crammed with six guns. She bought an expensive race horse, Venus, and whipped it up and down the streets, her angular features grimly set; Belle was a truly ugly woman with razor thin lips, beady eyes, and a sliver of slicked down hair slapped to her forehead.

When Reed was killed in a gun fight in August of 1874, Belle began living with an Indian outlaw named Blue Duck, who appeared about 1876. At this time she organized a band of horse thieves and they regularly raided the ranches and small towns through the Oklahoma Strip.

Then Sam Starr, a Cherokee Indian gone bad, arrived at Younger's Bend and Belle married him. Belle and Sam Starr embarked upon a rampage of horse and cattle stealing unequalled in the history of Oklahoma. She and her husband were arrested in 1883 and given six months in jail. Upon their release, the Starrs resumed their brigandry. They were again arrested in 1886, but the "hanging judge" for Fort Smith, Judge Isaac Parker, released them for lack of evidence.

One of the deputies who had arrested the pair felt that their trial had been a farce and, in December, 1886, started an argument with Sam Starr in a local saloon which ended when both men drew their guns and shot each other to death.

Belle Starr's paramour days were not at an end, however. She found a new lover, a Creek Indian named Jim July.

Belle Starr, the so-called "Bandit Queen," sporting a small arsenal. (Western History Collection, U. of Okla. Library)

He was wanted for robbery but Belle convinced him to turn himself in since the law had little evidence with which to convict him. He agreed and, on February 3, 1889, the pair headed for Fort Smith. Belle rode half-way to the town and then turned around to ride back to her home at Younger's Bend.

Alone on the trail, Belle was shot from her horse by an unknown gunman lying in ambush. Some said he was one of the many lovers Belle had discarded. Hours later, a traveler found Belle and took her home. She died in her daughter's arms. Pearl Starr had an elegant monument erected over her mother's grave with the following poem inscribed at its base:

"Shed not for her the bitter tear,
Nor give the heart to vain regret,
'Tis but the casket that lies here,
The gem that fills it sparkles yet."

STOKES, EDWARD S. ("NED")
Murderer • (? -1880)

Stokes was a minor robber baron who hitched his wagon to Big Jim Fisk, stock manipulator and Jay Gould's erstwhile partner in bilking Cornelius Vanderbilt of the $19 million Erie Railroad. Handsome, cultured Ned Stokes first came into business contact with Fisk through stock manipulations concerned with oil. He profited enormously but was not content with merely sharing in the spoils of Fisk's schemes; he stole Big Jim's ravishing mistress, Helen Josephine "Josie" Mansfield.

Josie had long been "Jubilee Jim's" mistress and he had squandered untold tens of thousands of dollars on her; her jewelry collection was the toast of New York's high society. (Fisk's wife Lucy didn't seem to mind since she publicly proclaimed that she "owned the man.")

Fisk, pompous and jealous, reacted angrily at losing his mistress to Stokes (whom he had brought to dinner one night at Josie's plush home). He accused Stokes of embezzling oil stock funds which they jointly owned. Stokes countered with a suit charging slander. Josie, who felt she was losing a fortune by throwing over Fisk for Stokes, then entered the battle and charged Big Jim with alienation of affections. Fisk sued Stokes for blackmail.

Stokes, on trial, bristled at the insulting questions put to him by Fisk's lawyer while on the stand. He was still seething as he downed a gourmet meal at Delmonico's on January 6, 1872 where he received word that he had been found guilty of blackmailing Jim Fisk.

Possessed of a violent temper, Stokes rushed to the street and caught a hansom cab to his hotel. There he pocketed a Colt revolver and went to see Josie Mansfield. Where was Fisk, Stokes wanted to know. The enterprising mistress had kept careful watch on the multi-millionaire's movements and told her paramour that Fisk would be at the Broadway Central Hotel, meeting a friend from Boston who was arriving that afternoon.

Ned went to the hotel and secreted himself at the top of its magnificent, richly-carpeted stairway. Fisk arrived there promptly at 4 p.m. dressed in his usual flamboyant cape and top hat, carrying a gold-knobbed cane. As the robber baron began to ascend the stairway, he saw Stokes on the top landing, pointing a revolver down at him.

"Now I have you!" Stokes yelled out.

Fisk gasped: "For God's sake, will no one help me?"

Stokes fired twice. The first shot only wounded Fisk superficially in the arm. The second bullet was lodged deeply in Fisk's ample stomach. Doctors refused to operate for fear of killing the patient. "Prince Erie," as Fisk was sometimes called, died hours later.

Stokes, quickly apprehended, was given three trials. At the end of the second trial a jury found him guilty of murder and he was given the death sentence. His deft lawyers used a legal loophole to win him a third trial where the verdict was reduced to manslaughter; he was sentenced to six years in jail.

Josie Mansfield, who had begged for her lover's life on the witness stand, did not wait for him. When Stokes was released from Sing Sing, she had already disappeared. Stokes died two years later, a broken, lonely man.

Miss Mansfield journeyed to Paris where, for a brief time, she was the rage of the City of Light, lecturing the French on matters of the heart. She died in 1931 in a small Left Bank flat with pictures of both Fisk and Stokes above her bed.

STORMS, CHARLES
Gunfighter • (? –1881)

Charlie Storms was a professional gunfighter who hungered after a reputation that would put him in contention with such top gunslingers as Bat Masterson and Wild Bill Hickok. Storms was sitting at the card table in Carl Mann's Saloon on August 2, 1876 in Deadwood when the cross-eyed lush, Jack McCall, walked up behind Hickok and blew out his brains, a wild act prompted by nothing more than drunkenness. (Hickok was uncustomarily sitting with his back to the door and was killed holding aces and eights, forever after known as "The Dead Man's Hand.")

Storms immediately took one of Wild Bill's famous pearl-handled pistols, a handsome .45-caliber single-action Colt, and kept it at his side till the day of his death. According to most reports, the weapon served more as a jinx to Storms than an asset. After several gunfights in Deadwood, Storms moved to Tombstone, Ariz. There, on the night of February 21, 1881, Charlie went up against diminutive but deadly Luke Short.

Short was a professional gambler and was employed at the time as a faro dealer in the Oriental Saloon. Storms, who had never met Short, thought of him as an undersized gunman with an inflated reputation. Emboldened by whiskey, Storms argued with Short at the gambler's table and then foolishly slapped the little man. A moment before Short went for his gun, his friend Bat Masterson leaped between the two adversaries.

Masterson convinced Storms to go home and sleep. Storms mumbled an apology to Short and walked away.

An hour later Masterson and Short were standing in front of the Oriental when Storms appeared. He grabbed Short by the arm as if to swing him around and into the street, while pulling Hickok's famed pistol from his scabbard. Masterson later stated that Storms "was too slow, although he succeeded in getting his pistol out. Luke stuck the muzzle of his own pistol against Storms' heart and pulled the trigger. The bullet tore the heart asunder, and as he was falling, Luke shot him again. Storms was dead before he hit the ground."

Luke Short was acquitted of the killing by a local judge on grounds of self-defense.

STOUDENMIRE, DALLAS
Gunfighter • (1843–1882)

BACKGROUND: BORN AND RAISED IN TEXAS. MINOR PUBLIC EDUCATION. SERVED IN THE CONFEDERATE ARMY DURING THE CIVIL WAR. MARRIED ISABELLA SHERRINGTON, 2/20/82, NO CHILDREN. ORIGINAL OCCUPATION, MARSHAL. DESCRIPTION: 6'2", BROWN EYES, AUBURN HAIR, HEAVYSET. ALIASES: NONE. RECORD: AFTER A SHORT BUT DISTINGUISHED CAREER AS THE MARSHAL OF EL PASO, TEX., STOUDENMIRE WAS REPLACED

When El Paso, Tex. was at the zenith of its gun madness, Dallas Stoudenmire, one of the most feared gunmen in the Southwest, was made its new marshal, April 11, 1881. In the year of his reign, Stoudenmire was involved in several shootings from which he emerged victorious. The marshal was a silent type who, like Wild Bill Hickok and Wyatt Earp, shot first and talked later.

While serving as marshal, Stoudenmire developed a feud with the Manning brothers—Dr. George, Frank, and James—who owned interests in almost all of El Paso's riotous saloons and one of the largest cattle ranches in Texas.

Stoudenmire and his close friend and one-time deputy, Doc Cummings, repeatedly claimed that the Mannings had hired gunslingers to kill them. Six days after he was made marshal, Stoudenmire, who was patroling the town's streets with Cummings, was shot at by assassins hidden in the darkness. Though he charged his assailants with two blazing six-guns (the marshal wore his pistols tucked into his belt, refusing to use holsters as being too cumbersome), Stoudenmire failed to capture anyone and received a slight wound in the heel.

On and off for a year, alleged Manning gunmen took pot-shots at Stoudenmire until he left El Paso to get married to pretty Isabella Sherrington in Columbus. Upon his return, the marshal learned that his good friend Cummings had been shot and killed in the Coliseum Saloon owned and operated by the Mannings. The brothers had been freed following this killing, their action termed self-defense. Cummings had come gunning for them, they insisted, and they had fired out of necessity.

Stoudenmire brooded over the loss of Cummings and took to heavy drinking. He became loud and threatened the Mannings with death on several occasions. The Vigilance Committee which had hired Stoudenmire suddenly lost faith in El Paso's fearless marshal and asked him to

Lawman turned gunfighter Dallas Stoudenmire of El Paso, Tex. (Western History Collection, U. of Okla. Library)

resign. He did, but he continued to hang about the saloons, cursing and insulting the Mannings.

Thoroughly drunk on the night of September 18, 1882, Stoudenmire staggered into Doc Manning's saloon and began to argue heatedly with the proprietor. (The feud had intensified to the extent where Stoudenmire and the Mannings had actually signed a truce months before.)

In the middle of their shouting match, Stoudenmire and Manning reached for their pistols. A Manning henchman, Walter Jones, attempted to stop the ex-marshal but was shoved aside. Manning fired a shot that was stopped by a packet of letters in the gunfighter's left breast pocket.

Stoudenmire fired and wounded Manning in the arm. Doc dropped his pistol and dashed forward, locking himself around the big ex-lawman, attempting to prevent him from firing another shot. The two men grappled and fought their way out of the saloon. James Manning then arrived, gun in hand, and fired two shots, the second entering Stoudenmire's head, killing him.

Doc Manning, enraged, leaped upon the dead man, and, grabbing one of Stoudenmire's own pistols, beat at the corpse's head with the gun butt.

The Mannings were exonerated once again. A judge called it self-defense.

STOUT, MARION IRA
Murderer • (? -1858)

Sarah Stout was anything but a fickle woman. Her strange allegiance to her criminal father and brother, both serving time in prison for robbery, was unswerving. The beautiful woman caught the eye of a Rochester, N.Y. man, Charles W. Littles. He courted the moody Sarah.

Before accepting Littles's hand in marriage, Sarah told him, in a rare burst of honesty, the truth about her relatives. Littles was in love. Nothing she could say or do, he vowed, would prevent him from wedding her.

A few years later, when Sarah's brother, Marion Ira Stout, was released from jail, a conspiracy immediately took place. Sarah was bored with her easy-going husband, she told Marion. There was a simple solution to that, Marion told Sarah. On the night of December 19, 1857 the brother and sister entered Littles' bedroom and, as he struggled to get out of bed, beat his head in with a hammer.

Both were arrested, tried, and convicted of the murder. Sarah was sent to serve a long term in Sing Sing Prison. Marion avoided returning to jail; he was hanged at Rochester, N.Y., October 22, 1858.

STOUT, PETER
Murderer • (? -1803)

A youth living in Dover, New Jersey, Stout was mad as a hatter. Murderous thoughts entered his mind at the slightest insult. One local lad, fourteen-year-old Thomas Williams, had passed a mild criticism about his appearance. Stout did not immediately react but, days later, he saw Williams on the street and engaged him in conversation. As the two walked along, Stout suddenly produced an axe and sank it into the boy's skull, killing him instantly.

Throwing down the murder weapon, Stout leaned forward, reddened his hands with blood from his victim's wound and smeared the gore all over his body. He then waited for a constable to arrest him.

After a speedy trial, Stout was hanged at Monmouth Court House, N.J., May 13, 1803.

STRANG, JESSE
Murderer • (? –1827)

Strang deserted his wife and child sometime in 1825 and went to live in Albany, N.Y., residing on the Van Renselear estate under the name Joseph Orton. He went to work as a hired hand for a neighbor, John Whipple. Elsie Whipple, the squire's wife, had a long history of promiscuity.

Only days after he went to work on the Whipple estate, Elsie enticed the young man to bed. Then she began to encourage Jesse to murder her husband. First the conspirators decided to kill their victim by giving him doses of arsenic (Strang purchased large amounts of poison on three separate occasions), but abandoned this idea and ultimately thought up a quicker death for Whipple.

The lovers decided to shoot Whipple through the glass of a window as he was preparing to retire for the night. For months, Strang practiced such a shot with an expensive rifle Mrs. Whipple purchased for him. On the night of May 7, 1827, Strang fired accurately and killed the unsuspecting husband.

A stray bullet fired by a passing drunk was the excuse Mrs. Whipple and Strang gave to authorities in explaining the squire's death. Oddly enough, Strang was a member of the coroner's jury and voted with other members a verdict of murder by "persons unknown."

Mrs. Whipple and Strang, however, could not stay apart, and suspicion against them grew. They were arrested and the weak-willed Strang soon confessed the killing to the Rev. Mr. Lacey, Rector of St. Peter's Church of Albany.

The lovers fell out at their trials. After his own conviction, Strang attempted to testify at Mrs. Whipple's trial. He figured that if the woman was convicted, his chances for commutation would be aligned with her own. The judge trying Mrs. Whipple, however, refused to allow the young man to testify and Elise was acquitted of the murder.

Strang was executed on the gallows in Albany August 24, 1827. Mrs. Whipple lived out her life in seclusion on her murdered husband's estate.

STRAWHIM, SAMUEL
Gunfighter • (? -1869)

Sam Strawhim earned his reputation as a gunfighter and killer in Hays City, Kan. just after the Civil War. He was a vicious, rowdy drunk who shot first and then asked the name of his victim. Hays was a wide-open cowtown for a number of years but a Vigilance Committee soon hired Wild Bill Hickok to keep the peace and the shootings abated. Strawhim was ordered to leave town and, angered by the directive, proceeded, with Joseph Weiss, to beat up a vigilante named Alonzo Webster.

Webster grabbed his pistol and shot Weiss; Strawhim fled, going to Ellsworth. The outlaw returned to Hays on September 27, 1869, still brooding about his exile. He entered Bittle's Saloon with about eighteen cowboys, old friends, and the mob began to shoot up the place. Bittles sent for Hickok, who arrived in a jovial mood.

At first, Wild Bill tried to joke Strawhim out of any gunplay. The gunfighter and his friends were then in the street, having taken all the saloon's beer glasses with them. Hickok ignored Strawhim's threat: "I shall kill someone tonight just for luck." The marshal smilingly collected several beer glasses from the drunken cowboys and took them back to the saloon. Strawhim followed him.

As Hickok stood at the bar, staring into a mirror, Strawhim threatened to break every glass in the place. Wild

Bill's lips curled into an ugly snarl, "Do, and they will carry you out." Hickok, watching in the mirror, saw Strawhim step behind him and reach for his pistol. The marshal whirled about, gun already in hand, and shot Strawhim dead.

SWEARINGEN, GEORGE
Murderer • (? -1829)

Rachel Cunningham was the most beautiful harlot in Washington County, Md. and her amorous adventures were not unknown to the local sheriff, George Swearingen. The sheriff cautioned her on several occasions to quit the area, but his arguments soon softened into love.

Swearingen was wealthy and married but, after openly taking up with Miss Cunningham, he neglected his estate and his wife. Nothing his friends could say could convince the sheriff to give up his mad romance. In the summer of 1829, Swearingen decided to do away with his wife. He took her riding and on the Hagerstown Road, he later claimed, she fell from her mount and was killed.

Authorities grew suspicious and Swearingen fled with his mistress to New Orleans. They were arrested there and returned to Maryland. Though the evidence was flimsy, after a brief trial the sheriff was convicted and sentenced to death for the murder. He was hanged at Cumberland, Md., October 2, 1829.

TALBOTT, CHARLES E.
Murderer • (? -1881)

Charles Talbott and his brother Albert had plotted the death of their father for several months. The old man was a tyrant who beat his wife, sons, and hired man unmercifully and at whim. One evening, after the Talbott brothers had waited until their father was about to retire for the night, Charles shot him to death with a hunting rifle.

They were quickly tried, convicted, and hanged.

TENTH AVENUE GANG

A band of robbers, the Tenth Avenue Gang operated throughout Manhattan during the 1860s and were led by Ike Marsh. This gang reached great notoriety in 1868 when Marsh and others stopped an express train of the Hudson Railroad and, after tying and gagging the express car guard, escaped with $5,000 in cash and government bonds.

The gang was finally absorbed by the Hell's Kitchen Gang led by Dutch Heinrich in the 1870s.

THOMAS, HENRY
Murderer, Burglar • (? -1846)

B urglary was Thomas's business and he worked his trade effectively for a number of years in the Ohio River country. While robbing the store of Frederick Edwards in Bourneville, O., on November 20, 1844, Thomas and his accomplices were interrupted when the proprietor burst in on them. Thomas stabbed Edwards to death with a hunting knife. He was captured and held on suspicion of murder days later.

While in jail, Thomas talked too much to a fellow prisoner, who informed authorities that the burglar had admitted the killing to him. This evidence was used to convict Thomas of Edwards's murder and he was quickly executed.

THOMPSON, BEN
Gunfighter • (1842–1884)

BACKGROUND: BORN 11/11/42 IN NOTTINGLEY, YORKSHIRE, ENGLAND. IMMIGRATED WITH FAMILY TO TEXAS IN 1849. MINOR PUBLIC EDUCATION. SERVED IN THE SECOND TEXAS CAVALRY DURING THE CIVIL WAR, WOUNDED IN 1863. MARRIED CATHERINE MOORE, 1863, ONE SON. ORIGINAL OCCUPATION, SALOONKEEPER. DESCRIPTION: 5'7", BROWN EYES, BROWN HAIR, STOCKY. ALIASES: UNKNOWN. RECORD: INVOLVED IN A NUMBER OF GUNFIGHTS, ALLEGEDLY KILLING TEN MEN BEFORE LEAVING TEXAS IN 1870; SHOT AND WOUNDED HIS BROTHER-IN-LAW, JAMES MOORE, IN 1864; CONVICTED OF ASSAULT AND ATTEMPTED MURDER, SENTENCED TO PRISON FOR FOUR YEARS; RELEASED IN 1866; INVOLVED IN SEVERAL GUNFIGHTS IN ABILENE AND DODGE CITY, KAN., SEVERAL KILLINGS CREDITED TO HIM; MURDERED, ALONG WITH HIS FRIEND JOHN "KING" FISHER, BY JOE FOSTER, BILLY SIMMS AND A MAN NAMED COY IN THE VAUDEVILLE THEATER IN SAN ANTONIO, 3/11/84.

Guns were Ben Thompson's way of life. Not long after his family immigrated to Texas from England, Ben began to practice shooting with an old six-shooter. By the time he was into his teens, he was considered an expert shot in Austin, his home town. He was involved in several gunfights before he was twenty, when he joined the Confederate Army, riding with the Second Texas Cavalry. Thompson was wounded in 1863, returned to Austin, and married pretty Catherine Moore.

His bride's brother, James Moore, was a man with a mean disposition, used to knocking his sister about. One day Thompson arrived home to find his wife unconscious. Moore had knocked her down and upon seeing Ben approaching, ran across an open field to escape. Thompson grabbed his gun and took off after his brother-in-law, wounding him in the leg.

Arrested by military authorities then in control of Northern Texas, Thompson was tried and sent to prison for four years. He was released in two years. Ben Thompson then became a roving professional gambler and gunfighter. His ability with a gun was demonstrated in a minor shootout in the small town of Ogallalie, Kansas in 1869. Thompson, wearing a black frock coat and sporting two pistols, was playing cards in the Crystal Palace. A young man entered the saloon, stood at the bar and began twirling his guns.

"The fellow was making a spectacle of himself," wrote noted Oklahoma lawman Jim Herron years later, "twisting his gun around and spinning it and pointing it at various men along the bar. Now this was something that a man never did in Texas or Oklahoma unless he was asking for trouble. . . . Suddenly I heard a shot, and this gun-flashing fellow let out a squeal like a javelina. His gun flew out of his hand and went clattering off across the floor, and as he grasped his hand in pain I could see he was minus a perfectly good finger for a bullet had hit him in his gun hand."

Ben Thompson had gotten up from his card game and fired a single shot from the end of the bar. Then he walked closer, blowing smoke from the muzzle of his pistol. "I never want to see you do a thing like that again, hear?" Thompson told the terrified cowboy.

Later, Thompson told Herron that he had no intention of killing the showoff. "I just wanted to slow him down a bit before he got himself into real trouble."

By 1871, Thompson had moved on to Abilene, Kansas and built up a lucrative saloon business there. He had a number of gunfights with gunslingers in Abilene from which he emerged victorious. Otherwise, his luck was poor. When his wife and son arrived in Kansas City to join him, he took them for a ride. The buckboard hit a hole in the road and spilled over. His son's foot was broken and his wife's arm was smashed, which later caused it to be amputated. Thompson himself suffered a broken leg.

Ellsworth, Kansas, another cowboy helltown, beckoned Thompson next. He plied his gambling trade there and often backed other gamblers in high stake monte games. One of these was John Sterling, who on August 15, 1873 won more than $1,000 playing monte while using Thompson's bankroll.

Sterling proceeded to get drunk on the money, not bothering to pay Thompson. Hours later, Thompson cornered Sterling in Nick Lentz's saloon and demanded his spoils. Sterling slapped Thompson in the face and Ben went for his gun. Before he could fire, policeman John "Happy Jack" Morco stepped between the two men.

Morco, who was later described by a historian as "an illiterate, surly fellow," had come to Ellsworth from California where, it was said, he had killed twelve men in separate gun duels. Morco persuaded Thompson to leave the saloon and "cool off." Ben went to Brennan's Saloon and waited. Minutes later he looked up from the bar to see Morco at the door of the tavern. With him, grinning, was Sterling.

"C'mon outside, Ben," Sterling said.

Thompson noticed both men were holding shotguns. He turned, dashed out of Brennan's, and ran to another saloon owned by Jack New, where he had left his pistol and rifle. His homicidal brother, Billy, an habitual drunk, joined him there carrying Ben's English-made $150 shotgun. The brothers stepped into the street. Bill Thompson stumbled and discharged one barrel of the shotgun, almost shooting a cowboy in the foot.

Ben Thompson shouted to Sheriff Chauncey B. Whitney, Sterling, and Morco: "We're going down by the railroad. More room there. Bring out your men if you want to fight."

Whitney walked up to the brothers and convinced them to settle the whole matter over a friendly drink in Brennan's saloon. The Thompsons had no sooner entered the bar when Ben saw Morco advancing toward him with a drawn pistol. Ben got off a quick shot as Morco dashed outside. Bill Thompson and Sheriff Whitney also ran outside.

Thinking the sheriff had trapped them, Billy Thompson turned his shotgun in Whitney's direction.

"Don't shoot!" Whitney yelled.

Billy Thompson fired both barrels at him from close range. With a scream, Whitney crumpled in the street and Billy Thompson ran back into the saloon to face his enraged brother. "For God's sake," Ben told his brother, "leave town, you have shot Whitney, our best friend."

Lifting a shot of rye to his lips, Billy Thompson said he would have fired "if it had been Jesus Christ." He then fled town.

Ben Thompson stayed in the saloon. Several friendly fellow Texans joined him. Ellsworth's Mayor Jim Miller begged him to surrender his guns and give up to the law. He refused. Miller then went outside where he saw several members of the town police force loading shotguns, preparing to shoot it out with Thompson. Miller fired them on the spot and Thompson then surrendered. He was soon released, after explaining that his brother had shot Whitney. "He was drunk and didn't know what he was doing."

Whitney gallantly supported this claim on his deathbed hours later, stating to friends: "He did not intend to do it. It was an accident . . . send for my family." (Billy Thompson was tried for the killing in September, 1877, but was acquitted; the shooting was ruled an accident.)

The biographer of Wyatt Earp insists that this gunfight was highlighted by Earp's appearance after Mayor Miller had fired his police force. According to this version, Miller ordered his deputies Ed Crawford, Charlie Brown, and Marshal J. S. "Brocky Jack" Norton to close in on Ben Thompson, who was menacing people with his shotgun from the platform of the Kansas Pacific depot. "Arrest that man," Miller reportedly called to his men. They did not move. "You're fired," Miller shouted angrily.

At this moment, a tall, mustachioed young man stepped from a nearby barber shop and said to Miller, "Can't a fellow even get a shave in this town without gunplay?" He was Wyatt Earp, soon to become legend. Miller shrugged helplessly.

"It's none of my business," Earp allegedly told Miller, "but if it was me I'd get me a gun and arrest Ben Thompson or kill him."

"I'll make this your business," Miller replied and tore the badge from Sheriff Norton's shirt and pinned it on Earp. "Go into Beebe's and get some guns. I order you to arrest Ben Thompson." Earp then obtained two second-hand .45s and walked across the plaza toward Thompson.

Biographer Stuart N. Lake wrote later that the two men glared at each other and that the following conversation took place while Earp stalked his prey:

Gunfighter Ben Thompson, who served briefly as a city marshal in Austin, Tex., was shot to death in a theater. (Kansas State Historical Society, Topeka)

"I'd rather talk than fight," Thompson said.

"I'll get you either way, Ben," replied Earp, still walking forward.

"Wait a minute," Thompson shouted. "What do you want me to do?"

"Throw your shotgun in the road, put up your hands, and tell your friends to stay out of this play."

"Will you stop and let me talk to you?"

Earp stopped walking.

"What are you going to do with me?" Ben Thompson asked.

"Kill you or take you to jail."

"Brown's over there by the depot with a rifle. The minute I give up my guns he'll cut loose at me."

"If he does, I'll give you back your guns and we'll shoot it out with him. As long as you're my prisoner, the man that gets you will have to get me."

Thompson threw out his gun. "You win."

If Earp truly got involved in the Thompson-Sterling feud

in Ellsworth, his appearance and backing down of Thompson was one of the great dramatic scenes of the Old West. However, no records, newspaper accounts, or official testimony exists to support this story, other than the heady narrative penned by Lake.

In addition to leading the fearsome Ben Thompson meekly to jail, Earp, in Lake's version, backs down an entire mob of Texans, including such notorious gunslingers as Cad Pierce, Neil Kane, John Good, and George Peshaur, who were bent on releasing Thompson.

After many years in Abilene, Ellsworth, and Dodge City, Thompson tried his hand at law enforcement, becoming City Marshal in Austin, Texas. He kept the job briefly, quitting when he became bored.

Though he survived many a gunfight, Ben Thompson was to be killed in a most inglorious fashion—shot to death while sitting in a theater seat, watching a song-and-dance act. He was attending a show with his friend John King Fisher in San Antonio when three gunfighters—Joe Foster, Billy Simms, and an ex-policeman named Coy—walked in and shot both men to death on March 11, 1884.

THORN, MARTIN GEORGE
Murderer • (1868–1897)

Police were baffled in June of 1897 when hunks of a body began turning up in the rivers about Manhattan. First a torso with a tattoo of a naked woman on its chest appeared wrapped in oilcloth. Next a pair of legs was turned in to police. The identity of the dissected corpse was impossible to determine.

Quite by accident, a reporter for the *New York World* heard two rubbers in a Turkish bath complaining that Willie Guldensuppe, a fellow worker, had failed to show up for a week. Knowing of the chopped up body the police possessed, the reporter asked: "Was your pal Willie tattooed?"

"Sure," one of them replied. "There was a pretty girl on his chest." The reporter obtained Guldensuppe's address—439 Ninth Ave.—and hurried there. He discovered that Mrs. Augusta Nack, who had immigrated from Germany several years before, an unlicensed midwife, ran the boarding house where Guldensuppe had lived.

Immediately following the location of Willie's address, a reporter for the *New York Journal*—both the *Journal* and the *World* were locked in desperate competition for such grisly stories—found a hardware merchant in Queens who stated he had sold an oilcloth to a woman who looked like Mrs. Nack. Police whisked the landlady to the station.

A buxom, pleasant-faced woman, Mrs. Nack was unperturbed. Police thought to shock her into a confession by seating her in a chair and then abruptly thrusting Guldensuppe's badly decomposed legs under her nose. "Are those Willie's?" she was asked.

Mrs. Nack never batted an eyelash. "I would not know as I never saw the gentleman naked."

This, of course, was far from the truth. Mrs. Nack, neighbors testified, had taken Willie Guldensuppe as a lover years ago. About ten months before his slaying, however, they reported a new tenant, one Martin George Thorn, had moved into Mrs. Nack's rooming house and into Mrs. Nack's bed, substituting for Mr. Guldensuppe.

There were reports of how the two men argued and fought. Mrs. Nack suggested to both men that further consternation could easily be avoided. All three of them would share the same bed, she stated. Guldensuppe declined and began to date another girl. Mrs. Nack felt Willie was slighting her and demanded Thorn kill him. (Another story had it that Thorn wanted to kill Guldensuppe because Willie had beaten him up in a bloody fistfight.)

Thorn and Mrs. Nack rented a farm in Woodside, a suburb of Queens. Mrs. Nack told Willie she intended to practice her mid-wifery there and lured him to the "baby farm" under the pretext of getting his ideas about setting up such a clinic, though Guldensuppe's experience as a rubber in a Turkish bath hardly qualified him as expert in such matters. Flattered, Willie journeyed to the Woodside retreat.

"Look around, Willie. Check everything for me like a nice fellow, will you?" Mrs. Nack asked. Guldensuppe wandered about the place, casually opening closets and idiotically staring at cobwebs while rendering such critical comments as "that's nice," and "that'll do."

One of the closets contained a surprise—Martin George Thorn. When Guldensuppe opened the closet where he was hiding, Thorn leapt out with a pistol in one hand and a dagger in the other. He first shot the beefy Guldensuppe and then stabbed him repeatedly until he was sure Willie was dead. Mrs. Nack appeared and she and her lover dragged the corpse into the kitchen.

There, Thorn carefully removed the head and went about slicing up the body in manageable chunks while Mrs. Nack obtained an oilcloth in which to wrap them. There was no sewer system leading from the Woodside cottage pipes, a fact Thorn overlooked when he turned on the taps to repeatedly wash his hands of blood while he butchered Guldensuppe's body.

Though Thorn and Mrs. Nack were suspected, they were not arrested immediately, even with the hot gossip of their neighbors sizzling police ears. A Woodside farmer noticed days later that his pure white ducks had turned pink. Upon investigating, he was shocked to find that a drainage pool near Mrs. Nack's cottage had turned red with human blood. The police had their murder scene and they also found in the cottage a saw and butcher knife caked with flesh and blood.

Both Thorn and Mrs. Nack were arrested and brought to trial. A barber testified that Thorn had bragged to him how he had murdered poor Willie and then cut him to pieces. The next day, Mrs. Nack abruptly stood up and described in detail how Thorn butchered her ex-boyfriend after shooting and stabbing him. She was so explicit in her description of the crime that several female members of the jury fainted and a mistrial was declared.

In the second trial, Thorn took the stand and told how

MURDERER OF GULDENSUPPE, MARTIN THORN, WILL PAY THE PENALTY AND BE KILLED TO-DAY.

Killer Martin Thorn and his dominating lover, Mrs. Augusta Nack, made the front page of the **New York World** in 1897 after murdering Willie Guldensuppe; Thorn went to the chair, Mrs. Nack got ten years in prison. (N.Y. Historical Society)

Mrs. Nack burst into his room one day in June, 1897 and shouted: "Willie's upstairs! I just killed him!"

The jury was sympathetic to Mrs. Nack even though the press universally branded her the catalyst of the murder. She was sentenced to twenty years in jail. Thorn got the electric chair, dying a few months later. When they strapped Martin George Thorn into the electric chair, he commented: "I have no fear. I'm not afraid." Then, "I am positive God will forgive me."

Mrs. Nack served only ten years of her prison term. When she was released she returned to her old neighborhood and opened a delicatessen which few persons patronized. She vanished before the First World War.

TINKER, EDWARD
Murderer, Swindler • (? -1811)

A captain of a small cargo schooner, Tinker plotted to defraud the company insuring his vessel. Two of his crewmen, Durand and Potts, were in on the plan but a third member, known only as Edward, was not. After scuttling his ship off Roanoke Island, Tinker moved to Newbern, N.C., so he could be near Edward in an attempt to convince him to support his story about losing his ship.

The young seaman seemed reluctant to testify for Tinker so the captain, under the ruse of a duck-hunting trip, shot Edward in the back, weighed down his body with rocks, and threw him into the sea. The body, however, floated back into Newbern harbor and the captain was arrested.

Tinker immediately sent off a letter to his co-conspirator Durand, pleading with him to blame Potts for the loss of his ship and the murder of Edward. The worst that could happen, Tinker pointed out, if Durand was convicted of perjury, was that he could lose a piece of his ear, an early practice by the courts.

Durand was having none of Tinker's involved schemes and informed authorities. The captain was taken to Carteret, N.C., and was there convicted of Edward's murder. He was hanged in September, 1811.

TRAVELING MIKE GRADY GANG

A group of mobile sneak thieves who plied their nefarious trade throughout New York City about the time of the Civil War, this gang included mountebanks like Greedy Jake Rand, Boston Pete Anderson, Hod Ennis, Eddie Pettengill, and, naturally, Traveling Mike, an infamous fence whose traffic in stolen goods approached, at times, that of Marm Mandelbaum, queen of the fences.

The mob hit it lucky when they entered the offices of the eccentric and penurious financier Rufus L. Lord. Though he possessed a fortune of more than $4 million, Lord's hole-in-the-wall office afforded him light from only one window. He was a thorny investor in stocks and bonds and his financial acumen was the talk of Wall Street. Personally, his mien could best be described as dingy. Lord clothed himself in rotting rags and torn slippers. To conserve expenses, he refused to have more than one candle burning in his offices at the rear of 38 Exchange Place.

On March 7, 1866, Traveling Mike and his minions confronted Lord, who was alone at his desk. Grady spoke of taking out a loan in the grand manner of a moneyed man. He airily prattled that a loan at twenty per cent would not be unreasonable. At this, Lord leapt to his feet and with quaking hands clutched Grady's lapels, demanding that he close the deal at once.

While thus distracted, Lord failed to see Pettengill and Anderson slip behind him and go to his burglar-proof safe. It was open, which was not unusual for Lord. Growing feeble-minded, he often left the safe open when leaving at night. He kept millions of dollars in cash and negotiable bonds inside.

Pettengill and Anderson removed a large tin box from Lord's safe while its owner urgently attempted to foist a loan upon Grady. The thieves then left. The effervescent Grady stated that he would return within an hour and sign the papers for the loan.

Upon opening the tin box, the robbers discovered

1,900,000 in cash and securities, the largest theft ever engineered by sneak thieves in the U.S. Almost all the bonds were negotiable. Every member of the gang retired on the spot except Traveling Mike, who continued selling stolen goods for years, proving he was just as parsimonious as Lord. The financier never quite recovered from the shock of the theft and installed a steel door in his office, where he died years later among his dusty money bags.

TULLY, SAMUEL
Murderer, Pirate • (? -1812)

Sam Tully was a thorough blackguard who worked on board the schooner *George Washington* under the alias R. Heathcoate, being sought in England for the murder of his father.

On January 21, 1812, Tully and his messmate, John Dalton, seized control of the ship while the captain was ashore at Cape Verde. They sailed the small craft to the West Indies and sank it near St. Lucie, but not before killing a protesting crewman, one George Cummings.

Both Tully and Dalton were captured and sent to Boston for trial. Tully shouted in court that he was compelled to take over the schooner because the captain was usually drunk and his seamanship would surely cause the deaths of the crew in any kind of storm. His arguments against the charges of murder and piracy fell on deaf ears and both he and Dalton were sentenced to death on the gallows.

The gallows scene in South Boston on December 10, 1812 was bizarre. Venders hawked hot pastries beneath the scaffold as thousands gathered to watch the two men die. An enterprising publisher named Coverly sold broad-

sheets on the case to the mob; he had to correct his pam
phlets which reported the execution of the two men, how
ever, because Dalton, at the last moment, was reprieved
Still the bloodthirsty crowd was not totally disappointed
Tully was hanged on schedule.

TURLEY, PRESTON S.
Murderer • (?-1858)

Drink was Preston Turley's downfall. His acute al
coholism caused him to be driven from the Bap
tist Church in Charleston, Va. (now West Virginia
The ex-minister hit the bottle harder than ever, encicin
his wife Mary Susan to join in his revels.

One late summer night in 1858, the couple began t
quarrel while both were well into their staggers. Turle
abruptly turned on his wife and, while raging scripture
strangled her in front of his three children.

Despite the witnesses, Turley attempted to conceal hi
wife's body by dumping her weighted corpse into th
nearby Coal River. He was quickly taken into custody an
sentenced to death.

On September 17, 1858, Turley addressed a large thron
for more than three hours, lecturing them on the wage
of demon rum. He was noticeably disappointed as th
hangman approached him with the noose. His death mat
tered little to him, it seemed, but the fact that his childre
had not come to see him die saddened him. He had repeat
edly encouraged them, in letters from jail, to attend th
ceremonies. One note stated: "Don't you want to go an
see Pa hung?"

TURNER, NAT
Murderer • (1800–1831)

In late August of 1831, a field slave foreman and Baptist preacher, Nat Turner, decided to revolt against his white masters, claiming to have had a vision from God who commanded him to free his people. Armed with knifes and hatchets, he and eight other blacks invaded his owner's house and hacked to death four adults and an infant.

Turner sent word to slaves on neighboring plantations throughout Southampton County, Virginia, to join him in his revolt. About sixty more slaves joined him and his small band and then began one of the most bloody uprisings ever witnessed in the antebellum South. The slaves took weapons and horses as they swept through each plantation, slaughtering every white person in sight.

Several blacks who refused to join Turner were beaten senseless and killed while shielding their masters with their own bodies. The burly foreman of one plantation, upon seeing his master knifed to death, strode up to Turner and said: "Now that you have killed him, you may kill me. I have nothing to live for."

Small children were tracked down in corn and cotton fields where they sought refuge; they were hacked to bits. The slaughter went on for forty-eight hours and caused the deaths of close to fifty whites.

While en route to the county seat, ironically named Jerusalem, Turner and his rebels stopped at the Parker plantation. Several of his men went into the plantation to recruit more slaves to the rebellion. Instead, they broke into the large wine cellar and proceeded to get drunk. Within an hour, Turner went into the cellar after them, exhorting them to continue along the bloodpath of their sacred revolution.

While Turner was thus occupied, a band of eighteen whites arrived at the plantation gates on horseback and

shot up the runaway slaves who were waiting there fo
their leader. Turner and his men rushed out of the win
cellar and drove them off, but it was clear that the white
had begun a ruthless counterattack. Word came to Turne
that troops were marching on his position; he and his mer
retreated. First they attacked a farm, but five whites, bar
ricaded inside, drove them off with fowling pieces. Hi
numbers reduced, the slave general fled with the remnant
of his army into the brush.

For three months white militiamen hunted Turne
throughout Virginia. Reprisals against anyone who ever
sympathized with Turner and his men were vicious and
quick. More than one hundred slaves were hanged, shot
or beaten to death. A few were drawn and quartered, thei
dissected bodies nailed to the entrance of certain slav
quarters as a warning.

Turner was finally apprehended along with eighteer
others in early November, 1831. He was condemned to
death. Before his public hanging, Turner confessed to hi
crimes. In describing the 48-hour bloodbath, he stated:

"I took my station in the rear and it was my objec
to carry terror and devastation wherever we went. I placec
fifteen or twenty of the best-armed and most to be reliec
on in front, who generally approached the houses as fas
as their horses could run.

"This was for two purposes—to prevent their [whites
escape, and strike terror to the inhabitants . . . I sometime
got in sight to see the work of death completed . . . viewec
the mangled bodies as they lay in silent satisfaction, and
immediately started in quest of other victims. . . ."

TUTT, DAVID (OR DAVIS)
Gunfighter • (? –1865)

Tutt had the reputation of a mean gunfighter a dozen years before he ran headlong into James Butler "Wild Bill" Hickok in Springfield, Mo. The cause of the argument between the two men is still uncertain.

Hickok had been recently mustered out of the Union Army and was apparently wooing a wild girl from the Ozarks, one Susannah Moore. Tutt, who was passing through town on his way West, was also attracted to Susannah's ravishing beauty. West, was also attracted to men quarreled over her while playing cards and that Hickok challenged Tutt to face him in the town square at high noon. Tutt accepted.

At about noon on July 21, 1865, Tutt, whose background indicated that he had shot several men in similar duels, began walking toward Hickok who stood passively waiting for him in the middle of the square. It was *the* storybook gunfight which Hollywood would ceaselessly employ a century later.

Tutt went for his guns first (he wore two) and began banging away at Hickok. His hurried shots went wide. Hickok, who was to dispose of a plethora of gunmen in future cow towns, then displayed the coolness under fire that would make him legend. While Tutt was slinging slugs at him, Hickok carefully and slowly drew his own pistol and, holding it with both hands, took deliberate aim and squeezed off one round. The bullet hit Tutt square in the heart from an estimated distance of seventy-five yards, killing him instantly.

UDDERZOOK, WILLIAM E.
Murderer, Swindler • (? -1873)

With his brother-in-law W. S. Goss, Udderzook entered into a plot to defraud an insurance company of $25,000. The Goss home—a small cottage in Baltimore, Md.—was burned to cinders in early 1873 and Mrs. Goss immediately pressed the Baltimore insurance company for payment, claiming her husband had been consumed by the flames.

The insurance company investigated and found the remains of a man who was totally unrecognizable. Company officials immediately smelled fraud, thinking the cadaver to be a corpse stolen from a nearby medical college (a technique perfected years later by mass murderer Herman W. Mudgett), but could prove nothing. The company refused to pay off and Mrs. Goss sued.

Though the jury awarded the sum to the bereaved Mrs. Goss, the insurance firm appealed. Authorities wanted time to find the living Goss, whom they suspected was in hiding. They were right. Udderzook had been secreting his brother-in-law in dozens of places for weeks, compelling

Goss to don ridiculous disguises complete with flowing red beards, frocks, wigs, and false faces.

When the insurance detectives appeared to be catching up with the pair near Chester, Pa., Udderzook decided to make Goss's demise a reality. He beat Goss to death, and hurriedly buried the body in a wooded area. The grave was soon found and Udderzook was apprehended.

He was sentenced to death on the gallows. Before he was hanged Udderzook wrote an emotional appeal, requesting that his body be buried as close to that of his brother-in-law's as possible—"that our bodies may return to the mother dust, and our spirits may mingle together on the bright, sunny banks of deliverance, where pleasures never end."

VAN VALKENBURGH, ELIZABETH
Murderer • (? -1846)

Mrs. Van Valkenburgh became annoyed with her husband and spiked his tea with arsenic—which killed him. She was indifferent at her trial, claiming that she had poisoned her husband to cure him of his drinking.

In addition to the murder of John Van Valkenburgh, Elizabeth admitted to killing a former husband in the same fashion and for the same reasons. It was never learned whether or not zealous temperance leaders were ever reached for comment on Mrs. Van Valkenburgh's drastic measures to reform drunks.

Elizabeth was hanged January 24, 1846 in Fulton, N.Y.

VASQUEZ, TIBURCIO
Murderer, Bandit • (? -1875)

A robber since his teens, Tiburcio Vasquez was released from San Quentin in 1870 and immediately launched a five-year spree of holdups in Southern California. Amazingly, Vasquez's dozens of robberies never ended in violence. This changed on August 26, 1873 when, with a band of men, the outlaw invaded the hamlet of Tres Pinos (also called Paicines), looting the town and killing three unarmed residents: George Redford and two others named Davidson and Martin.

Giant rewards were offered for the capture of Vasquez and dozens of posses combed the Cahuenga Pass, his reputed hiding place. Before his capture, Vasquez hit yet another town, Kingston, robbing the local hotel and all the stores. As he and his men made for their mountain hideout, they robbed several stages and travelers.

A posse led by George Beers, a sharpshooter, cornered the band in Cahuenga Pass (now the site of Hollywood) and shot it out with the outlaws. Beers brought down Vasquez himself with a shotgun blast but the outlaw leader lived to face trial for the murders of the three Tres Pinos men. He was found guilty and sentenced to hang.

His execution took place at San Jose, Calif., March 19, 1875.

California bandit Tiburcio Vasquez. (Denver Public Library)

WADDELL, REED
Swindler • (1859-1895)

Waddell was the son of a wealthy Springfield, Illinois family. He was college trained and was expected to enter the family business. Gambling and confidence games, however, were the primary interests of Waddell, and he was ostracized by his family for the many scams he perpetrated in Springfield. Journeying to New York, Waddell was the first to employ the gold brick con game.

He had a lead brick triple gold-plated and made up with a rough finish. A hole was cut out of the brick and a gold plug inserted. The brick was stamped "U.S." in the same fashion the United States Assayer's Office marked authentic gold bricks. With this device, Waddell approached the gullible and offered to sell his brick, a family keepsake, he said, to shore up debts. If the sucker was suspicious, Waddell dug out the gold plug and suggested the dupe check it with a jeweler. Invariably, he did and was amazed to find out that the metal was, indeed, solid gold.

Waddell sold his first gold brick for $4,000. Inside of

ten years, the sharper made $250,000 through the sale of his spurious bricks. He moved to Paris to fleece more suckers but was killed there in March, 1895 by gambler Tom O'Brien in an argument over a rigged banco game.

WARD, RETURN J. M.
Murderer • (? -1857)

Ward was a brutish, illiterate, and psychotic giant of a man who made life unbearable for his petite wife, Olive. The woman had been beaten numerous times by her cretinous husband and, to spare herself further agony, moved away from his Sylvania, Ohio home.

At his pleading, the woman returned for a brief visit in early 1857, whereupon Ward killed her. He hid her body under the bed for safekeeping and neighbors, aroused at Mrs. Ward's disappearance (she had informed them of her worst fears before rejoining her husband), charged Ward with the killing but failed to find Olive's body after searching the house. Apparently it occurred to no one in the search party to look under the bed.

As soon as the suspicious crowd departed, Ward rushed to the bedroom, dragged his wife's corpse forth and dissected it in the kitchen with an axe and carving knife. He threw the bloody pieces into the open hearth and burned them.

Ward then cleaned out the fireplace the next day and placed the ashes by the steps of his front door (as stated, he was none too bright). Neighbors inspected the ashes and found parts of Olive's jaw bone. Ward was arrested and tried.

At his trial, the killer insisted that he struck his wife only after she had inflicted a terrific blow on him (the jury roared with laughter), and that he had accidentally killed her. In his panic, Ward claimed, he cut up the body and attempted to dispose of it by burning it in the fireplace. The murderer's vivid description of how he minced Olive's torso was so sickeningly detailed that the jury condemned him halfway through his testimony.

Before he was hanged, Ward admitted killing at least two other persons near Richland, Ohio.

WATSON, ELLA ("CATTLE KATE")
Cattle Thief • (1866-1888)

Ella Watson thrived in the broad expanses of Wyoming's cattle ranches near Rawlins. Born to a prosperous farmer in Smith County, Kan., she had run away from home and worked as a dancehall girl in Denver, where she married at eighteen. Her husband, however, was a woman chaser and she soon left him. Ella then drifted to Cheyenne and then Rawlins, Wyo. where she worked in a bar as a shill.

Clever Jim Averill, who had moved West after allegedly receiving a diploma from Cornell University, spotted Ella in the Rawlins saloon and soon asked her to move to Sweetwater where he ran a post office and bar operation. He would back her in a brothel, he said, and they would split the profits.

Ella agreed and arrived in Rawlins in early 1888. A local paper described the 26-year-old woman as having "a robust physique," and being "a dark devil in the saddle, handy with a six-shooter and a Winchester, and an expert with a branding iron."

She would soon get plenty of practice with the branding iron. Averill, who wrote vituperative letters to local papers in protest of the cattle barons and their evil ways, began to steal cattle on a wholesale basis, keeping them penned up in a corral next to Ella's bordello. Ella, practically surrounded with cows, came to be known as "Cattle Kate."

On several occasions, local cattlemen spied their brands on cows in Kate's pens but were driven off when Kate appeared brandishing a rifle. In July of 1888, a large vigilante group showed up at Kate's bordello and caught her off guard. She fought wildly and then asked, "Where are you taking me?"

"To Rawlins," one of the men shouted.

"You can't do that!" she screamed.

"Why not?"

"I haven't got my print dress on, that's why not!"

They loaded her in a wagon and drove off to Jim Averill's ranch which was a half mile distant. There they took Averill prisoner and he was thrown into the wagon alongside Kate. As the cowboys rode along toward a remote canyon, it became apparent that they weren't headed for Rawlins. One of them mumbled something about lynching Cattle Kate and Averill but they were unconcerned. They laughed and joked as they rode along, poking fun at the riders galloping next to them.

Reaching the Sweetwater River, the cattlemen stopped. They fixed ropes around the necks of Cattle Kate and Averill. "Jump," one rancher told Averill as he was standing on a boulder, the rope around his neck attached to a limb of a cottonwood tree.

Averill smiled. "Stop your fooling fellows," he said.

They weren't fooling. One man came up and pushed Averill into space and another shoved Cattle Kate from her rocky perch. Both fought for their lives with unbound hands. "The kicking and writhing of those people was awful to witness," one newspaper reported.

Days later the bodies were taken down and seven of the lynching party were arrested. They posted bonds for each other but never faced trial. One of the vigilantes felt a tinge of remorse and later told a reporter: "We didn't mean to hang 'em, only scare 'em a little."

WEBSTER, JOHN WHITE
Murderer • (? -1850)

Amerca's first "classic" murder, which focused national attention on distinguished educator Dr. John White Webster, was for all practical purposes brought about through an act of unpremeditated wrath.

Dr. Webster (M.A., M.D., Harvard) was a corpulent, ineffectual-looking man who peered mildly over loose-fitting spectacles, but he was also a much-respected professor of chemistry and mineralogy at the Massachusetts Medical College during the 1840s. Webster's office was directly below that of Oliver Wendell Holmes (who would testify at his trial, as would Drs. W. T. G. Morton and C. T. Jackson, discoverers of ether, and Jared Sparks, President of Harvard and one of George Washington's biographers).

The professor was not the reclusive type, but gave handsome parties and delighted in long, sumptuous meals brightened with the best wines and illustrious company of Boston intellectuals such as poet Henry Wadsworth Longfellow. His expensive tastes were costly to the point where Webster spent far beyond what his annual salary of $1,200 would allow. Such extravagances compelled Webster to seek financial aid in the form of loans. First he borrowed $2,432 from a local group of lenders. He next went to an opulent member of this group, Dr. George Parkman, and borrowed an additional $400.

Parkman was an odd creature, tall, gangling, razor-thin, with a jutting, squared-off jaw (he was called "Chin" by students), pointed nose, and small, squinty eyes. A graduate of the University of Aberdeen, Parkman had given up medicine to become one of the school's wealthiest landlords. Though miserly, Parkman ostentatiously donated the ground on which the Massachusetts Medical School stood and for whom the Parkman Chair of Anatomy was established (occupied at one time by Oliver Wendell

Holmes). Parkman was not so generous with those to whom he lent money, particularly with the pudgy-faced Dr. Webster. Parkman originally loaned Webster money in a sham spirit of friendliness. This attitude soon dissolved when, in the fall of 1849, the rod-like Parkman entered Webster's classes wearing a stovepipe hat and a long, black frock coat to goad him with sarcastic remarks while the professor attempted to deliver lectures.

Webster ignored Parkman; he also ignored the loan he promised to repay. On one occasion, Parkman told Webster: "The world does not owe you a living." Webster only smiled good naturedly and walked away. Parkman continued to hound Webster. The money shark learned that Webster had accumulated more than $1,000 after selling his valuable minerals collection. Still no payment came to him from the professor.

Parkman's dark mood became even blacker on November 23, 1849 until he worked himself into an indignant rage, raced to the college grounds, and entered Webster's office.

"Have you got the money?" Parkman demanded of Webster.

"No, I have not," the professor replied.

Parkman was beside himself with anger. "I got you your professorship and I'll get you out of it!" This was patently untrue but at this impassioned juncture, Parkman actually believed he was responsible for Webster's appointment.

The threat was too much for Webster. "I felt nothing but the sting of his words," the professor wrote later. "I was excited by them to the highest degree of passion." Webster grabbed a heavy piece of kindling wood from a pile near the fireplace and crashed it down on Parkman's head with great force. The blow crushed Parkman's stovepipe hat and his head. He collapsed to the floor, bleeding from the mouth.

Parkman was sprawled on the floor for ten minutes while Webster frantically used spirits of ammonia and other drugs to revive him. It was hopeless. Parkman was dead. And it was murder, Webster realized with a shudder.

The professor was a practical man. There appeared to him no reason why he should face such a charge. The solution was simple—merely dissect and destroy Parkman's

This early drawing illustrates Webster's killing of Dr. Parkman. (N.Y. Historical Society)

body. Calmly, Webster dragged the corpse into his washroom after locking all the doors. There he labored long to lift the body into a sink and then, using a butcher knife (careful not to employ any of the dissecting knives) meticulously cut up his creditor's body.

The college janitor, Empraim Littlefield, was a born meddler. He had witnessed an argument between Parkman and Webster weeks before, at which time Parkman dunned Webster for the money due him. He had watched the determined Parkman enter the college grounds on the day of the murder and go into Webster's office. He checked the doors when Parkman did not reappear, only to find himself locked out.

Entering another office, next to Webster's assay furnace, Littlefield felt the wall. It was scalding hot. Webster had built a fire so intense that the brick wall backing the furnace burned to the touch. On the other side of that wall, Webster was burning Parkman's head and other sections of his body.

Three days later, November 26, 1849, a reward of $3,000 was offered for the return of Dr. Parkman. Authorities believed him kidnapped and held for ransom, such was his vast wealth. Janitor Littlefield suspected something else.

He tried to inspect Dr. Webster's dissecting vault where bones were stored. It was locked.

The enterprising janitor then spent two days removing parts of a wall, brick by brick, surrounding this chamber. In an eerie midnight scene, Littlefield finally broke through and, holding his oil lantern through a small aperture, spied the bloody pelvis and parts of a leg belonging to Dr. Parkman. He scurried off to babble his story to officials.

Webster was arrested and an investigation of his premises revealed a thigh and thorax secreted in a tea chest, bits of bone lodged in the grate of the furnace and, most damning of all, Parkman's identifiable teeth intact at the back of the furnace.

While Webster was being taken to jail, he gulped down a vial of strychnine which he had prepared for just such an occasion. He had developed a nervous stomach, however, and could not hold the poison.

His trial was a national spectacle. The press heightened the drama by devoting pages and pages to the case. Thousands journeyed to Boston from as far as New Orleans to view the murderer. So many visitors arrived that the judge ordered that spectators could only sit in the gallery during the proceedings for a period of ten minutes (and they were timed) in order to enable all to enjoy the macabre scene. In this way, more than 60,000 bug-eyed spectators visited the trial.

Webster's only defense was that he had acted out of anger and that he had not intended to kill Parkman. The dissecting and hiding of the body convinced the jury otherwise and he was convicted and sentenced to death. Dr. Webster was hanged in August, 1850.

WESTERVELT, WILLIAM
Kidnapper, Murderer • (1831- ?)

Early in 1874, a discharged New York cop, William Westervelt, arrived in the quiet community of Germantown, Pa. After making several inquiries as to the financial status of grocer Christian Ross, he departed. Though Ross owned an impressive-looking mansion, he was not as well-to-do as Westervelt was made to believe by gossipy neighbors.

Mistaking Ross for a rich man, Westervelt sent two of his confederates, infamous burglars Joseph Douglass and William Mosher, to Germantown to kidnap Ross's youngest son, four-year-old Charles Brewster "Charley" Ross, and bring him to New York where he would be held for ransom.

On July 1, 1874, Douglass and Mosher abducted little Charley from in front of his home on the pretext of taking him to Philadelphia to buy fireworks for an upcoming Fourth of July celebration. He was never seen again but reports have it the boy was delivered to Westervelt and held in New York while negotiations went on for the delivery of the ransom money, $20,000.

Christian Ross was told to pack the money in a suitcase and then board a specific New York-bound train. He was told to stand at the end of the platform car and toss the suitcase from the train when he saw a series of lights flash along the way. He followed these instructions, but all the way to New York, Ross saw no lights as he stood on the back platform of the car. The car was jammed with detectives, a fact Westervelt may have learned.

New York police authorities, by checking handwriting samples in their files, identified the ransom notes as having been written by William Mosher, a habitual burglar. Ironically, Westervelt, who was Mosher's brother-in-law, was called in by police to help. After several meetings it was obvious that Westervelt could not produce his brother-in-law. Then, on December 14, 1874, Mosher and Douglass were caught in the act of burglarizing a Brooklyn home and both were shot while resisting arrest.

With his dying breath, Mosher admitted to kidnapping Charley Ross. "We done it," he said. "We did it for money."

Westervelt was subsequently identified as having been in Germantown asking strange questions about the Ross family. He was brought to Philadelphia and there stood trial for the kidnapping. A woman identified him as being on a trolley car with little Charley but the ex-cop would admit to nothing, repeatedly stating his innocence. He was tried, found guilty of perpetrating America's first major kidnapping, and sentenced to seven years of solitary confinement which he served. Upon his release, Westervelt completely disappeared.

Underworld reports had it that Westervelt took the Ross child to New York and held him there while attempting to collect the ransom money. When the intensive manhunt for the child began and publicity on the case became widespread, he panicked and drowned the boy in the East River.

WHITE, ALEXANDER
Murderer • (1762-1784)

White immigrated from Tyrone, Ireland to Boston where he fell in love with a local girl. He proposed marriage but soon realized that in his impoverished state he could ill afford a bride. To solve his dilemma, White, who worked as a seaman aboard a cutter, tried to rob his captain, killing him in the process while their ship was anchored in Cow Harbor, Long Island, N.Y.

A passenger witnessed the murder and escaped White's blade by diving overboard and swimming to shore where he made a report to harbor authorities. The seaman was arrested and quickly convicted of the killing and of piracy. He was hanged at Cambridge, Mass., on November 18, 1784.

WHITE, JOHN DUNCAN
Murderer, Pirate • (? -1826)

White, alias Charles Marchant, was wanted for several robberies in New England. He and his partner, Winslow Curtis, alias Sylvester Colson, signed on board the *Fairy*, a merchant vessel, in 1826 to avoid the pursuit of authorities.

While bound for Gottenburg, White and Curtis revolted and killed Captain Edward Selfridge, only 23, and first mate Tom Jenkins, throwing their bodies overboard. The two mutineers then sailed the *Fairy* to Louisburg, Nova Scotia and sank it.

The two pirates were soon captured and brought to Boston for trial. They were found guilty and sentenced to death. On the night before the execution, White hanged himself in his cell; Curtis mounted the scaffold the next day and died on time.

WILBER, LEWIS
Murderer • (1816-1839)

Riverboat life on the Erie Canal was exciting and adventuresome to many early American pioneers, but it was routine and boring to Lewis Wilber. He had worked the boats for several years and was on board the *Oliver Newbury* heading West when he struck up an acquaintance with 53-year-old Robert Barber, a passenger who climbed aboard at Utica, N.Y., August 29, 1837.

Barber told Wilber that he was on his way to Buffalo where he intended to get married. Wilber smiled and nodded approvingly. The two, according to the other thirty-odd passengers, became great friends. When the boat stopped at New Boston for supplies the next morning, the two men got off and strolled leisurely into the woods talking in animated fashion.

Four miles upstream, Wilber, alone, climbed back on board the *Oliver Newbury*, such was the snail's pace of the tow boat. When questioned as to Barber's whereabouts Wilber explained that the older man had decided to walk to Syracuse. Barber's corpse, horribly cut to pieces, was found almost eight months later.

Wilber was remembered by the passengers and he was traced by lawmen to the Ohio River Valley where he was arrested and returned to New York for trial. Though he confessed to the murder, Wilber never volunteered his reasons for killing Barber.

The murderer was executed on the gallows October 3, 1839 at Morrisville, N.Y.

WILD BUNCH, THE

When the West as the outlaws knew it began to collapse like a Chinese magic box in the 1890s, the remnants of the robber bands straggled and romped toward their last bastion: Hole-in-the-Wall, an almost impenetrable and natural fortress of deep gorges, high cliffs, and rocky retreats that straddled the Wyoming,

Colorado, and Utah state lines. Outlaws came there from all points of the land.

Some drifted in, crime weary and looking for a place to rest, even to permanently settle. Others roared into Hole-in-the-Wall to recruit gang members for sallies and raids into more civilized areas. Under the pressure of tens of thousands of settlers, farmers, and town-builders, the bandits were being penned in, like the Indians, sectored off into invisible reservations.

Before their demise, the outlaw gangs lashed out viciously in a decade-long battle with the forces of the law, a battle that reached across the plains of ten states. The victims were trainmen, bankers, and cattle ranchers, who were robbed by ravaging bands that left hundreds killed, wounded, and crippled. It was the last fling of the bad man on horseback, the last stand of a violent and uncompromising breed known as The Wild Bunch.

Here are the men who rode in and out of Hole-in-the-Wall for thirty some odd years, all of whom could be termed loosely or specifically members of the Wild Bunch:

—Dave Atkins, train robber and murderer from San Angelo, Texas. Originally a farm hand, Atkins turned to crime early in his twenties. Pinkerton archives described him as having a "round face, thick lips . . . drops his head when talking . . . peculiar slouchy walk."

—Jack Bennett, who often brought supplies to his outlaw friends living in Hole-in-the-Wall. Bennett was caught after a shootout with a posse and was hanged from the crosspieces at the entrance of the Bassett ranch in March, 1898.

—Sam Carey, called "Laughing Sam," was anything but congenial. A meanstreaked bandit with an ugly knife scar under his right eye, Carey was one of the first outlaws to use Hole-in-the-Wall as a hideout in the 1880s. He had murdered several men by the time he embarked on a bank robbing career that led him through Wyoming, Montana, and South Dakota. With him rode the Taylor brothers and professional train robbers Bud Deslow and H. Wilcox.

Laughing Sam's robbery of the Spearfish bank in South Dakota was almost a repeat of the disastrous raids led by Jesse James at Northfield and the Daltons at Coffeyville.

He alone escaped a citizen's ambush as the gang emerged from the bank, riding back to the Hole more dead than alive. A cowboy surgeon removed three bullets from his badly scarred body and Laughing Sam rode out again the next week to rob a train.

—William Tod Carver, one of Butch Cassidy's original riders, who rode with Butch and the Sundance Kid on a half dozen train robberies.

The Wild Bunch arrived in Fort Worth, Texas, and thought it would be fun to sit for a formal photograph; they are (standing, left to right) William Carver, Harvey Logan ("Kid Curry"), and (sitting, left to right) Harry Longbaugh ("The Sundance Kid"), Ben Kilpatrick, and the impish Butch Cassidy. (Pinkerton, Inc.)

—Joseph Chancellor, a Texas-born bandit who first earned his reputation as a gunfighter and bankrobber in Oklahoma before moving to Hole-in-the-Wall. Chancellor had also served time in the Santa Fe, N.M. Penitentiary (released January 28, 1897) for rustling. He arrived in the Hole about 1904. This 37-year-old bandit was described by Pinkerton archivists as being nervous. "Constantly gets up two or three times during the night to smoke. Uses brown cigarette paper. Fingers stained from the use of this paper. Never drinks or chews tobacco."

—William Cruzan, 33 years old by the turn of the century, an ugly-tempered pistol-whipper who had served four years in jail for rustling and robbery. A lone wolf bandit, Cruzan raided several banks in the Dakotas, Wyoming, and Colorado before he was gunned down.

—George L. "Flat Nose" Curry (George Parrott), once described as "the largest rustler in Wyoming." Also known as "Big Nose" Curry, this bandit served as a Western Fagin to the Logan brothers, Harvey, Lonny, and Johnny (another Logan brother, Henry, did not take up the outlaw trail). He also rode with Butch Cassidy as did Harvey Logan, in many raids. Logan's dog-like idolatry for George Curry caused him to adopt the name Kid Curry.

After participating in several bank and train robberies in the Southwest following the turn of the century, George Curry rode back to the Hole-in-the-Wall and began rustling cattle. He was caught red-handed while changing a brand by the sheriff of Vernal, Utah.

Instead of surrendering, Curry leaped on his horse and galloped off. The sheriff gave chase and for ten miles, the two men exchanged shots that boomed and echoed across the plain. A lucky shot hit Curry in the skull and he dropped from his saddle—dead.

The residents of Castle Gate, Utah rushed to the outskirts of their little town where Curry had been slain. Outlaws, like the buffalo, were becoming increasingly rare and some of the citizens enthusiastically sought souvenirs of this memorable pursuit and capture. They took out hunting knives and stripped away Big Nose George Curry's flesh from his chest. One ambitious townsman made a pair of shoes from the flesh. Another swatch wound up as a good luck charm and was carried from vest to vest through generations of outlaw *aficionados.* The final possessor of the skin swatch, before these gruesome artifacts were turned over to a Western museum, was a Professor Reed of the Wyoming University at Laramie.

—Frank "Peg Leg" Elliot, a 21-year-old bank robber, was first arrested with Robert Eldredge in October, 1891. Elliot and Eldredge were caught robbing a train and shot to death by a posse.

Dave Lant. (Pinkerton, Inc.)

Harry Tracy. (Pinkerton, Inc.)

—O. C. "Camilla" Hanks, also known as "Deaf Charley," was one of Butch Cassidy's original Wild Bunch. Hanks rode alongside Cassidy, Kid Curry, the Sundance Kid, Bill Carver, and Ben Kilpatrick in almost every raid the Wild Bunch committed.

Hanks was a short, squat outlaw from Las Vegas, N.M., where he murdered a man in a bar fight. In his twenties he robbed and killed in Utah and Montana under the alias Charley Jones. He was captured by a posse in Teton, Mont. in 1892 just after robbing a Northern Pacific train at Big Timber, Mont. Sentenced to ten years in jail at Deer Lodge, Hanks was released on April 30, 1901 and promptly rode to Hole-in-the-Wall where he joined Butch Cassidy and went on to rob trains at Tipton, Wyo. and Wagner, Mont. He was later shot and killed.

—Swede Johnson, an insane killer who pulled his six gun at the slightest insult. Johnson first appeared in Hole-in-the-Wall in 1898 and became friendly with arch killers and robbers Dave Lant and Harry Tracy, who was known as the "Mad Dog" of the Wild Bunch. Three months after his arrival, Johnson exploded when Willy Strang, a seventeen-year-old cowboy, kiddingly dumped a pitcher of water on him. Johnson jumped up and emptied his six gun into the boy. He, Tracy, and Lant were tracked down for this murder and Johnson was sent to Wyoming State Prison for life.

—Ben Kilpatrick, "The Tall Texan," was, next to the Sundance Kid, Butch Cassidy's top man. He was a mediocre gunfighter but nerveless when it came to robbing banks and trains. When Butch and Sundance fled to South America, Kilpatrick, using the alias Benjamin Arnold, struck out on his own. Laura Bullion, alias Della Rose, went with him. She was the last in a line of cowgirls who followed Kilpatrick's outlaw trail.

Both Kilpatrick and Laura Bullion were captured by police detectives in St. Louis on November 8, 1901. Found in their luggage was $7,000, part of the money Kilpatrick had helped Butch Cassidy to liberate from a Great Northern train at Wagner, Mont., on July 3 of that year.

The Tall Texan admitted taking part in the Wagner robbery, and on December 12, 1901 he was sentenced to fifteen years in the federal penitentiary at Atlanta, Ga. Laura Bullion was convicted as the gang's accomplice and drew a five year sentence in a Tennessee women's prison.

Released on June 11, 1911, Kilpatrick resumed his old ways, a trainrobber out of his own time. He didn't last long. On March 14, 1912, when Kilpatrick and Howard Benson, another ex-convict from Atlanta, walked into the baggage car of the Pacific's Sunset Flyer, they learned that the old times were gone forever.

Resistance to armed bandits before the turn of the century had been unthinkable. But feisty David A. Trousdale, the baggage car guard, was not impressed by Kilpatrick and Benson who demanded he turn over the money in the safe. The two first attempted to dupe Trousdale.

"I'm a Union Pacific detective," Benson told him when they entered the car. "We just got wind of a robbery attempt on you."

Trousdale began to reach for his rifle when Kilpatrick poked his own rifle in the guard's stomach, saying, "Don't try it, young fellow."

The nervy guard, through a ruse, got Kilpatrick to turn his head and when he did so, Trousdale brought an ice mallet down on his skull, killing him with one blow. He then grabbed the Tall Texan's rifle and shot and killed Benson.

"They thought they were such smooth workers at the game," Trousdale told reporters later. "But it made me sore the way they acted, so I decided to take some of the conceit out of them . . . I am more worried about what to do with the vacation and the reward the company has given me than I am about killing those two."

A more humiliating end never befell a Western bad man.

—Elza Lay was another one of the hard-core members of the Wild Bunch who rode with Butch Cassidy on almost all of his robbery sorties. Following the disappearance of Cassidy and Sundance, Lay was trapped by a posse in Clayton, N.M. and tried to shoot his way to freedom. He killed a sheriff in the attempt but was knocked senseless by gun butts and thrown into jail. He was sentenced to prison for life in the Santa Fe Penitentiary.

—Jesse Linsley, a horsethief and ex-convict, appeared

briefly at Hole-in-the-Wall in the 1890s after committing some minor robberies. Linsley disappeared at the turn of the century.

—Harvey Logan, better known as "Kid Curry," was the real killer of the Wild Bunch, a ruthless gunslinger whose leadership abilities were marred by his quick temper and total reliance upon a six gun. One of four brothers, Logan came from Dodge, Mo. and gained Western fame in his early twenties as one of the most feared gunmen alive. He could not outdraw Sundance but was a deadly marksman. He killed eight men in street duels before joining the Wild Bunch.

Logan wore a pearl-handled Peacemaker with a fourteen inch barrel, and he used it often. Taught to rustle cattle by George Curry, Logan soon graduated to robbing banks and trains. He appeared at Hole-in-the-Wall with gunmen Bob Lee and Jim Thornhill about 1896, the same time his leader, Butch Cassidy, arrived there fresh from serving a two-year prison sentence. Logan participated in every major robbery committed by the Wild Bunch and it was often that Cassidy had to stop Kid Curry from needlessly killing train guards.

When Cassidy and Sundance left for South America Logan promised to join them, but he went on to rob banks and trains and by 1901 was the most hunted outlaw in America. He was trapped in a Knoxville, Tenn. poolroom in the fall of 1902, and was wounded as he attempted to escape squads of policemen. He was identified as the infamous Kid Curry by Pinkerton detective Lowell Spence.

As he was being taken to jail, five thousand people people mobbed the police van to get a look at him. But Curry's mind was on Spence.

"Some day I'll kill that man," Logan told one of his captors. "He's very troublesome."

Logan was imprisoned in 1902 but escaped from the Knoxville Jail on June 27, 1903. Pinkertons led by Lowell Spence and other law enforcement officers trailed Logan all the way to the Rockies in Colorado. There Logan formed a new band of robbers and stopped a train in Parachute, Colo., taking a small amount of money from the express car. Two days later Logan and his men were trapped in a dead end canyon by a large posse.

Tom O'Day. (Pinkerton, Inc.)

While jumping up and running for the cover of a large boulder, Kid Curry was wounded in the shoulder. The lawmen heard one of the outlaws call to him: "Are you hit?"

After a long silence, Kid Curry answered: "Yes, and I'm going to end it here." With that Harvey Logan, the most feared member of the Wild Bunch, sent a bullet into his left temple and died.

—James Lowe was a 32-year-old train robber who was in and out of Hole-in-the-Wall during the waning years of the Wild Bunch. He was killed in 1910.

—Tom O'Day, a cowboy from Wyoming, turned to crime in the late 1890s, centering his exploits on bank robbery. He sometimes rode with Butch Cassidy but preferred to be on his own. He was finally captured in Casper, Wyo. on November 23, 1903 while herding stolen horses through the center of town. He was given a long prison term.

411

—Will Roberts, also known as "Dixon," specialized in train robbery and was one of the last important outlaws to hide out in Hole-in-the-Wall.

—Harry Tracy, the most brutal member of the Wild Bunch, preceded Butch and his boys to Hole-in-the-Wall by two years and was addicted to murder. Tracy was sent to the Colorado State Prison at Aspen for life with Dave Lant, convicted with Swede Johnson for killing Willy Strang in 1898.

Tracy escaped from the Aspen jail on June 9, 1902 with Dave Merrill. Somehow, Tracy got his hands on a rifle and began picking guards off the prison wall. He killed one and wounded three. Then he and Merrill, using a wounded guard as a human shield, broke through a gate and dashed to freedom.

They traveled to Oregon, stealing guns and ammunition in Salem, and robbing a carriage in Portland. Hundreds of soldiers were put on their trail. Tracy and Merrill went into the woods and headed for Washington.

Tracy appeared alone in a small fishing town on Puget Sound on July 8, 1902. He had killed Merrill. While the two men were being hunted, they had taken refuge in a barn. There Tracy found a newspaper and began to read. He came across a story that reported Merrill had informed on Tracy years ago, a fact unknown to Tracy, in order to receive a lighter sentence for a robbery they had both committed. Laying aside the paper, Tracy reached over and strangled his fellow escapee to death.

Commandeering a motor launch in a fishing village, Tracy ordered the captain to pass close to the McNeil Island Penitentiary which jutted from the middle of Puget Sound.

"For God's sake, why?" the Captain asked.

"I want to pick a few guards off the wall," Tracy replied. The outlaw thought better of the idea when it occurred to him that the guards might fire back and possibly kill him. He ordered the captain to take him to Seattle. There he tied up the boat's crew and began walking inland. He bummed his way through Washington, begging meals from farmers.

The soldiers and possemen were still tracking him in August, 1902. Tired, hunted like an animal in alien territory, Tracy decided to turn about and make a fight of it. He hid in a tall stand of timber and traded shots with lawmen for several hours. As the sun began to set, Tracy realized his position was hopeless. Like Harvey Logan, he preferred to end his own life rather than return to prison.

At dusk, Harry Tracy put his six gun to his temple and fired.

The possemen listened for a while and then one said, "I guess he's through." They closed in, a hundred men gripping rifles, and stepping carefully around tall trees and through thick underbrush. Tracy was lying in a clearing with a pistol still gripped in his stiffened hand. He had pulled his trousers up to his knees to display his worn out cowboy boots, the dead Western outlaw lying in the woods of Washington, far from his native plain.

It was all over with the Wild Bunch.

[ALSO SEE Butch Cassidy *Bloodletters and Badmen*, Book 2.]

WITTROCK, FREDERICK
Trainrobber • (1858-1921)

He was a victim of the potboilers and lurid dime novels churned out during the early 1880s to puff the imaginary exploits of Jesse James. Meek and mousy Fred Wittrock voraciously consumed any and all such blood-curdling accounts of Western bandits, spending more time on this literature than at his uneventful job as a clerk in a St. Louis store.

In November, 1886, his mind exploding with heady tales of robbery, Wittrock stopped the St. Louis and San Francisco flyer as it was slowing down to enter the St. Louis yards. He was masked with a black bandanna and he held two menacing six-guns. Within minutes he successfully escaped with $10,000 taken from the Adams Express Company's safe.

Wittrock returned to his job and whiled away the hours reading newspapers to see if detectives had picked up any clues from his great train robbery. They hadn't. Wittrock decided to help authorities and sent a letter to the *St. Louis Globe*, telling the paper that "the outlaw's tools" could be found in a St. Louis baggage room.

Detectives found the pistols, bandanna, and a copy of a dime novel with Wittrock's home address written on its cover. They tracked him down and arrested him. As they were leading him away, Wittrock asked deputies to please refer to him as "Terrible Fred," his much-feared underworld name.

Wittrock served a long prison term and was released to live out his life as a retired bad man, much like Al Jennings, spinning impossible yarns about himself for young school children who stared open-mouthed and believed.

WOOD, ISAAC L.
Murderer • (? -1858)

Isaac Wood was a ruthless but careless murderer. His brother David owned a huge estate at Dansville, N.Y., but never lived to enjoy it. David Wood died unexpectedly in May, 1855, struck down by a strange illness. His wife Rhoda and her three children died of the same illness short months later.

The illness had been administered to the family in the form of arsenic by Isaac Wood, who promptly looted the estate once the members died. He moved to New Jersey, where he cold-bloodedly killed his wife and child and then moved on to Illinois.

Before leaving Dansville, Isaac, as administrator of the Wood estate, leased his brother's home to a man named Welch. The new tenant discovered three packs of arsenic in the barn wrapped in official papers, papers that had been exclusively in the possession of the estate's administrator, Isaac.

Wood was tracked down and brought back to New York for trial. He was speedily convicted and executed July 9, 1858 at Geneseo, N.Y.

BLOODLETTERS AND BADMEN
Jay Robert Nash

A definitive collection—in three volumes—of the most notorious men and women in American history from the eighteenth century to the present. A connoisseur's treasury of crime and excitement, suspense and nostalgia. "A monument to American misbehavior."—*New York Times Book Review*

___**Book 1:** **Captain Lightfoot to Jesse James**
(I32-137, $4.95, U.S.A.)
(I32-138, $6.25, Canada)

___**Book 2:** **Butch Cassidy to Al Capone**
(I32-140, $4.95, U.S.A.)
(I32-141, $6.25, Canada)

___**Book 3:** **Lucky Luciano to Charles Manson**
(I32-142, $4.95, U.S.A.)
(I32-143, $6.25, Canada)

To order, use the coupon below. If you prefer to use your own stationery, please include complete title as well as book number and price. Allow 4 weeks for delivery.